CREATIVITY
And Its Cultivation

CREATIVITY

AND ITS CULTIVATION

ADDRESSES PRESENTED AT THE

INTERDISCIPLINARY SYMPOSIA ON CREATIVITY

MICHIGAN STATE UNIVERSITY

EAST LANSING, MICHIGAN

HAROLD H. ANDERSON, EDITOR

HARPER & ROW, PUBLISHERS

New York and Evanston

Library of Congress catalog card number: 59–7049

CONTENTS

Contents

CONTRIBUTORS

HAROLD H. ANDERSON, *Research Professor of Psychology,* Michigan State University, East Lansing, Michigan.

ALDEN B. DOW, *Architect,* Midland, Michigan.

HENRY EYRING, *Dean of the Graduate School,* University of Utah, Salt Lake City, Utah.

ERICH FROMM, *Director, Department of Psychoanalysis,* Medical School, National University of Mexico; *Professor of Psychology,* Michigan State University, East Lansing, Michigan.

J. P. GUILFORD, *Professor of Psychology,* University of Southern California, Los Angeles, California.

ERNEST R. HILGARD, *Professor of Psychology; Associate Director, Laboratory of Human Development,* Stanford University, Stanford, California.

HAROLD D. LASSWELL, *Professor of Law and Political Science,* Yale University, New Haven, Connecticut.

ABRAHAM H. MASLOW, *Professor of Psychology and Chairman of the Department,* Brandeis University, Waltham, Massachusetts.

ROLLO MAY, *Psychologist, Psychoanalyst,* New York City.

MARGARET MEAD, *Associate Curator of Ethnology,* American Museum of Natural History, New York City.

HENRY A. MURRAY, *Professor of Clinical Psychology,* Harvard University, Cambridge, Massachusetts.

CARL R. ROGERS, *Professor, Departments of Psychology and Psychiatry,* University of Wisconsin, Madison, Wisconsin.

EDMUND W. SINNOTT, Dean of the Graduate School; Director of Shef-
field Scientific School; Director, University Division of the Sciences;
Sterling Professor of Botany, Emeritus, Yale University, New Haven,
Connecticut.

GEORGE D. STODDARD, Dean, School of Education, New York University,
New York City.

PREFACE

Creativity is a subject of wide interdisciplinary interest. The purposes of these Symposia are to define and refine the concepts of creativity from a variety of approaches; to suggest criteria for recognizing the process of creativity as seen in the biological, social, and natural sciences; to discover or invent units or common denominators for evaluating the process of creativity from these several perspectives; and within the realm of human behavior to identify and attempt to assess those qualities of human relating that facilitate and those more easily discerned characteristics of human relating that restrict the process of creativity.

These Symposia are sponsored by the various colleges, divisions, schools, and departments of Michigan State University and are made possible through a grant for a program of Research on Creativity.

The above statement was prepared for the printed program of the Interdisciplinary Symposia on Creativity. It is a statement of aims for a lifetime of research rather than a hope of achievement through a series of addresses. It was presented as an ideal, as a constellation in the sky to give direction.

The speakers were given an open invitation to discuss creativity as a broad general topic to be developed from their own perspectives and experience. They were selected for the breadth, variety, and depth of their interests and backgrounds. The addresses are interdisciplinary by design. There are regrettably areas of thought not included which any reader will note. Chapters by two invited speakers who were unable to come are included. J. P. Guilford wrote his chapter specially for this volume. Material on our topic by Carl R. Rogers is reprinted from *ETC.: A Review of General Semantics* by permission.

In creativity we are dealing with a topic that is both old and new. Many civilizations have evolved their own stories of creation. The records of early thoughts about creation which are available to most persons in our culture are found in the first chapter—the very first chapter—of Genesis. In this sense creativity is old.

The thoughts about creativity which we are discussing in these

Symposia are not old; they are new. They represent, however, only a different perspective or a recent perspective on natural phenomena and human behavior that in themselves are as old as our history records. The transition from the story of Creation in the first chapter of Genesis to the perspectives on creativity of today would make one of the most fascinating stories of the evolution and development of human thought. That story unfortunately is not told here. It is alluded to in one or two of the chapters. In the Old Testament man had not discovered himself as an individual. Today, thousands of years later, man is only beginning to discover the profound meanings of the individual person. In the Old Testament man was not creative; only God was creative. Until two or three centuries ago the notion that man—any man—could be creative in thought and in action was regarded as blasphemy. This transition in human thinking which is taking so long—so many centuries—is itself a lesson in human creativity.

In the Old Testament Creation took six days, and in this sense it was a process; nevertheless, the story essentially represents static, finished, completed, and closed Creation. The possibility of openness of creation, the thought that God may still be creating the heavens and the earth, was not left to future generations.

For centuries the Greek philosophers, who made such a great impact on modern Western thought, sought the absolute, the fixed, the final, the unchangeable. Even two thousand years later, da Vinci, having seen fossil shells from the sea embedded high in the Alps, noted in his diary some of the perplexities about his own perceptions. Against this historical background, it is not surprising that it took so long for Darwin to appear with a concept of movement—a concept of something that was not absolute, something that was not fixed, something that could emerge, evolve, and yet still have infinity as a goal.

What is new in creativity today is the creativity in man himself, with the new dignity which this confers, and the creativity in man's recognition of the process and openness in the cosmos.

What is new in Creativity is the growing realization, the emerging discovery, of the tremendous unsuspected potentialities in the creativity of man, in the nature of human resources, in the meaning of respect for the individual. Such a discovery, which has been taking on meaning since the Renaissance and which is still in process, may prove as significant as Darwinian evolution or the discovery of atomic energy. With detached unanimity, the authors of the chapters in this book are struggling to add to this meaning.

We have historical examples of the courage and strength required in seeing things for oneself, and of the difficulty involved in rejecting the contradictory traditions of the past. Five hundred years ago the world was flat. To most persons it looked flat. People were taught that it was flat. People wanted it flat. They governed their lives in accord with a flat world. Most people lived and died accepting the traditions of partial, inadequate, and erroneous observations, being careful not to risk falling over the edge. To a few simple observers, however, such as Leonardo da Vinci and Cristoforo Colombo, the world was not flat. The phenomena that today are used by a ten-year-old child to explain the roundness of the earth were available for observation five hundred years ago. The shadow of the earth on the moon, the masts of distant ships, the positions of the stars, were all there. But five hundred years ago it was difficult to observe exactly or to integrate such observations into a consistent hypothesis regarding the shape and behavior of the earth. The gradually emerging discovery, demonstration, and acceptance of this one fact in geography, the roundness of the earth, has taken a matter of centuries. The resulting adaptation of man to living in a round world has been accompanied by a revolution in his life and thought.

There are many ways in which the world of today is warped, distorted—flat. There are many ways in which we behave according to the misperceptions of the past. There are many ways in which we do not know the shape of things before our very eyes. Today the phenomena of human behavior are before us, available for all to see. Today parents fondle and flog their children; teachers encourage and harass their pupils; nations fight their neighbors and change their loyalties overnight. Most people continue to be bewildered by the apparent inconsistencies and contradictions in human motives. The earnest groping for a better understanding, the striving for a vigorous and harmonious relationship with others, and the search for social well being are probably as old as biological protoplasm itself. Two or three hundred years of groping toward an understanding of man's creative Self and of man's integrating relating with his fellow man is a short time indeed.

Creativity, the emergence of originals and of individuality, is found in every living cell. In psychology, we still talk about individual differences in a rather static, cross-sectional way. We are just beginning to think of individual differences in a moving, changing, progressing, interacting way, a way we are beginning to call *dynamic*. This flow and interweaving of individual differences is, by definition as well as by discovery the process of emerging originals, creativity. Creativity is in each one of us.

That is to say, creativity was in each one of us as a small child. In children creativity is a universal. Among adults it is almost nonexistent. The great question is: What has happened to this enormous and universal human resource? This is the question of the age and the quest of our research.

The research program on creativity, for which the Symposia served as background, has three projects. The first is to bring to completion a study of children's judgment of social conflict and social problem solving. This is a cross-national study based on data regarding over nine thousand children in seven countries: Germany, England, Norway, Sweden, Finland, Mexico, continental United States and Puerto Rico. It was designed to test certain hypotheses about an environment propitious for social invention and creative, constructive problem solving in situations of interpersonal conflict (Anderson and Anderson, 1954b). The materials, the *Anderson Incomplete Stories*, devised for this research, describe parent-child, teacher-child, and child-child situations. The second project is designed to describe and assess the early expressions of spontaneity and social reactions in infants, their interaction with persons and things in the environment, and the human facilitators and restrictors of expressions of spontaneity and creativity in infants. The third project is similar to the second in purpose and plan, although wider in methodological scope. It is a study of creativity in bright elementary school children.

It is a pleasure to thank the members of The Interdisciplinary Planning Committee who worked with me in arranging the Symposia on Creativity: Milton Cantor, History; Paul J. Deutschmann, Communications Research Center; Gil Edson, Continuing Education Service; Lloyd C. Ferguson, Microbiology and Public Health, Division of Biological Science; John A. Garraty, History; Alma M. Goetsch, Art; John W. Hoffman, Engineering Experiment Station; Stanley J.

Idzerda, Honors College Program; David Krathwohl, Bureau of Educational Research; Joseph G. La Palombara, Political Science; Louis L. McQuitty, Psychology; Branford P. Millar, English; Jack J. Preiss, Sociology and Anthropology; Robert J. Rentschler, Continuing Education Service; Bruce Smith, Political Science; John C. Speck, Jr., Chemistry; and Lewis K. Zerby, Philosophy.

The Symposia on Creativity were held between the dates of April 19, 1957, and July 9, 1958. When the first symposium, conducted by Eyring, Sinnott, and Fromm, had been arranged, the Committee decided to supplement it by two panel discussions on creativity to be held the following month. Each of these meetings was addressed by three members of the faculty at Michigan State University. It is a further pleasure to acknowledge the cordial participation of these six colleagues: Robert S. Bandurski, Botany and Plant Pathology; S. Howard Bartley, Psychology; Allen Leepa, Art; Donald J. Montgomery, Physics and Astronomy; Erskine V. Morse, Microbiology and Public Health; and Lewis K. Zerby, Philosophy.

I am pleased now to acknowledge indebtedness to my wife, Gladys Lowe Anderson, who has been a colleague with me in all phases of this research.

HAROLD H. ANDERSON

September 15, 1958
East Lansing, Michigan

CREATIVITY
And Its Cultivation

I

Scientific Creativity

HENRY EYRING

EACH person is born into an environment with a language and culture that provide a more or less complete world view. He usually assumes, correctly, that his first conflicts with the notions he has learned will be resolved when he understands the accepted views better. Sooner or later, however, he comes up against glaring inconsistencies which bring his conceptual world into serious question. The necessary reconstruction is the beginning of a creative process limited only by the expertness of the innovator and the time devoted to it. This intellectual construction of a world picture is an extremely important aspect of scientific creativity.

OPERATIONAL CHARACTER OF SCIENCE

Beginning chemistry sparked one of these earliest re-evaluations for me. Professor Tartarian, an excellent teacher at the University of Arizona, nevertheless presented the chemistry of copper in a didactic fashion with little regard for the experimental evidence for his revelations. It was a matter of real satisfaction when I finally realized that copper is simply a name useful in describing a certain collection of experiments; that chemistry includes many processes not represented in the chemistry of copper; and that the experiments reported in the literature might, or might not, be reproducible. Thus science became operational, something to be tried over again if questions remained.

RECURRENCE AND THE IDEA OF VARIABLES

As soon as one gets to the point of making systematic observations the question arises as to what observations are worth recording. Clearly, any actual event is extremely complicated; if described in sufficient detail, it is unique in the history of the world and will never recur. Such a detailed view of things can help us to understand neither the future nor the past, in their nonrecurring aspects. Only those aspects of a situation which recur can give us useful insight. Thus, in science, whether or not we say it, we always mean that, in comparing two events, we examine certain special aspects of the situation which are changed while everything else that *matters* is kept the same. Thus we have forced upon our attention the idea of variables which influence events.

TIME AS A VARIABLE

Early in this process we are obliged to give a meaning to time. The conception of elapsed time resolves itself into the recognition of change. Time is measured by counting the number of recurrences of some cyclical process. The usefulness of the conception of the uniform flow of time becomes apparent as soon as it is clear that many seemingly independent cycles have durations which are in fixed proportions to each other. This correlation between the duration of isolated events is simplest to understand when we consider identical systems. Thus, either of two ammonia molecules invert 2.39×10^{10} times per second, as can be shown by microwaves, because they are identical and there is no reason for them to behave differently. This orderly periodicity of an almost endless variety of events is a verifiable and exciting fact of nature. We might, with Newton, think of a uniform flow of absolute time in which all these events are taking place, or we might think that there is a correlation between durations because one periodicity is in fact determined by all the others. The theory of relativity forces the latter conclusion, since it states that relative velocity of two systems shifts one frequency with respect to the other. As always, however, this result arises from a conscious choice of theoretical construct. One has elected to treat the velocity of light as the same in the resting and in the moving system, and let the moving clocks and moving meter sticks change their values in the appropriate way for this to happen.

POSITIONAL COORDINATES

The Foucault pendulum with its bob at the end of a long wire vibrates on a near-frictionless support and oscillates in its fixed plane in space as the earth turns under it. With the disappearance of the ether and Newton's absolute space, cosmologists are faced with the problem of what determines the inertial coordinates for the pendulum. Again one adopts the view which is consistent with relativity that the coordinate system for one body is determined by the rest of the bodies in space. It is interesting that the laws of Newtonian mechanics, relativity, and quantum and statistical mechanics are relations between these space and time coordinates, together with such derived properties as energy and momentum.

SOME FACTORS IN DISCOVERY

Newton could arrive at his law that, in the absence of such things as viscous resistance, the mass of a body times its rate of change in velocity is equal to the force acting on it only by ignoring Aristotle's incorrect notion that force is always required to keep a body moving at a constant velocity. Newton's task was made more difficult because in certain circumstances Aristotle's law is actually true. For example, force is required to propel a body at constant velocity through a viscous medium. This is illustrative of the enormous complexity of natural phenomena. Creativity is rarely a single flash of intuition; it usually requires sustained analysis of a great many observations to separate out the significant factors from the adventitious. A keen observer once said of Einstein that part of his genius was his inability to understand the obvious. Rejection of superficial explanations of one's own as well as of others is prerequisite to understanding. To reach a correct solution efficiently also requires unconcern for all except the truth. Science practiced to bolster a faulty hypothesis rather than to test it objectively is often worse than useless.

SOME CHARACTERISTICS OF THE EFFECTIVE INNOVATOR

Undoubtedly the prospective scientist should arrange to be born with the right genes. Anyone who has examined the variations to be found among individuals with ostensibly equivalent training cannot escape this conclusion. Even the gifted individual, however, requires a stimulating environment, including freedom from distractions which deflect attention from the question at issue, and freedom from an authoritarian society which prevents unbiased inquiry. He profits likewise from congenial surroundings and stimulating company. He should preferably be completely at peace with the world except for the violent conflicts characterizing the problem engaging his attention. Thus he needs to be independent of all types of vicious circles which deflect attention from the problem at hand. The lone wolf has solved many problems, but an increasing number of scientific enterprises are becoming highly cooperative and require social integration. No degree of talent can compensate for an impossible personality inside the large scientific laboratories which are doing an ever increasing proportion of the creative work of the world.

THE CREATIVE PROCESS

No serious investigator need ever be without a suitable problem appropriate to his talents. Thus every field either (1) is well understood, in which case a book can be written about it, (2) consists of uncorrelated experimental and theoretical material suitable for a review article, (3) contains certain experiments in need of theoretical explanation, or (4) needs critical experiments in order to settle knotty questions. Only lack of interest or of time or an overwhelming ineptitude deters the prospective investigator from the creative process. Usually the excuses given for failure betray an amazing inventive talent and a vivid imagination. Such brilliant efforts are worthy of better causes. On the other hand, a genuine tragedy is presented by the brilliant mind with a critical faculty so far outrunning creative imagination that the unhappy possessor is forever condemned to bitter sterility. How often such cases are really incurable and how often cooperation, encouragement, and the elimination of the effects of hypercritical companions can work a cure is a question of the greatest importance.

Creativity is manifested at many levels and takes a variety of forms. An exciting variety is the recognition of analogies. Thus a fruitful new field was born when Van't Hoff, long ago, recognized that large molecules confined to one side of a membrane by their inability to permeate it nevertheless sucked the solvent through from the other side because of the tendency of the large molecules to expand the space available to them, just as a confined gas would do. As a result, the laws of gases were taken over intact and applied to interpret osmotic pressure. The faculty for recognizing such an analogy resembles the ability to recognize a recurrent musical theme running, with variations, through a composition. After the variations are stripped away the recurring pattern is recognized for what it is.

Still another such example is the recognition of the thermodynamic equivalence of a molecular-sized hole in a liquid to a molecule in the gas phase. Thus it costs the same amount of energy to vaporize a molecule as it does to create a molecular-sized hole in the liquid. Furthermore, holes in the liquid and molecules in the gas dart around with the same speed and abandon so that each possesses the same entropy. It follows from thermodynamics that two such species with the same energy and the same entropy will be equally abundant. Thus we can say that in a cubic centimeter of the vapor there are just as many molecules as there are molecular-sized holes in the liquid. Thus the sum of the densities should be a constant and we have a deep insight into the famous law of rectilinear diameters of Cailletet and Mathias. Because holes smaller than molecular size also accumulate in the liquid, the sum of the densities of gas and liquid actually decrease slightly with temperature in a linear fashion. This picture of holes in liquids led me not only to the above explanation but also to a detailed theory of the liquid state, including both thermodynamic properties and molecular transport. Similar considerations involving this concept of duality between particles and holes pervade a great deal of particle physics. The idea of duality between points and lines is an extremely fruitful analogous concept in mathematics.

Idea-Generating Concepts and Intuition

From time to time exciting new principles are required to explain experimental facts. Not infrequently the concepts have been guessed at for ages, but until the proof of their correctness is available such guesses can only be suggestive and are often ignored. A famous example is the insistence of Democritus and Lucretius that matter is composed of discrete particles. The peculiar shapes of the particles were supposed to account for differences in properties of the different substances. More than a millennium later, evidence had finally accumulated that elements combined in definite proportions and that, when the same elements formed a second compound, the ratios of the amounts of the elements were in simple multiples of those found in the first compound. Dalton marshaled the evidence and was able to show convincingly that this evidence required the conception that the elements are formed of discrete particles—atoms—which are combined in various proportions to form a variety of compounds. Which was the discovery—the intelligent guess of the principle or its proof? Here the answer is unmistakable. The inspired guess bore no fruit through the centuries, whereas the principle, once proved, was immediately fruitful. A characteristic feature of a good proof is that it can be repeated and understood. People who have been right in a scientific matter and yet have been generally ignored by other competent scientists usually lacked sufficient proof.

It is interesting to consider what qualifications make for scientific intuition. The familiar story of the race horse that was lost is instructive. The lost horse was sought for all day by the entire town, unsuccessfully. On the second day the village fool went out and in an hour returned with the horse. In response to inquiry as to his procedure, he explained that the first day he sat and thought what he would do were he a horse. On the second day he went to the point where he himself would have gone. The horse was there.

Another example of an idea-generating concept may be instructive. The activated complex in the theory of chemical reactions is an example of such an idea-generating concept. The atoms in molecules are held together by chemical bonds. These bonds consist of two electrons shuttling back and forth between a pair of atoms, much as two baseballs might be kept in the air by passing them between two players. Mesons hold nucleons together in the nucleus in an analogous manner. This shuttling back and forth of the electrons lowers the electronic kinetic energy with no corresponding rise in potential energy. The lowering of kinetic energy arises because the lower electronic path constitutes an increase in wavelength and hence a decrease in frequency, and therefore of energy. A chemical reaction between two pairs of bonded atoms occurs when they crash into each other with such great force as to forget to whom they belong; subsequently they separate and combine with new partners. Concurrently, the electrons alter their path to circulate about the new partners. The crowding together of the two pairs of bonded atoms in the activated complex results in one electron pair being pushed into a higher energy state. The high-energy electron pair, as a result of this promotion in status, avoids running into the other electron pair which completely preëmpts the lowest state of the four-atom system. This general result that one pair of electrons having opposite spins fills up a state is known as the Pauli principle.

The metastable, intermediate state between reactants and products, as was indicated, is called the activated complex. A clear visual picture of the activated complex requires an understanding of the potential energy surface in configuration space. A sufficient number of the interatomic distances of the complex to fix its configuration are plotted. These distances are taken normal to each other and to the energy coordinate of the system in hyperspace. Such a plot yields a potential energy surface in configuration space. The resulting surface has the features of an ordinary landscape, with the low valleys corresponding to stable chemical compounds. These valleys are connected by passes through which the reactants pass into the new valley-forming reaction products. The activated complex is much like an ordinary molecule except for the internal translational degree of freedom corresponding to the passage over the potential barrier in configuration space. Transit across the barrier is so fast that the activated complex survives only a kinetic jiffy (10^{-13} seconds at ordinary temperatures). As a result, its properties must be deduced from quantum mechanics or from reaction rate data. Its fleeting existence precludes direct measurement. With this conception of the activated complex, reaction kinetics is finally systematized to the same extent that equilibrium theory is systematized by thermodynamics.

The velocity of any reaction at unit concentration of reactants takes the form $k' = \kappa \frac{kT}{h} K^{\pm}$, where $K^{\pm}$, like any equilibrium constant, fixes the concentration of activated complexes, $\frac{kT}{h}$ gives their rate of decay, and κ is the fraction decomposing which do not immediately reconstitute themselves. This rather technical theory is outlined here because it is the point of departure for understanding all chemical changes and is also an example of creativity falling within the author's experience.

It is perhaps instructive to detail the genesis of the activated complex concept as I recall it. Fritz London in 1928 suggested an approximate way of constructing potential surfaces in configuration space using the quantum mechanics. In the spring of 1930, following a modified procedure, I laboriously constructed such a surface for the reaction of a hydrogen atom with a hydrogen molecule, in collaboration with Professor Polanyi. It occurred to me that, if the potential surface for three atoms colliding along a line were constructed to scale, a ball rolled on this model surface would mimic the behavior of the three-atom system. The next time I met with Professor Polanyi at his home in Zehlendorff, Dr. Wigner was there, and I spoke of this concept. Dr. Wigner said, "That is a beautiful idea." He proceeded to sharpen this concept in an addendum to a paper by Polanyi and me, and, in 1933, with Pelzer, he extended his ideas into a statistical mechanical calculation of the rate of the hydrogen reaction, using the potential surface Polanyi and I had calculated. In 1935, after much labor, I gave the generalized version of reaction rates, introducing the idea that the activated complex is like an ordinary molecule, except for a fourth translational degree of freedom. Polanyi and Evans followed this with a lucid treatment emphasizing pressure effects.

Several points are interesting in this bit of history. First, had there been some easy way to calculate potential energy surfaces, I would probably not have labored over them to the point where the concept of a ball rolling through the saddle point was hammered into my consciousness. Secondly, although the potential surfaces one can construct are very rough, and the purist suffers when he uses them, still they provided the bridge one must use to cross over into the field of general reaction rate theory. When quantum mechanical methods yield better surfaces, this progress will eventuate in a refinement rather than in any major change in our concepts of reaction rates.

This experience highlights certain conclusions. First, the innovator must usually find his way by means of unfinished bridges. Also, in science as elsewhere, the blazed trail precedes the broad highway. Finally, the development of the theory of absolute reaction rates illustrates another fact observed many times before. One's successes are always related to and built upon the findings of others. Creativity in science, as with most human enterprises, prospers most in a friendly atmosphere of cooperation.

THE CREATIVE ENVIRONMENT

It seems clear that difficulties never stopped really interested investigators from doing research. There is always a way. My own experience at the Universities of Arizona, California, Wisconsin, Princeton, and Utah and at the Kaiser-Wilhelm Institute in Berlin served to confirm this belief. Comparing the various backgrounds that encouraged such creativity, I recall how, at Arizona, Ernest Anderson worked early and late singing hymns and extracting the various sugars from the gums of all kinds of desert plants, while Professor Douglas intrigued the world with his tree ring dating. Later, at Berkeley, in G. N. Lewis's laboratory, there was no place for scientific onlookers. Everyone did research and comparatively little teaching. My only formal course in chemistry for the Ph.D. degree was thermodynamics. This was in spite of the fact that my earlier training was in mining engineering and metallurgy rather than chemistry. The preliminary examinations were perfunctory, but the minor in mathematics involved taking a substantial amount of class work. In spite of a belief in light teaching loads for professors, it was recognized by Lewis that freshmen at the beginning of their careers respond to expert teaching. This teaching was provided through the general chemistry lectures given by Joel H. Hildebrand. In addition, every professor was expected to teach one laboratory section of freshman chemistry. In this way, even the freshmen were thrown into the company of accomplished scientific investigators. The results on the students were interesting to watch. Some students certainly elected chemistry as their life's work who would otherwise have passed it by.

The stream of outstanding physical chemists turned out by the G. N. Lewis school at Berkeley includes three Nobel prize winners. The success at Berkeley has frequently been cited as establishing the superiority of a system in which the entire emphasis was on research to the exclusion of course work. This too-facile explanation leaves out of account the significant fact that Lewis's fame and the high quality of his staff attracted a substantial fraction of the best talent available. With such a student personnel, most systems would have succeeded. The fact remains, however, that at Berkeley graduate students mingled with outstanding scientists who entertained no doubt that intelligent research was the most important activity in the world. This contagion infected everyone. Individual success in research was accompanied by a shedding of any undue veneration for the embalmed science of the past. Seminars led by Lewis were always exciting, even when the blackboard could be seen but dimly through the blue haze of tobacco smoke exhaled by the addicts.

Another point was significant. The new graduate student was given keys to all the stockrooms. This was in fact a presentation of the "keys to the city." With this handsome gesture went a few words on acceptable conduct. So far as I remember, people responded to this generosity admirably. The chemistry department at Berkeley was, in fact, a society of scholars. Successful research was the badge of honor. To not attempt research was unthinkable. The research atmosphere provided at Berkeley has probably rarely been equaled. Granting this, I, nonetheless, would have added a few more courses and made the preliminary examinations more searching.

Wisconsin in 1927 was good, but different. It was much more decentralized. Daniels and Adkins, among others, were nuclei around whom good men gathered. Courses were more numerous and preliminary examinations harder. The research fund provided by Steenbock's patents on food irradiation paid for research fellowships and equipment. In its best fields Madison rivaled Berkeley.

Geheimrat Haber's Institute in the Kaiser Wilhelm Institute of 1929 also sparkled. Haber's poor health did not prevent his making incisive comments, and he surrounded himself with such top European scientists as Freundlich, Polanyi, Bonhoeffer, Fritz London, and Eugene Wigner. The facilities were good and the personnel the best. Again there were freedom, encouragement, and good library facilities. Chemical research at Dahlem was high adventure.

A stimulating year in Berkeley, 1930 to 1931, was followed by fifteen years at Princeton. Here one saw again an exciting research center not quite like anything that had gone before. A quota system restricted graduate students in chemistry to twenty-five. This could be stretched to thirty students. An excellent supply system provided everything needed to work with by signing it out. Seminars were frequent and lively. H. S. Taylor was particularly effective in focusing discussions on the essential point in any scientific discussion, and everyone entered freely into the discussions. More course work was required than at Berkeley, and Ph.D. preliminary examinations were more searching.

The graduate students again were excellent, since only about ten could be accepted from a hundred very good applicants. Here again, everything that would stimulate the creative process was used.

The last eleven years at Utah have been concerned with setting up a Ph.D. program and watching it grow. Because the foundation had been well laid earlier, this has been a pleasant, successful operation. Our program more nearly approximates that at Princeton than the one I knew at Berkeley. About fifty Ph.D. candidates in chemistry work as teaching fellows, as research fellows, or on various supported projects. Again, the creative atmosphere aimed at is one of friendly, active cooperation.

The Future Outlook for Creative Investigation

Chemical investigation in this country has been stimulated tremendously by the money invested in research by government agencies and by the high income tax laws which prompt industry to strengthen their position by plowing back into research some of the profits that would otherwise be partly taxed away anyway. Our present tremendous research effort should, in the best interests of society, be doubled; nonetheless, we are witnessing out of it a material advancement never even imagined before. Even to madmen it must be clear that worldwide cooperation in creative research can solve all our economic woes and that following any other course will lead the world to destruction and unimaginable human misery. To be optimistic of continuing success in the current tremendous creative effort requires only the faith that mankind is not insane. With the unlocking of atomic secrets man has acquired the capacity to make the world uninhabitable. Society cannot now allow power over atomic forces to fall into the hands of any single individual, since in that case human existence will hinge on the slender thread of one man's sanity. Genuine democracy with its checks and balances has an urgency about it in these days of mortal peril which never existed before. Society will succeed in continuing its creative advance because the alternative to this is irreversible disaster to everyone.

2

The Creativeness of Life

EDMUND W. SINNOTT

ALFRED NORTH WHITEHEAD once remarked that the psychical is the creative advance into novelty. Ralph Lillie (1945) went still further. "Inertia," said he, "is primarily a physical property, a correlate of the conservation which is a recognized character of the physical as physical. In contrast, the psychical, being a factor of novelty, is the *anticonservative* property in nature." In other words, mind is the source of creativity.

The creativeness with which we are here concerned goes back to that memorable time when evolutionary change shifted from a biological to a cultural basis as man's mind reached the point where memory, reason, and imagination made possible the accumulation of experience and the exploration of the truly new. The progress which resulted was far more rapid than mere biological advancement had ever been, for it did not have to be built into the genetic constitution of our race. It resulted in the radical changes—almost explosively rapid in terms of geological time—which have marked man's history ever since and which we like to call the progress of civilization. Such creative change, however, results in gains which may be only temporary, since acquirements of this sort are not inherited. In our pride of accomplishment we should remember that we are removed from barbarism by only a single generation. The results of our progress must therefore be recreated in every individual during his own life. Although each generation has to start afresh, it has the great advantage that it can, if it will, begin a new creative advance unhampered by the follies and prejudices of the past.

In what way, we may ask, does such a creative advance arise? Whence comes a new idea? How is the fabric of custom and habit so rent that something emerges which we have never known before? I should like to suggest that this problem involves not only the origin and nature of mind but something deeper still—the character of life itself. It is *life* which is anticonservative, original, creative. The basis of our problem lies not so much, I think, in psychology or philosophy as in biology. Let us consider what evidence there may be for this conclusion.

The great lesson to be learned from evolution is the continual emergence of new kinds of organisms. That man has arisen from the beasts is surely important to know, and that all living things are related to one another by virtue of a common ancestry; but the distinctive feature of the evolutionary process is that it brings forth biological novelties—new forms, types, and patterns hitherto unknown on earth and (still more important) holding promise of greater changes yet to come. Organic evolution is as truly a *creative* process as the one described in the first chapter of *Genesis* and the seventh book of *Paradise Lost*. From the simple forms of life in the primordial seas long before Cambrian time to the extraordinary richness and variety that it reached in the preglacial world, there was a magnificent progression, reaching one climax after another; a vast diversity of living things, even the fragmentary fossil remains of which fill us with wonder at the teeming fecundity and originality of life.

Compared to this creativeness of life, the history of the inorganic world seems sterile and monotonous. So far as we can determine, the chemical elements in the stars are like those here on earth. Some evolutionary progression there must have been among them, from helium to uranium. Whether this was gradual or whether it all happened in a stupendous explosion in the first half hour of time, as Gamow would have us believe, no one can be sure. At best only some ninety-two elemental forms of matter exist, surely a slight enough diversity compared to the wealth of differences in living things. Molecular variety is somewhat greater, but the complexity of inorganic chemistry is far less than that of organic.

The physical state of the planets has also doubtless changed somewhat, and in our solar system they show specific differences which may well be still more numerous in the planets related to other stars than ours. The stars themselves pass through a cycle of change from youth to old age. Even among the galaxies there is some diversity.

In general, however, the lifeless universe seems to have kept on doing the same sort of things age after age, making atoms, molecules, worlds, stars, and galaxies without number. Cosmogonists have little evidence that, aside from its constant expansion, the universe is changing very much. One major act of creation may still be taking place if the simplest sort of matter is continually being produced from nothing, as some maintain, but this would also seem to be a monotonous process. Sunsets and rainbows are not new on this old earth, but life is.

How, in the midst of this inorganic sameness, life began, we do not know. By chance collisions, molecules of greater size and complexity may have appeared until at last one of them developed the means for incorporating into itself the substance of another and thus learned to eat. Such a molecule and its descendants may have been the first of living creatures. A large molecule that much resembles a virus particle has already been synthesized. At least the protagonists of "spontaneous generation," a subject in disrepute since Pasteur's day, again are active, though the origin of life is still far from explained.

Whatever its source may have been, life is based on chemical substances which are rather easily broken down and rearranged. This instability, channeled in certain directions by nature's selective action, is the source of that variability and creativeness by which life differs from lifelessness and which makes possible evolutionary change.

But it is not this sort of creativeness with which the present discussion is chiefly concerned. We are interested here not so much in the genesis of new organisms as in the genesis of new ideas; not in organic evolution but in creative imagination. Surely, it may be argued, these are very different things, since one is in the realm of the physical and the other of the psychical. I should like to suggest that these two realms may be much closer together than is commonly believed. There is a basic similarity between them which indicates that they are really two manifestations of the same phenomenon—life itself. If this can be established, the problem of creativeness at every level may be studied as a biological one, in the widest sense, and against a much broader background than that provided by psychology or philosophy alone.

LIFE IS ORGANIZATION

The similarity between the mental and the physical goes back to the essential quality of life. This does not inhere, it seems to me, in any particular substance or combination of substances, or in any specific trait such as growth or reproduction or irritability. It is to be seen, instead, in the regulatory and organizing quality all living things display which results in their essentially purposive character, both in development and behavior. Living things are *organisms*. An organism is, first of all, an organized system of structures and activities. It is not a sprawling mass of semi-independent parts and processes but is held together under a coordinating control. This system is far more significant than the materials of which it is composed.

Such an organized system may be seen at various levels, beginning even in an individual cell. A typical plant cell, for example, has a cellulose wall, a large central vacuole full of water with a few substances dissolved in it, and a layer of what is commonly regarded as "living" protoplasm. Ninety per cent of the latter is water, however, and the rest is made up chiefly of protein molecules. None of these components, outside the cell, possess a vital spark. Life comes from the relationships between them.

The organism itself is far larger and more complex than this, but it is the same sort of organized system. Food enters it and is built into it, each bit incorporated into a particular structure and occupying a precise position in the whole. As tissues wear out, matter leaves the organism again. Studies with atoms "tagged" by isotopes have demonstrated this continual "turnover." It does not change the living system, however, for by a series of regulatory processes the organism maintains itself.

LIFE IS A SELF-REGULATING PROCESS

The same tendency to maintain a norm is to be seen in physiological activities, where various sorts of processes are kept at a steady state in what is now familiarly known as homeostasis. Each keeps in balance with the rest. Regulations in bodily structure and in physiological function are hard to distinguish from each other. Both are under protoplasmic control, and it seems reasonable to regard both as manifestations of the organizing and regulatory character of living systems.

Use of the word homeostasis to describe such biological activities is, however, somewhat misleading, since it suggests that the maintenance of a constant or static condition is the essential quality of an organism. Actually, the norms of these organized systems are continually changing, and a living thing is constantly *developing*. New qualities emerge in it. This process is most conspicuous in its early stages and slows down at maturity; but every organism has a life cycle beginning with the fertilized egg, reaching its climax with reproductive maturity, and then passing through later stages to old age and death.

Development is not an aimless affair; each stage follows precisely its predecessor. The science of embryology is the study of this regular progression. If one examines an organism, particularly a dead specimen, its appearance is of something complete and static. Actually, however, a living thing may well be called a slice of space-time, for it is continually changing and unfolding. Nevertheless, through all this alteration it maintains its own particular identity, its own organized unity. Each organism has its particular series of norms, its special cycle of progressive and creative development. Continual change is the keynote of this cycle; not unguided change but change that moves toward a very definite end—the mature individual and the completion of the cycle. The characters of the organism are inherited ones, to be sure, determined by particular genes in the constitution of the individual, but what is inherited is not single traits but a series of developmental steps by which definite goals are reached.

This conclusion is further emphasized by facts revealed through the experimental study of embryology. The normal course of development toward a particular end can be blocked and altered in various ways, as by removing certain parts of the growing system, placing it under abnormal situations, or even disorganizing it completely. Under these conditions the organism shows a persistent tendency to restore lost parts, reorganize itself, and achieve the end it would have reached if unimpeded.

The literature of experimental embryology is full of examples of this self-regulation. Everyone has seen how the growing shoot-tip from a plant, cut off and put into water or moist sand, will regenerate its lost root system. Not only will isolated bits of stem do this but often leaf stalks, flower stalks, or bits of the leaf blade. Many cases have been found where an entire plant will grow from a single cell, and presumably every cell has the power to do this if proper conditions could be provided. As long as these structures are parts of a living system, each will perform its particular and proper function in that system, but if it becomes separated it tends to recreate another whole.

Various organs of animals, if removed, will be restored—crab claws, appendages of amphibian larvae, tails of worms, eyes of snails, and many others. In very early stages the embryo may be cut in two and each part will then grow into a whole animal instead of half of one. One of the most dramatic cases of regeneration has been found in certain sponges, where the whole body may be completely broken down into its constituent cells by being gently squeezed through a fine-meshed piece of cloth. These cells, if they have access to each other, will before long begin to fuse into small and then into larger groups, and finally will organize themselves again into the body of a sponge.

Not all plants and animals can restore missing parts and reorganize new wholes, and this power is best shown in early developmental stages. Increasing differentiation results in gradual loss of regenerative potency, especially in animals. This capacity is so widespread, however, that it seems clear that something representing the whole organism, specific in its character, is present in every cell of the body and ready, should occasion require and favorable conditions occur, to proceed in its own cycle of creative change and form a new, organized whole again.

This tendency in every living system to integrate its materials and processes in conformity with a norm which it persistently seeks to reach emphasizes the essentially teleological character of development and function. The unity of the organism seems to inhere in the end toward which it is moving rather than in any fixed course for reaching that end, for the end may be gained not in any single linear progression but in a variety of ways. This quality was termed by Driesch (1929) equifinality.

The interesting fact from the point of view of our discussion is that no sharp distinction can easily be drawn between the regulation to organized ends shown in embryological development and physiological processes on the one hand and in instinctive behavior on the other. All of these are activities of protoplasm, the first building matter into a growing system, the second controlling its activity within the system, and the third moving the system as a whole in the process of behavior. Instinct shows the same equifinality as does embryology, since, although the conditions under which an instinctive act is performed are almost always different, the objective of the act is nevertheless attained—the building of a nest, the seizure of prey, or the escape from danger. The end to be gained and not the precise steps toward it dominates the organized pattern of behavior.

A comparison has often been made between this biological goal-seeking and the purposiveness which in man we recognize as a character of mind, a psychical process. Though there is no time for it here, a strong argument can be made, I believe, for the conclusion that mind itself is *that which directs behavior in conformity to ends set up in the organism*, especially in the brain. More than simple reflex action is here involved. A given stimulus does not lead invariably to the same response, for the response will be such as will tend to achieve the particular pattern or norm established in the living system at the time.

This conclusion that mind is an aspect of biological goal-seeking maintains that all ideas originate as purposes, as aspects of a normative behavioral pattern. Primitively, every purpose leads to a *bodily* act. Where this is inhibited for any reason the purpose remains but is transformed to a desire or some other sort of *mental* act, culminating in the higher sorts of mental phenomena. These acts are not isolated events but are related as parts of a mental pattern that suggests the physical pattern of embryology.

Such a conception puts "mind," of a sort, into all animals and even into plants, and makes it coextensive with life. It regards life as teleological in character—not the naïve and false anthropomorphic sort of teleology sometimes evident, unfortunately, in biological teaching, but teleology which emphasizes the normative, self-regulatory quality of life as an organizing force. It looks on motivation as the result rather of pulls toward goals than of pushes and drives. Space is lacking here to develop this idea more fully and to answer objections to it, but a strong case for it can be presented.

CREATIVITY AS A QUALITY OF MIND

After this more general biological excursion, we are now ready to return to the problem of creativeness as a quality of mind. Creativeness is related, presumably, to the richness and variety of mental life. If biological goals are the basis of mind, however, they evidently must be far more diverse than those which govern the single-track goal-seeking of embryology. The complexity of mental life is so great that one may have difficulty in accepting the idea that mental activity, the stream of constantly changing thoughts and images, is a manifestation of the same sort of normative behavior evident in the more slowly paced activities of the body in its development and functioning. We may agree that mind is creative, but what creativeness can there be in these general processes of biology save the slow genetic changes in evolution? The fecund creativeness of man's mind seems so unlike this as to constitute a completely different order of things.

CREATIVITY AS RESPONSE TO ENVIRONMENT

This objection, though obvious and important, can be answered. The life of the mind, like all life, certainly has its basis in the genetic constitution of the individual, but its changes are not dependent on genetic change. Rather are they the result of the enormously varied responses of a given genetic constitution to environmental differences. We must remember that much of the variety of all organic life is due to environmental variety. What a given hereditary factor determines —and this is too often overlooked—is not a particular characteristic of body or function or behavior, but a particular response to a particular environment. A specific genetic constitution determines not a single trait but a repertoire of reactions to a wide series of possible environmental stimuli. In each environment the norm or goal may be different.

A certain type of primrose, for example, produces red flowers if grown at low temperatures, but white ones at higher ones. Its flower color is certainly an hereditary trait, but what is inherited is not a particular color but a particular norm of reactivity to temperature by the pigmentation process in its flowers. The pattern expressed in the shape and veining of the wing in the vinegar fly, *Drosophila*, is inherited, but flies of the same genetic constitution may produce wings of markedly different character if they spend their pupal life under different temperatures. Each is as "normal" as the other, but the norm of development is different in every case. Many examples of this variety of response to temperature and to many other sorts of environmental factors have been found.

Bodily traits in general, however, are relatively constant under a wide range of environments. Behavioral characteristics, on the other hand, although certainly possessing an hereditary basis, are far more plastic and variable in their response. The norms to which behavior conforms are not nearly as rigid as bodily ones and may be radically changed by factors in the outer or the inner environment. An animal fully fed will respond very differently to the sight of food from one that is hungry. Its behavioral goals in these two states are quite unlike. A bird in which certain glandular secretions have reached a given level will start to migrate and its urgency in seeking this instinctive goal may be so strong as to overcome all other instincts.

Where its inner state is constant its outer environment may be changing and this also modifies the pattern of behavior which the organism seeks to attain. In von Frisch's (1939, 1950) fascinating story of the language of the bees, for example, the author shows how a single bee, by communicating information to his colleagues, may modify their behavior. If he has discovered a rich supply of nectar of a particular kind he returns to the hive. The other bees can tell by odor the flowers from which he has come, and by a specific series of motions he also tells them not only in what direction the treasure lies but how far away it is. The bees rush out to find it and soon begin to bring the nectar home. The behavior pattern of each has been set up in its nervous system for that day by a stimulus from the discoverer bee. Tomorrow the goal may be a different one, and the next day different still. Above these temporary goals is the transcendent one of finding nectar and bringing it back to be stored up within the hive. Below them, in turn, are those briefer ones which draw the bee from flower to flower in response to its sensations of smell and sight. In each bee there is an end, enduring or temporary, to which the pattern of its behavior conforms.

This hierarchy of goals is subject to continual modification by inner and outer factors. As a result, the psychological life, so to speak, of this little animal, far from being a fixed and sterotyped one, shows a considerable degree of diversity. This diversity originates not simply in the variety of stimuli it receives from its environment but also in the continual changes which these bring about in its organized pattern of behavior.

Among mammals, mental life is much more complex, for memory and learning have emerged and become important parts of it. Mental patterns here are still more plastic and may be greatly modified by experience and learning. A hungry fox trotting through the woods comes on the trail of a rabbit. His continuing goal, to satisfy his hunger, now is sharpened to the more specific one of catching this particular rabbit. His behavior is largely instinctive, but if he is a wise fox experience has improved his skill in hunting. His memories of the thicket where a hound once almost seized him or of the bar-way where a hunter shot at him or of the point on the path where a trap once caught his mate all modify the way in which he seeks to realize the end of catching the rabbit and having him for dinner. The fox probably has no stream of conscious ideas in these matters, but his memory of former experiences modifies his behavior and enriches and complicates its pattern. His major goal of satisfying his hunger may change as the season comes to seek a mate or to pursue game for his cubs instead of for himself, and these changes further enlarge the pattern of his goal-seeking.

THE HIGHER LEVELS OF CREATIVITY IN MAN

Man has emerged into a much higher behavioral level than any other animal can reach. His memory is far more extensive. By this means and the invention of speech and written symbols he is able to use the accumulated experience of the past. Most of his goals are now fulfilled not by bodily actions but by mental ones. To gain knowledge is now one of his great ends. By seeking relationships between facts, he learns to recognize general uniformities and to relate particulars to them, thus acquiring ability to reason. He can prove that Socrates, being a man, must be mortal since all men are so. Thus he has come to deal in abstractions.

His inner environment is vastly richer than that of a beast, and, as society develops, his outer environment becomes far more complex also. All these diversities, like the far simpler environmental changes at the embryological and instinctive levels, modify the goals that are set up within his living system. The interpretation of mental life, how-ever rich and complex, as the seeking of a wide variety of changing goals in the organized pattern is therefore a defensible one. Conscious-ness, so often involved with the concept of mind, is a problem by it-self which need not, I think, concern us here. Conscious purpose, desire, thought, is the *subjective experience* of behavioral goals set up in the living system to which our actions continually seek to conform.

IMAGINATION

But there is one important element that must be added to this con-cept of the human mind, particularly as we consider its creativeness. The multiplication of man's behavioral goals and the increased com-plexity of his psychological patterns have enriched his mental life, but something else has been acquired during his upward progress. Gaining the power to accumulate experience and to reason was not enough to make him truly man. Another quality was necessary—the great gift of *imagination*. This is perhaps man's most distinctive trait, for it makes possible his creativeness. Here at last, we finally come more closely to grips with the theme of this study.

To achieve his goals, to satisfy the pattern of the desires that arise in him from the interaction between his wide genetic capacity and the increasing complications of his environment would not have been enough to account for the tremendous acceleration in man's progress since he became man. Frequently, human advancement has been stalled because something essential for its further development was missing. Sooner or later there was born in someone's mind a new idea which supplied the necessary element. Hence must have come the use of fire, communication by written symbols, the invention of the wheel and the bow, domestication of animals, and many more. These doubt-less had no sudden origin but were the products of many minds; but they were all novelties that could not have appeared unless there had been someone who could *imagine* a situation never yet experienced, who could picture in his mind something he had not seen.

THE PROCESS OF CREATIVITY

The problem of creativeness comes down at last to that of how these new ideas have their origin. Much thought has been given to this matter by psychologists and other students of the creative process.

Two major methods appear to be operative. One is primarily deductive—creativeness by direct frontal assault. It consists in marshaling the widest possible array of facts and ideas and then carefully searching for heretofore unrecognized relationships between them. This seems to be the method used by Edison, for example, in making his inventions, and by Einstein in the development of his theoretical ideas. But we can be sure that this is not the way in which at least the first steps in creativity, in either science or the arts, have generally been taken.

It is much more common for a new idea to arise almost spontaneously in the mind, often seemingly out of nothing and at a time when a person may be thinking of something quite different. A famous instance is the way in which one of Henri Poincaré's (1913) insights into mathematics came to him. He had been struggling for days with the problem of functions, to no conclusion. One night after drinking black coffee and being unable to sleep, ideas rose in his mind, he says, in crowds, colliding, sometimes interlocking, and finally making some stable combinations from which he discovered the existence of the Fuchsian functions. Shortly afterward, while on a geological excursion and with no thoughts of mathematics in his head, as he put his foot on the step of an omnibus the idea flashed into his mind that the transformations he had used were identical with those of non-Euclidean geometry, a profound insight.

Another notable example often cited of the solution of a scientific problem without conscious effort is Otto Loewi's proof of the chemical mediation of nerve impulses. This came to him vividly in a dream, but on awaking he could not remember the details of it! The next night, fortunately, the dream was repeated. This time, before going to sleep again he recorded it fully and in the laboratory the next day performed the critical experiment that proved the truth of the solution thus given him.

Lovers of A. E. Housman (1933) have read his essay on *The Name and Nature of Poetry* in which he describes how his verses often arose in his mind. "As I went along," says he, "thinking of nothing in particular, only looking at things around me and following the progress of the seasons, there would flow into my mind, with sudden and unaccountable emotion, sometimes a line or two of verse, sometimes a whole stanza at once, accompanied, not preceded, by a vague notion of the poem which they were destined to form part of. Then there would usually be a lull of an hour or so, then perhaps the spring would bubble up again."

Many poets have experiences such as these. Robert Frost told a friend of mine about one of his. One winter evening the poet had opened his front door and strode out into the snowy darkness for a breath of air when there came into his mind the whole of that lovely poem "Stopping by Woods on a Snowy Evening." The strange pattern of rhymes continued in his mind through the verses as he wrote them down, and to bring the poem to a close he had to break the rhythm in the final quatrain.

Many other cases such as these are described in Ghiselin's (1952) book, *The Creative Process*, in Hutchinson's (1949) *How to Think Creatively*, and in other places. This sort of creativity is not common, but it is certainly far from rare. It has been found among all sorts of men and women who are faced with the need—sometimes the consuming, passionate desire—to gain a new insight into truth or beauty, to solve a problem in science, to bring to life a painting out of pigment, oil, and canvas, or to set a poem down in words.

Such inspirations, it is well recognized, rarely come unless an individual has immersed himself in a subject. He must have a rich background of knowledge and experience in it. In science, he must be laboring to find the answer to a problem or to bring a mass of apparently unrelated facts in his mind into a unity; in art, he must be dreaming and pondering about a painting or a piece of music which he feels is there but cannot quite be brought into existence; in poetry, he has an intense preoccupation with something beautiful but still vague which he is trying eagerly to express. He is wrestling to bring into actuality these cloudy, half-formed products of his imagination. Often along the way he will jot down notes or sketches or snatches of music or single lines of verse or a half-written story, steps toward the completion of his still inchoate theme. Then, in a time of relaxation or when something else is actively occupying his mind, the answer which he seeks, or at least the creative nub of it, will come sauntering into his mind as if spontaneously.

Sometimes, as we have seen, the whole answer to a scientific problem may thus appear, or the outline for an entire story, or a substantial bit of verse; but more commonly the initial inspiration is only the start and must be followed by long hours or days of labor in revising and reorganizing and completing the original flash of insight. Nevertheless, without this flash the creative process might never have been able to get started.

THE UNCONSCIOUS

What relation can there be, we now may ask, between the organizing, regulatory, goal-seeking processes in which we have sought the origin of mind and these creative activities which are man's particular glory? Evidently such creative imagination is especially active at the mind's unconscious level. Here mental work is being done. Here, quite without conscious participation, choices are being made and ideas fitted together into patterns. ̄

Psychology has little to tell us yet of what is happening here. In dreams and half-dreaming states the mind is filled with a throng of images and fantasies. The whole unconscious presumably is occupied with such, their source lying in memory and the experiences of the past and perhaps also directly in the processes of life itself. Here, we should remember, is the place where matter, life, and mind are most inextricably mixed. Here the natural tendencies and predilections of living stuff come to expression. More than all, I think, here the organizing power of life fashions into orderly patterns the floating fantasies of the unconscious mind. Here, if anywhere, new patterns may be created.

All this sounds rather vague and mystical, and it does indeed touch on a frontier where almost nothing now is certainly known. It is not pure speculation, however. The creative processes that must be taking place in the unconscious may not be different from those in the conscious mind. A scientist, faced with a problem, marshals all the facts he can find that bear on it. Many relations among them seem meaningless, and such he rules out. Others have significance, and finally, by rearranging and organizing the facts, he is able to build a consistent pattern of ideas and to form a theory. Many psychologists believe that something not unlike this is taking place in the unconscious when an individual has been pondering a problem and seeking to solve it in his conscious mind. Among the throng of random images and ideas, the unconscious mind rejects certain combinations as unimportant or incompatible but sees the significance of others. By its means, order—

intellectual, aesthetic, perhaps spiritual order—is here distinguished from randomness. Thus the unconscious mind is able to solve problems and to lay at least the foundation for the construction of a poem or a work of art. These are new creations. They might have been produced by the conscious mind and often have been, through sheer force of mental labor; but the reason that such a frontal attack often fails seems to be that the free association, present in the unconscious, is blocked in various ways and the really creative new relationships therefore are not seen.

One must recognize the operation in the unconscious of such an organizing factor, for chance alone is not creative. Just as the organism pulls together random, formless stuff into the patterned system of structure and function in the body, so the unconscious mind seems to select and arrange and correlate these ideas and images into a pattern. The resemblance between the two processes is close. The concept is worth considering that the organizing power of life, manifest in mind as well as in body—for the two are hardly separable—is the truly creative element. Creativity thus becomes an attribute of life.

That mind actually does possess some such organizing power as this is suggested by the conclusions of gestalt psychology. I am not competent to discuss these nor is this volume the place to do so, but it seems clear that mind, or whatever its physical correlate may be, when confronted with the throng of unassociated stimuli pouring into it from the organs of sense, is able to organize them, largely without conscious effort, into patterns or Gestalten. Mind has a truly morphogenetic quality about it. The patterns it makes are new things, not repetitious of something in the past. This specifically creative ability of mind should not be forgotten in any consideration of creativity in general.

For the unconscious thus to build something new requires an incentive, a goal to be achieved. In this strange creativeness we seem faced with a much less concrete sort of goal than the ones discussed earlier—a seeking not for food or for a mate or for preferment or to enjoy the pleasures of a game or the more refined ones of listening to a symphony, but for something still inchoate, unformed, which is seeking, so to speak, to reach expression. The invariable precursor of unconscious creativity is a strong conscious desire for something—the solution of a problem or the construction of a work of art when only hints or cloudy outlines are in the mind. This eager search is often accompanied by wrestlings of the spirit which leave the seeker exhausted and spent, but when he abandons it, the search is still pursued at the lower unconscious levels of his mind and there it often is successful. In such cases we seem to be witnessing not the operation of an *established* norm but its actual *creation*. The living system here is exercising its ability to integrate and organize a pattern out of formlessness, an achievement which rational thought, being somewhat removed from its primitive living source and bound with habit and convention, may be incapable of doing.

An act of unconscious creativeness is dramatic and conspicuous but relatively rare. It is difficult, however, to draw a line between such a process and others much more common, products of the conscious mind which we call acts of *creative imagination*. Here the unconscious may have a share, also, but the process is in consciousness. From this comes the creation of most works of art, at least in their final state, and the solution of most scientific problems. It is the mark of genius.

But how, in turn, can we distinguish between the constructive processes of the creative imagination and that image-forming which is such an important part of all mental life from childhood to old age? Imagination of this simple kind seems to be a characteristically human trait. Indeed, it is necessary if reason is to be fruitful, for most reasoning processes require assumptions, if nothing more, and these are constructive acts of the imagination.

The imaginative process doubtless did not come into being suddenly, but probably arose when man began to contemplate the possibility of achieving one goal rather than another. Perhaps when he first recognized the significance of the concept "if," it was born. At any rate, its development seems to have gone hand in hand with that of rationality. These primitive forms of imagination, we can agree, are potentially creative though often not actually so. They have led, however, at the higher levels of man's mind, to what seems a truly creative process.

CONCLUSION

What, then, may we conclude as to the biological basis of creativity? Simply this, I think: that *life* itself is the creative process by virtue of its organizing, pattern-forming, questing quality, its most distinctive character. In living things below man and in man's bodily structure, life is tied to a conservative and relatively rigid physical basis in the genetic constitution of the individual, necessary if the world of organisms is not to become mixed and chaotic. But when this same organizing quality is applied to behavior, its products are much more various; and when it operates in the unthinkable complexity of the human brain, with its billions of neurones and almost countless number of synapses, the possibilities of new mental patterns are almost infinite. Gerard (1946) has well described this situation in his essay, "The Biological Basis of Imagination." Says he, "By such various mechanisms, then, great masses of nerve cells—the brain as a great unity—act together; and not merely do two or a billion units sum their separate contributions, but each is part of a dynamic fluctuating activity pattern of the whole. This is the orchestra which plays thoughts of truth and beauty, which creates creative imagination. . . . What a beautiful basis for making new gestalts or recombinations of sensory material!"

Here is the field where the creative imagination operates, whether in the conscious or the unconscious mind. Imagination, we may say, is simply the basic formative quality of life, emerging at this highest level from its former dependence on a rigid material basis and free to express itself in high creativity. The material for these expressions, these new norms and patterns, may exist in many forms—in pigments on canvas, in musical notes, in words, or simply in ideas. However creativity may manifest itself in the affairs of men, it is in this inherent creativeness of life, I believe, that its ultimate source is to be found.

Such is my thesis. For some, the suggestions here presented will have little appeal. It is unorthodox biology that I have presented. Many biologists will look with disfavor on an extrapolation of the fact of organization, real though it is, into the realm of purpose and thus of mind, and they will be likely to regard as useless the attempt to see in it the germ of creativity. Psychologists, particularly of the tougher-minded sort, will criticize the argument as naïve and as offering to our understanding of creativeness little that is constructive. I cannot help feeling, however, that the roots of the various problems that have been discussed here will finally be found in an understanding of the nature of life. Biologists, like all good and conservative scientists, have hesitated to plunge into speculations which verge on the metaphysical, for both speculation and metaphysics are terms somewhat in disrepute in scientific circles today. But problems such as this one of creativeness are so involved with life that students of the science of life, whether they like it or not, are going to be impelled more and more to try to make some contribution toward their solution, if only to state the problems in more precise form. This chapter is a tentative step in that direction.

3

An Architect's Views on Creativity

ALDEN B. DOW

No MATTER where we may look, the process of creativity is at work. It may be in the growing of a plant, erosion of a mountain or the swelling of the sea. All is change, all is individual, and everywhere is creativeness.

You may casually observe that the daisies in a field are all alike, but on closer observation find each one an individual, each a product of this force we call creativeness.

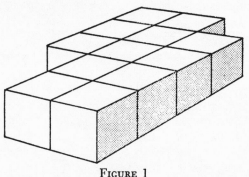

FIGURE 1

To demonstrate how this is possible, I call your attention to the cubes in Figure 1, which are all identical. They represent certain structural elements in, say, the daisy. It is the nature of these particular elements to combine with each other with their faces adjoining and the corners matching. Thus, as long as there is only this one structural element in the development of a system, the resulting form is rectangular in character.

But suppose that one of these structural elements is not a pure cube, or that another cube element of larger size must live with the others, as in Figure 2. As you will observe, this upsets the purity of

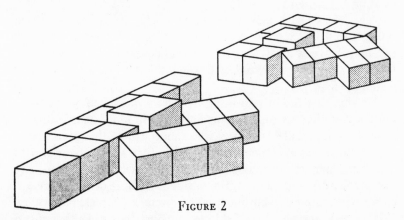

FIGURE 2

the structural system, so that just one element of this odd size can introduce the possibility of a variety of forms. The greater the variety of structural elements that enter into the total composition, the greater the variations possible in the developed form.

Atoms themselves are made up of particles wildly racing around an orbit, striking and bouncing here and there, producing a form never the same for any two instants. Thus in nature there are never two identical building blocks, and therefore never two identical structures. For this reason I am not surprised at the creativeness or individuality found in natural structures. I am amazed, however, that with all this creative ability nature is willing to conform just enough to produce a thing that we can recognize as a common daisy. If the building blocks are similar, I can see how there would be a common kind of character among individual forms. For example, a house built of bricks is a brick house, and a house built of wood is a wood house. This, no doubt, is what we call genetics, but it does not account for the similarity of the forms of all daisies. The reason, I presume, is that the daisy, in order to survive, must conform to specific outside influences or forces, such as water, wind, sunlight, minerals, gravity, insects, and many more. The effect of these outside forces on the final form excites my curiosity. I suspect that, within limits, the greater the number of influences or outside forces, the less individuality is displayed in the final form. I admit that I have only weak arguments to support this thought. I mention it only because the thought has, for me, some exciting implications.

Now, let us take a look at the human being. Physically, he is not unlike the daisy. Some of us may look alike to the casual observer, but no mother ever mistakes the identity of a twin, and if you want to make a permanent record of this identification, you need only to record the fingerprints.

Knowing that the human being is such an individual physically, it must follow that his thinking apparatus is also individual. With this view in mind, I fail to see why we cannot assume that each person is by nature a creative personality. Rather than worry about how to make him more creative, we should take this quality for granted. The real problem is to discover what outside influences or forces prevent creativeness, or prevent anyone from becoming a complete personality.

It seems to me we are guided in our productiveness in either of two ways—by the narrow deadening boundaries of conformity, or by the intellectual or spiritual guidance of truth or principle. Conformity seems to be the tool of fear or ignorance, whereas principle is the process of love or growth. It is important to realize that conformity must be taught, whereas truth and principle are ultimately learned.

I am disturbed, in current society, by the growing tendency to accept direction through conformity. Too often it is the philosophy of bigness. Government subsidies rarely contain a creative force. Their purpose is to bring about conformity in order to satisfy an emergency, and many businesses become sterile in this kind of atmosphere. I would like to call your attention to the great number of graphical prediction charts that are being shown to us these days, all based upon blind conformity. I received such a chart from a paint organization the other day. It plotted the most popular colors starting with the year 1945 and, by continuing the direction of these lines through 1957, anticipated the popular colors for 1958. The predictions are probably correct. The fallacy lies in the uncreative approach to the use of color. It is like the blind leading the blind.

My father used to criticize such an approach in this way—he would say—"Never copy. If you cannot figure out a way to do a thing better than it has been done before, don't do it, for otherwise you are just inviting cut-throat competition." This is another way of saying that blind conformity is deadening. The faults of this kind of conformity do not apply only to business. I believe that the majority of life's unpleasantnesses can be traced to the influences of conformity. The man who hates his job is contributing nothing, he is a blind conformist. (There is a great difference between blind conformity and the kind of conformity we mean when we speak of conforming to a truth or principle.)

If we are going to grow into the great creative people we must become in order to maintain our standard of living, we must actively express our beliefs in truths and principles. The most important thing we can do is to develop a faith in the wonderful potentialities of the individual human being. This human being is not the complete individual that I have implied. He does have certain qualities and abilities which are in a measure common to all. In order to review these qualities, I want to outline an analysis I made of myself some years ago. It came about because of one of those very blue Mondays.

Everything seemed to be wrong. My office was off the beam, my clients were off the beam, my family was off the beam, and I was not too sure just which beam I was trying to ride. I sat down at my desk and said, "What in the world am I trying to do?" And I came up with an answer that somewhat surprised me. I said that I was looking for a "way of life." So I wrote down on a piece of paper, "Way of Life."

And then I asked myself, "What is a way of life?" It seemed that, whatever it was, it had to please me and it also had to please my neighbor. Thus I concluded that a way of life was made up of a balance with myself on one side and the group on the other side. I called this Individual Rightness, and Social Rightness, and my diagram looked like Figure 3.

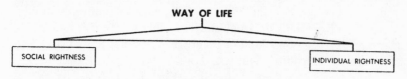

WAY OF LIFE

SOCIAL RIGHTNESS　　　　　INDIVIDUAL RIGHTNESS

FIGURE 3

Then I asked myself, "What is social rightness?" It seemed to me that when things were right with the group, it was a matter of morals, therefore, under social rightness I put the word "Morals." "What are morals?" I asked. They seemed to be made up of another balance, with "Ethics" on one side and "Conscience" on the other, as in Figure 4. Ethics seemed to spring from our social heritage, which gives

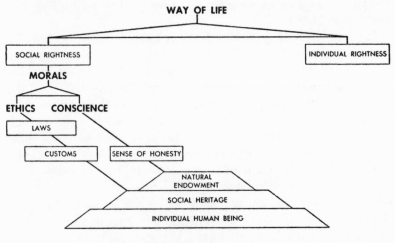

FIGURE 4

us customs and laws. Conscience seemed to develop from our natural endowment, through a sense of honesty. I find that some people doubt that the sense of honesty is a natural endowment. We know this must be true, because without it we could not exist. A child has a keen sense of his mother's truthfulness; a man depends upon the honesty of his neighbor.

Now let's take a look at Individual Rightness. When are things right with me? When I can say, "This is a beautiful solution," or sing, like that cowboy in *Oklahoma*, "Oh, what a beautiful morning," I certainly have individual rightness. In other words, it is a matter of beauty, a very personal kind of beauty, but still it is aesthetics. Therefore, below individual rightness, I wrote the word "Aesthetics," as in Figure 5. Then I asked myself, "What produces aesthetics?" It seemed to be a matter of two things—"Creativeness" on one side and

"Taste" on the other. Creativeness develops from our natural endowment through our peculiar ability to think and our particular talents. Ability to think, of course, has nothing to do with capacity of the mind for thought or what we call IQ. It is a pure expression of the individualism of every mind, and when this is combined with that individual's particular talent, which is also individual, a combination of forces exists which, if not diverted by a requirement for conformity, cannot help but be original. This originality, however, is useless to

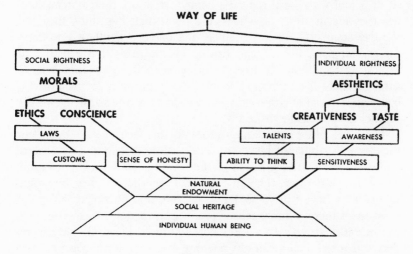

FIGURE 5

this individual unless he is capable of weighing the value of this idea as opposed to another. This is the function of taste, acquired through the sensitivity and awareness which comes from our social heritage.

We now have a diagram that is in balance and it tells us some interesting things. For example, by referring to this diagram, I find that on a blue Monday I am out of balance. My thoughts are all on the side of social rightness, and all I have to do to bring my spirits out of this miserable existence is to do something over on the individual rightness side of the scale. My actions may not make any practical sense to anyone including myself, but the very doing of something for myself seems to bring my whole self back into balance.

I understand that the majority of patients in mental hospitals live a life on the social rightness side of this scale. All of their thoughts or worries involve their relation to the group or to an individual. It is interesting to note that people living entirely on the side of individual rightness have no concern for the group and are those who today are filling our jails. Living too much on either side of this scale, one is a problem not only to oneself but to Society as well.

I cannot help but believe that this diagram explains some of the problems we are having with teenage delinquents. All day long they sit in school with social rightness being forced into their systems. Unless they are in athletics, which calls upon their ingenuity, they end the day completely out of balance, and one can hardly blame them for grabbing the hot-rod and tearing up the road. It is a matter of expressing their individualism, or bringing their system into balance through individual rightness. The school pressure is to make him a completely *social* or conforming being while his true self demands the balancing individual rightness.

There are other signs which point to this lack of balance in our society. It is displayed by some of our painters, sculptors, musicians, and even a few writers. Much of their work is void of care or significance. It is little more than an emotional excursion. If they are experiments, they have real value, but I am sure that historians will point to many of these commercialized products as the unconscious outward expression of the need for individual rightness. Please do not misunderstand me. I believe in abstractions, but they must contribute as much as possible to our living experiences. In other words, they must have integrity.

These days we hear a great deal of talk about a shorter work week and the necessity it will create for more recreational facilities. Naturally, recreation plays its part in balanced living, but it is national suicide to refer to it as the great need simply because we have so much free time on our hands. This free time, which was once productive, must be revived in all areas of creativity, otherwise we will be swallowed by some more aggressive society. It might do some good to change recreational needs to the healthier name, "creational" needs.

Referring to the diagram again, I would like to point out that social rightness is passive and individual rightness is active. The latter, I believe, is stimulated by a love for what you are doing, whereas social rightness is a matter of keeping peace in the family. It seems to be the leveling device. All individual advances come from the individual rightness side of this scale, and social rightness distributes the results.

Now, suppose we are in balance—where do we go from there? I think the next step is a matter of a desire to grow. I call it an affection for an idea. If you have this affection, this desire to grow, you must know something about the natural influences and forces involved.

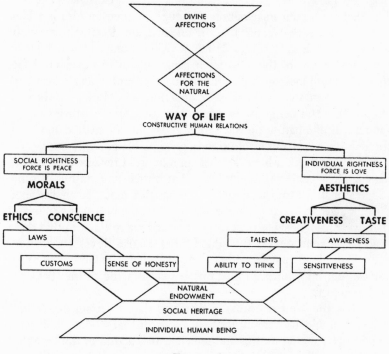

FIGURE 6

Therefore, it seems that the next step in this diagram (Figure 6) is to have an affection for the natural. Having this affection is quite different from knowing the facts of the subject. One knows people whose minds are filled with factual material but who have never created anything. It is far more important or creative to have an affection for the idea that 2 plus 2 equals 4 than to have a mind that says, "This is a fact."

For example, I find in my own business of architecture that it is dangerous to do too many schools or buildings of a similar type one after the other. It means filling your mind with the facts of one particular problem and then by force of habit applying the same ideas without reason to the new problem. This does not lead to a practical creative solution.

Since the beginning of history, man has been intrigued with the idea that growth can extend beyond this physical existence. The very fact that he has an imagination that suggests such an idea is a kind of proof that says it is possible. In this diagram, I called this area of growth "Divine Affections." What it really means, I do not know, but I find it one of the most fascinating parts of this diagram. I feel that we should look upon it as the source of all truth and all creativity.

When I first started the practice of architecture, I came to the conclusion that the designing of a building was a simple process of reasoning. All one had to do was gather all the facts together, and then, through reasoning, out would come a good building.

One day, after finishing sketches for a house, I reviewed my reasoning for the scheme. Although I could at least invent reasons, it came to me as a shock to realize that the things that made this house good did not start with reason. Ideas seemed to come out of the blue and then were recognized as reasonable. This led me to the idea that there must be different ways of thinking. I listed them as three.

First, the kind that says 1 and 1 make 2. It is the kind of thinking you can put into words. I called this factual thinking, or the "Science" of the subject.

Next is the kind of thinking that says that a certain flower in a bouquet should be here rather than there; or that to dig a hole with a shovel you should do this and not that. It is a kind of thinking that is just as real to you as the first kind; however, you are unable to put it into words. I call it personal thinking, or the "Art" of the subject.

Finally, there is the kind of thinking that gives you an answer when least expected. You have been working on a problem for days and cannot find a satisfactory solution. Then, while at the breakfast table, with no apparent thought of the idea on your mind, suddenly the answer appears. This, I believe, is called "Intuitive Thinking." The most valuable thing about it is that, as far as you are concerned, it is a truthful and new idea. Someone else may have thought of it before, but as far as you are concerned, it is an original. For this reason, and because it is an honest thought unruled by conformity, it is the most valuable kind of thinking and more should be done to stimulate its development.

As a step toward this development, it seems to me that it would help us if we all clearly realized that there are different kinds of thinking. Then we should look for ways to stimulate the most valuable kinds.

Again I would like to quote my father. He said an inventor must have this attitude, "No matter what he sees, it is just the thing he has been looking for." I would also like to quote my friend, Michael Church, of the University of Michigan. He tells how as a boy he was going to take a trip across the country. Before leaving, his father said this to him, "No matter what you see, look at it with this point of view in mind: 'I'll never see this again.'" I think these are both stimulating points of view.

There is a real force for creative thinking that I find few people aware of. I first became acquainted with this force in high school in a physics class. It is found in Newton's law of motion: "For every action there is an equal and opposite reaction," as illustrated in Figure 7. When I first heard this law of motion, it impressed me as being not only a physical law but a social law as well. Then I began to wonder how there can ever be any progress if this is the way people behave.

I worried about this for many years, and finally the thought came to me that this was not only a physical law but also the way animals behaved. It says that if I push down on this table with a force of ten

ACTION ►◄ REACTION

Figure 7

pounds, the table pushes back with a force of ten pounds. Or, for example, a goat with an idea meets another goat; they lock horns, and there they stand until one collapses. All wars and brutal fights involve this principle. This, however, is not the way a thinking or creative man conducts himself (Figure 8).

He begins an idea knowing full well there is going to be a reaction; consequently, he waits until this reaction is formed and then he

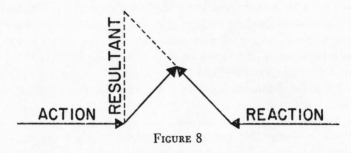

changes his course. As the diagram shows, the reaction must then follow, and the resultant of these two forces becomes greater than the original force. In other words, the original idea, when confronted with the reaction, absorbs some of the reaction idea with its own and thereby makes the final idea a combination of ideas, which in truth is a new idea. Naturally, the greater the intelligence displayed in the action and reaction, the more valuable the resultant idea.

A motion picture I made a few years ago provides an example of how this works. It illustrates how this idea can be applied to creating fun. While I was visiting Higgins Lake, in Michigan, some friends who had been living in Japan called on us, fully dressed in Japanese costume. We were delighted with these clothes as well as the stories they told of Japan. More friends joined the party, and then a reaction started. We decided to invent our own Japanese costumes. The results were quite successful. All of this led to another action. I decided it was time to get out the movie camera. Without any thought in mind as to a plot or sequence, I started taking pictures. When these were developed, the reaction was the beginning of a story. I took a few more pictures to round out the idea and this is the result. As I said before, this shows how action and reaction can be applied to having the best kind of fun. This picture was inspired by an action. It begins and ends with a reaction. This has led me to believe that, as a rule, comedies start and end in a reaction, whereas tragedies start and end in an action. The reaction leaves you satisfied, and that is usually the objective of a comedy. On the other hand, an action always leaves you with the desire for the reaction. When a composition is ended in this way, the real ending is left to the imagination of the reader or observer, which, generally speaking, is the objective of a tragedy.

In a democratic society, action and reaction is not only the rule but also the most important value of the democratic process. It is the active, creative force of a democracy and the great weakness of a society ruled by rigid conformity. Does it always produce the best idea? Sometimes not. On the other hand, I find that in my own profession it is more apt to produce an idea superior to the original. This, as I said before, is a matter of the intelligent understanding of what makes quality, or what is value.

I find myself asking the question a hundred times a day, Is this a good or bad idea? Or, What's good about this idea? Or, What's bad about it? Can the weak values be separated from the strong values? I believe they can, and in the process of doing this we learn about values or what makes quality.

I have a little test I like to use which divides quality into three parts: (1) honesty, more than sincerity; (2) humility, ability to give and take gracefully; and (3) enthusiasm, ardent pursuit of expression.

First, is this thing honest? And do not confuse this with sincere. We can accept sincerity as honesty in a child but not in a mature man, for sincerity allows for ignorance, and honesty can be nothing but truth. Honesty, as a specific property of quality, is difficult to define; however, I believe that everyone is born with an affection for truth, so that with little practice you can learn to detect it in its multiple forms.

Second, a thing of quality must also have humility. By this, I mean the ability to give and take gracefully. It seems to be a combination of justice, respect, and love. A building that has humility must contribute something to the land it sits on, and the land in turn must contribute to the building. A person who has humility contributes something to an acquaintance, and in turn he takes something from that acquaintance. A bouquet sitting on a table, if it has humility, contributes something to the table, and the table in turn contributes to the bouquet. One is enhanced by the other. It is not the same bouquet if it is placed elsewhere.

Third, quality must have enthusiasm; call it the ardent pursuit of expression. It is that property we call sparkle or liveliness in a person, or richness in a fabric or piece of architecture. For example, if it is a building serving a complex of services, it is not just a box with a hole in the side labeled "Entrance." The building itself must reflect its multiple services and through architectural expression one is led to the entrance. This quality exists in a person if he has a variety of approaches to his subject and is interested in all subjects. If it is the bouquet on the table, it has variety.

Of the three properties of value, honesty, humility, and enthusiasm, I find humility the most precious.

In our household we have found this test to be of value in many ways. Not long ago after finishing dinner, I said to my wife, "My, that was a good dinner," and our daughter, Barbara, spoke up and said, "Father, do you mean it had H, H, and E?" (Honesty, Humility and Enthusiasm.) We enjoy discussing things we read and see on the same basis. It is fun and creative to be able to pinpoint the weak or strong qualities of a movie, concert, or almost anything using this triad.

Now I have given you a variety of thoughts on the subject of creativity, which I take for granted is the production of something pleasing to human beings. There is an antipode of creativeness which fills the vacuum where there is no creativity. This is destructiveness. We have all seen this in the behavior of our children. If a child is not doing something creative, such as building with blocks, he is apt to be pulling the furniture to pieces. This is destructiveness filling the vacuum where creativity should be. More should be said about destructiveness, but it is not the subject of this paper.

Here we are interested in the constructive side of creativeness, and, after all these words, I wonder if it cannot be reduced to just one word—care. I believe that any fine thing must above all else reflect human care, and when this care is uninhibited by conformity and is really profound, it is creative.

One summer while we were at the Interlochen Music Camp in Michigan, Mrs. Dow visited a class in ballet dancing and heard the instructor tell his young pupils, "Please remember that naturalness is not art." He meant that although it might be natural to walk across the floor flat-footed, with one's arms swinging this way and that, it does not reflect human care.

Several years ago I picked up a piece of ivory that was obviously a scrap piece broken off from some larger section of the tusk. This piece of ivory measured about four inches long, one and one-half inches wide, by one-half inch thick. It was irregular in shape, in fact ugly.

But the artist who chose this piece of ivory for a carving took such exquisite care in the forming of a face on its side that I now consider this a prize possession. With great care he transformed what was meaningless into a thing of the greatest meaning, beauty, and I believe this beauty is the reflection of his great affection or love. I cannot question its honesty, humility or enthusiasm. It has them all.

So we might say that, if we are going to be creative, all we need is to develop a deep sense of care. First, however, we must have a purpose or a way of life that is commensurate with human needs. I believe that my outline for this is sound. It says that human life has no boundaries provided it recognizes the wonderful and beautiful potentialities of the individual human being.

4

The Creative Attitude

ERICH FROMM

In TALKING about creativity, let us first consider its two possible meanings: creativity in the sense of creating something new, something which can be seen or heard by others, such as a painting, a sculpture, a symphony, a poem, a novel, etc., or creativity as an *attitude*, which is the condition of any creation in the former sense but which can exist even though nothing new is created in the world of things.

The first kind of creativity, that of the artist, is conditioned by a number of factors; by talent (or, if you like, you may say also, by the genes), by study and practice, and by certain economic and social conditions which permit a person to develop his talent through study and practice. In this chapter I shall deal not with this kind of creativity but with the second, the *creative attitude*—or, as we might also say, with *creativity as a character trait*.

What is creativity? The best general answer I can give is that creativity is the ability *to see* (or to *be aware*) and *to respond*. This answer may seem to describe creativity in simple terms. Many people will say: "If that is creativity, then certainly I am creative, for I am aware and respond to things and to people. Am I not aware of what happens on the way to my office? Do I not respond with a friendly smile to the people I come in contact with, or do I not see my wife and respond to her wishes?"

Indeed, this is what most people believe, and yet their idea is erroneous. In fact, it would be much closer to the truth to state that most people are not aware of, and do not respond to, anything. Obviously, in order to proceed, we must examine what goes on in the process of seeing and responding, and what makes the difference between creative and noncreative attitudes.

Let us assume that a person sees a rose and states: "This is a rose," or, "I see a rose." Does he really *see* a rose? Some do indeed, but most do not. Then, what is the experience of the latter? I would describe it this way: they see an object (the rose), and state that the object they see falls under the concept "rose," and hence that they make a correct statement in saying: "I see a rose." Although it seems that the emphasis in this statement is on the act of *seeing*, it is really on the act of cognition and verbalization. The person who thus states that he sees a rose is actually stating only that he has learned to speak, that is, to recognize a concrete object and to classify it under the proper word for its class. Seeing, here, is not really seeing, but an essentially mental act. What, then, is seeing in the real meaning of the word?

Perhaps I can explain it best by mentioning a concrete example. A woman who had been preparing peas in the kitchen enthusiastically tells a friend whom she sees later in the morning: "I experienced something wonderful this morning; I saw for the first time that peas roll." Many people, on hearing this, would feel somewhat uncomfortable and begin to wonder what is the matter with the woman who says this. They take it for granted that peas roll, and their only surprise is that somebody can be surprised at it. But what *they* really experience in seeing peas roll is a confirmation of the mental knowledge they have that a round body rolls on an inclined and relatively smooth surface. This fact of seeing peas roll is just a confirmation of knowledge, rather than the full perception of rolling peas by the whole person.

It is striking to see the difference between this kind of adult behavior and the attitude of a two-year-old child toward a rolling ball. The child can throw this ball on the floor again and again and again, seeing it roll a hundred times, and never be bored. Why? If seeing a ball roll is merely a mental act confirming the knowledge that balls roll, one experience is enough. There is nothing new in the second and third and fiftieth experience. In other words, one gets bored in seeing it again and again; but for the child this is primarily not a mental experience but a delight in really *seeing* the ball rolling, a delight which many of us still feel when we watch a tennis game and see the ball bouncing back and forth. If we are fully aware of a tree at which we look—not of the fact that this is correctly called a tree, but of *this* tree, in its full reality, in its suchness—and if we respond to the suchness of this tree with our whole person, then we have the kind of experience which is the premise for painting the tree. Whether we have the technical skill to paint what we experience is another question, but no good painting is ever done unless there is first a full awareness and responsiveness toward the particular object.

To view it from still another angle, in conceptual knowledge the tree we see has no individuality; it stands there only as an example of the genus "tree"; it is only the representative of an abstraction. In full awareness there is no abstraction; the tree retains its full concreteness, and that means also its uniqueness. There is only this one tree in the world, and to this tree I relate myself, I see it, I respond to it. The tree becomes my own creation.

What we experience when we see people is not customarily different from what we experience when we see things. What goes on when we believe we see a person? We see, first of all, marginal things. The color of his skin, the way he is dressed, his social class and education, whether he is friendly or unfriendly, useful or not useful. What we want to know first is his name. The name permits us to classify him, just as we classify the flower by saying that it is a rose. The way we perceive him is not too different from the way in which he perceives himself. If we ask him who he is, his first answer will be to tell us that his name is Jones, and if we show that we do not feel fully informed about him yet, he will add that he is a married man, father of two children, and a doctor. Anyone who even then does not feel that he knows this man is obviously lacking in perspicacity, or inordinately intrusive. We see in the concrete person an abstraction, just as he sees an abstraction in himself and in us. We do not want to see more. We share the general phobia of being too close to a person, of penetrating through the surface to his core, and so we prefer to see little, no more than is necessary for our particular dealings with the other person. This kind of marginal knowledge corresponds to an inner state of indifference in our feeling toward the other person.

But this is not all. We do not see the person only marginally and superficially. In many ways we also see him unrealistically. We see him unrealistically in the first place because of our projections. We are angry, project our anger at the other person, and think *he* is angry. We are vain and perceive *him* as vain. We are afraid and perceive him as afraid. And so on. We make him the coat-hanger for the many suits which we do not like to wear ourselves, and yet we think this is all he, and are not aware that these are only the clothes which we put on him. Aside from projecting, we do a lot of distorting with the other person, because our own emotions make us incapable of seeing the other person as he is. The three most important facts which lead to this result correspond to the three basic "sins" in Buddhist ethics: greed, folly, and anger. It is needless to explain that, if we greedily want something from another person, we cannot see him objectively. We see him distorted by what our greedy expectation wants him to be, our anger forces him to be, or our folly imagines him to be.

To see the other person creatively means to see him objectively, that is, without projections and without distortions, and this means overcoming in oneself those neurotic "vices" which necessarily lead to projections and distortions. It means to wake up fully to the awareness of reality, inside and outside of oneself. To put it in other words: only if one has reached a degree of inner maturity which reduces projection and distortion to a minimum can one experience creatively.

The experience of seeing the reality of a person occurs sometimes as a sudden and surprising experience. I have seen a person a hundred times, and suddenly, when I see him for the hundred and first time, I see him fully, I feel as if I had never quite seen him before. His face, his movements, his eyes, his voice assume a new, more intense, more concrete reality by the difference between his new view and the previous one. I learn the difference between seeing and seeing. The same happens with well-known scenery or a well-known painting or any other well-known object.

To see a person or a thing in this sense of utmost reality is the condition for giving a realistic response. Most responses are as unreal and purely mental as most awarenesses. If I read in the newspaper of a famine in India, I hardly respond, or, if I do respond, I do so with a thought; with a thought that it is too bad, with a thought of regret, or even a thought of pity. It is different if I see a person suffering in front of me. There I react with my heart, with my hands and my legs. I suffer with him, I have the impulse to help, and I carry out the impulse. Even when confronted with the concreteness of another person's suffering or another person's happiness, however, many people react only marginally. They "think" the proper feeling, they do the proper action, and yet they remain distant. To respond in a realistic sense means that I respond with my real human power, that of suffering, of joy, of understanding, to the reality of the "object" which experiences something. I respond to the person as he is; to the experience of the other person as it is. I respond not with my brain or my eyes or my ears. I respond as the whole person I am. I think with my belly. I see with my heart. When I respond to an object with the real powers in me, which are fitted to respond to it, the object ceases to be an object. I become one with it. I cease to be the observer. I cease to be the judge. This kind of response occurs in a situation of complete relatedness, in which seer and seen, observer and observed, become one, although at the same time they remain two.

CONDITIONS FOR CREATIVITY

What are the conditions of the creative attitude, of seeing and responding, of being aware and being sensitive to what one is aware of? First of all, it requires the capacity to be puzzled. Children still have the capacity to be puzzled. Their whole effort is one of attempting to orient themselves in a new world, to grasp the ever-new things which they learn to experience. They are puzzled, surprised, capable of wondering, and that is what makes their reaction a creative one. But once they are through the process of education, most people lose the capacity of wondering, of being surprised. They feel they ought to know everything, and hence that it is a sign of ignorance to be surprised at or puzzled by anything. The world loses its characteristic of being full of wonder and is taken for granted. The capacity to be puzzled is indeed the premise of all creation, be it in art or in science.

The French mathematician Poincaré expressed this succinctly. "Scientific genius," he said, "is the capacity to be surprised." Many scientific discoveries are made in just this manner. The scientist observes a phenomenon which many others have seen before him without being puzzled, without stopping to be surprised. He has the capacity to be surprised; the obvious becomes a problem, his mind starts working, and this is the beginning of his discovery. What makes him a creative scientist is only partly his ability to solve the problem. It is to a large extent his ability to be puzzled by what the average scientist takes for granted.

The second premise for the creative attitude is the ability to concentrate. This is a rare ability in our Western culture. We are always busy, but without concentration. When we do one thing, we are already thinking of the next thing, of the moment when we can stop doing what we are doing now. We do, if possible, many things at the same time. We eat breakfast, listen to the radio, and read the newspaper, and perhaps at the same time we carry on a conversation with our wife and children. We do five things at the same time, and we do nothing. Nothing, in the sense that we do it as a manifestation of our real powers, of which we are the masters. If one is truly concentrated, the very thing one is doing at this moment is the most important thing in life. If I talk to someone, if I read something, if I walk—whatever it is, if I do it in a concentrated fashion, there is nothing more important than what I am doing in the here and now. Most people live in the past or in the future. But there is no past or future as a real experience. There is only the here and now. Quite obviously, there can be no true awareness and no true response except in the here and now, that is to say, in the attitude of full commitment to whatever I do, see, feel at this very moment.

Speaking of what "I" do and feel raises another problem, namely, that of the experience of "I," of the experience of self, which is another condition of the creative attitude. It is true that the word "I" is one of the last words a child learns in the development of his capacity to speak, but once he has learned it, he uses it glibly. In expressing an opinion, for instance, we say, "I think" this or that. If one analyzes this opinion, however, one might discover that the person only voices what he has heard from someone else, what he has read in the newspaper, what he was taught by his parents when he was a child. He is under the illusion that it is he who thinks of this, when actually it would be more correct if he said: "It thinks in me." He has about the same illusion a record player would have which, provided it could think, would say, "I am now playing a Mozart symphony," when we all know that we put the record on the record player and that it is only reproducing what is fed into it.

What holds true of thinking is true of feeling. Let us assume that we ask a person who attends a cocktail party how he feels, and he answers, "I feel fine; I feel very happy." Yet, when we see him leave the cocktail party, he may suddenly look sad, feel tired; he may have a dream the following night which is nothing but a nightmare. Had he really felt happy? If we examine the phenomenon, this would appear to be true: he saw himself drinking, smiling, talking among other people who drank, smiled, and talked, and he concluded from that that he must feel fine and be happy, just as everybody else did. He may *feel* sad, bored, indifferent, but he *thinks* the feelings which are put into him by the situation, by the expectations of the appropriate feeling on this occasion.

The sense of *I*, or the sense of self, means that I experience myself as the true center of my world, as the true originator of my acts. This is what it means to be original. Not primarily to discover something new, but to experience in such a way that the experience originates in me.

To feel a sense of self, a sense of identity, is a necessity for every human being. We would become insane unless we had such a sense of self. But this sense of identity differs according to the social structure of the culture in which we live. In a primitive society, where the individual has not yet emerged as an individual, the feeling of "I" can be described in terms of "I is we." My sense of identity exists in terms of my being identified with the group. As man proceeds in the process of evolution and emerges as an individual, his sense of identity becomes separated from that of the group. He as a separate individual must be able to feel "I."

There is a great deal of misunderstanding about this sense of self. There are some psychologists who believe that the sense of self is nothing but a reflection of the social role which is ascribed to him, nothing but the response to expectations others have about him. Although it is true that, empirically speaking, this is the kind of self most people in our society experience, it is nevertheless a pathological phenomenon, the result of which is deep insecurity and anxiety and a compulsion to conform. One can overcome this anxiety and compulsive conformism only by developing the sense of self which I have been discussing before, where I experience myself creatively as the originator of my acts. This, however, does not mean at all that I become egocentric or narcissistic. On the contrary, I can experience myself as "I" only in the process of my relatedness to others or, to refer to our main topic, on the basis of a creative attitude. If I am isolated and unrelated, I am so full of anxiety that I can not possibly have a sense of identity and of self. What I experience in this case is rather a sense of proprietorship over my person. I feel then, "My home is my castle." My property is me. All that I possess, including my knowledge, my body, my memory—this constitutes me. This is not an experience of self in the sense described above, namely, the self as agent of creative experience, this is an experience of self based on a sense of holding on to my person as a thing, as a possession. The person with this kind of attitude is in reality a prisoner of himself, shut in and necessarily frightened and unhappy. In order to acquire a genuine sense of self, he has to break out of his person. He has to give up holding on to himself as a thing and begin to experience himself only in the process of creative response; paradoxically enough, if he can experience himself in this process, he loses himself. He transcends the boundaries of his own person, and at the very moment when he feels "I am" he also feels "I am you," I am one with the whole world.

Another condition of creativeness is the *ability to accept conflict and tension* resulting from polarity, rather than to avoid them. This idea is very much in contrast to the current climate of opinion, in which one attempts to avoid conflict as much as possible. All modern education tends to spare the child the experience of conflict. Everything is made easy, everyone is tolerant. Ethical norms are leveled out in such a way that there is rare occasion to experience conflict between desire and norm. There is a general superstition that conflicts are harmful, and that hence they should be avoided. The opposite is true. Conflicts are the source of wondering, of the development of strength, of what one used to call "character." If one avoids conflicts, one becomes a smoothly running machine, where every affect is immediately leveled off, where all desires become automatic, where all feelings become flattened out. Not only are there conflicts of a personal and accidental nature, as it were; there are conflicts deeply rooted in human existence. I refer here to the conflict between the fact that, at the same time, we are tied to the animal kingdom by our body, its needs, and its final destruction, we transcend the animal kingdom and nature through our self-awareness, imagination, and creativeness.

We represent all potentialities the human race has or will ever have, and yet in this short life we realize only an infinitesimally small part of these potentialities. We plan and foresee, and yet we are subject to accidents which are completely independent of our will and planning. To be aware of these conflicts, to experience them deeply, to accept them not just intellectually but in feeling, is one of the conditions for creativity. To deny them or to experience them only intellectually leads to marginal and superficial experience, which excludes creativity. It must be added here that we try to ignore not only conflicts but also polarities. These polarities exist in many levels. They are found individually as polarities of temperament. Socially the most important polarity is that between men and women. What have we done with it?

In a false concept of equality, which amounts more and more to a concept of sameness, we have reduced this polarity. Inasmuch as man in modern society transforms himself more and more into a thing, men and women are transformed more and more into things, and hence the polarity between them becomes increasingly reduced. Men and women are practically the same, and their difference remains important only in the purely sexual sphere. In this process erotic attraction, which is a result of the cosmic polarity between the male and the female poles, is greatly reduced in intensity. Love is transformed into pleasant comradeship and loses the truly erotic and passionate character which is the very source of its creativeness. We have, indeed, witnessed a great advance in modern culture in the achievement of equality between the sexes, and we have made rapid advances even in the achievement of racial equality. But we cannot be quite proud of this achievement. Although in one sense it is obviously good, we have paid for it by the neglect of true differences and polarities. Originally the idea of equality meant that we are all equal in the sense that each man is a thing in itself and must not be made into a means for the ends of others. Or, to put it into religious language, that each man is a child of God, and no other man must be a god or master to him. Equality meant that we each have the same human dignity in spite of the fact that we are different; it meant the right to develop one's differences, and yet the principle that no one has a right to use differences for the exploitation of others. Today, *equality means sameness*. It means not to be different from the herd, and the general fear is that differences would threaten equality. I am sure that only if this point of view is overcome, if sameness is replaced again by true equality, can creativity develop.

There is another way in which the condition of creativeness can be phrased. I refer to the *willingness to be born every day*. Indeed, birth is not a single process taking place when the child leaves its fetal existence and starts to breathe by itself. This event is not even as decisive as it seems in a biological sense. Although the newborn child breathes by itself, it is just as helpless and dependent on mother after birth as it was when it formed a part of her body. Even in the sense of biological development, birth has many steps. It begins with leaving the womb; then it means leaving mother's breast, mother's lap, mother's hands. Each new ability, the ability to talk, to walk, to eat, means at the same time leaving a former state. Man is governed by a peculiar dichotomy. He is afraid of losing the former state, which is one of certainty, and yet he wants to arrive at a new state which gives rise to the possibility of using his proper forces more freely and more completely. Man is always torn between the wish to regress to the womb and the wish to be fully born. Every act of birth requires the courage to let go of something, to let go of the womb, to let go of the breast, to let go of the lap, to let go of the hand, to let go eventually of all certainties, and to rely only upon one thing: one's own powers to be aware and to respond; that is, one's own creativity. To be creative means to consider the whole process of life as a process of birth, and not to take any stage of life as a final stage. Most people die before they are fully born. Creativeness means to be born before one dies.

The willingness to be born—and this means the willingness to let go of all "certainties" and illusions—requires *courage* and *faith*. Courage to let go of certainties, courage to be different and to stand isolation; courage, as the Bible puts it in the story of Abraham, to leave one's own land and family and to go to a land yet unknown. Courage to be concerned with nothing but the truth, the truth not only in thought but in one's feelings as well. This courage is possible only on the basis of faith. Faith not in the sense in which the word is often used today, as a belief in some idea which cannot be proved scientifically or rationally, but faith in the meaning which it has in the *Old Testament*, where the word for faith (*Emuna*) means certainty; to be certain of the reality of one's own experience in thought and in feeling, to be able to trust it, to rely on it, this is faith. Without courage and faith, creativity is impossible, and hence the understanding and cultivation of courage and faith are indispensable conditions for the development of the creative attitude.

Let me say again that creativity in this sense does not refer to a quality which particularly gifted persons or artists could achieve, but to an attitude which every human being should and can achieve. Education for creativity is nothing short of education for living.

5

The Nature of Creativity

ROLLO MAY

WHEN we look over the studies and writings on creativity in the psychological field, the first thing that strikes us is the paucity and inadequacy of the work. In academic psychology after the time of William James and during the first half of this century, the subject has been generally avoided as unscientific, mysterious, disturbing, and too corruptive of the scientific training of graduate students. Or, when some studies of creativity actually were made, they were in peripheral areas which creative people themselves felt really had next to nothing to do with creativity. Fortunately, during the last ten years a change has been occurring. Such works as Wertheimer's *Productive Thinking* (1945, 1959) mark one evidence of the shift, and the interdisciplinary investigations of creativity at several universities are another evidence.

In psychoanalysis and depth psychology the situation has been almost the same. Whereas psychoanalysts and other psychologists working clinically in psychotherapy have made a number of studies of creative activity, most of them are also felt by artists and other creative persons to have almost nothing to do with what the creative persons themselves recognized to be going on in their creative moments.

I well recall an incident of some twenty years ago which brought vividly home to me the oversimplification and inadequacy of the depth-psychological theories of creativity. One summer I was traveling with a group of seventeen artists through central Europe, studying and painting peasant art. While we were in Vienna, I procured an invitation from Alfred Adler, whom I had known and whose summer school I had attended, to bring the group of artists to his home for a private lecture. In the course of his lecture to the group in his parlor, Adler touched upon his *compensatory theory of creativity*. This is, briefly, that human beings produce art, science, and other aspects of culture to compensate for their own inadequacies. The figure of speech of the oyster producing the pearl to cover up the foreign body of the grain of sand intruding into its shell is often cited as a simple illustration. Beethoven's deafness was one of the many famous examples which Adler could cite, showing how highly creative individuals compensated for some defect or organ inferiority. Adler also cited sociological data to indicate how the race of man as a whole developed culture and civilization to compensate for man's relatively weak position on this unfriendly crust of the earth. Then Adler, having entirely forgotten he was addressing a group of artists, looked around the room and remarked, "Since I see that very few of you are wearing glasses, I assume that you are not interested in art." The oversimplification of this theory of compensation never was more dramatically exposed! The theory does have some real merit and is partially true. But its error is that it does not deal with *the creative process as such*. Compensatory trends in myself or yourself will influence the forms or degrees our creating will take, but they do not explain the creativity itself. Compensatory needs will influence the particular emphases in science or culture, but they do not explain the culture as such. I learned, thus, early in my psychological career to regard current theories explaining creativity with a good deal of skepticism. And I learned always to ask the question: Does the theory deal with creativity itself, or does it deal only with some artifact, some partial, peripheral aspect of creativity?

The other most widely current psychoanalytic theories about creativity have two characteristics. First, they are *reductive*. That is, they reduce creativity to some other process. Secondly, they generally specifically make it an expression of *neurotic* patterns. The usual definition of creativity in psychoanalytic circles is "regression in the service of the ego." The term "regression" immediately indicates the *reductive* approach. I should like to disagree firmly with the implication that creativity is to be understood by reducing it to some other process, or that it is essentially a neurotic process. Certainly, creativity is associated with neurotic problems in our particular culture—Van

Gogh was psychotic, Gauguin seems to have been what we would call schizoid, and obviously creativity (and originality) are associated with persons who do not fit into the culture. But this does not at all mean that the creativity itself is the *product* of the neurosis or illness. The above association of creativity with neurosis led to the dilemma which all of us have at one time argued, namely, if by psychoanalysis we cured the artists of their neuroses, would they no longer create? This false dilemma, as well as many others, arises from the reductive theories. Furthermore, if we create out of some *transfer* of affect or drive, as implied in sublimation, or as a by-product of an endeavor to accomplish something else, as in *compensation*, does not our very creative act then have only a pseudo value? We must indeed take a strong stand against the implications, however they may creep in, that talent is a disease and creativity a neurosis.

WHAT IS CREATIVITY?

Whenever we face the question of defining creativity, therefore, it is important to make the distinction between pseudo forms of creativity, that is, creativity as a superficial experience, as a "frosting" to life, as aestheticism on one hand, and actual creativity on the other. Actual creativity I define as the process of bringing something new into birth. This distinction is between art as artificiality on one hand and true art on the other. It is a distinction that artists and philosophers have struggled to make clear all through the centuries. Plato, for example, put his poets and his artists down in the sixth circle of reality, because, he said, they deal only with appearances and not with reality itself. He was there referring to art as the frosting of life in contrast to the real food, art as decorative, a way of making life prettier, a dealing with semblances rather than with reality itself. But in his later beautiful dialogue, the *Symposium*, he described what he called the *true artists*, namely, those who bring into birth some new reality. These poets and other creative persons are the ones who express *Being itself*, he held. Or, as I would put it, these are the ones who enlarge human consciousness. Their creativity is the most basic manifestation of man's fulfilling his own being in his world.

Now we must make the above distinction sharp and radical if our inquiries into creativity are to get below the surface. We are not dealing with hobbies, with do-it-yourself movements, holiday painting, or other forms of filling up leisure time, particularly on the part of the indolent classes. Nowhere has the meaning of creativity been more disastrously lost than in the idea that it is something you use only on Sundays. Any penetrating explanation of the creative process must take it as the expression of the normal man in the act of actualizing himself not as the product of sickness but as the representation of the highest degree of emotional health. And any enduring description of creativity must account for it in the work of the scientist as well as the artist, the thinker as well as the aestheticist, and must not rule out the extent to which it is present in captains of modern technology as well as in a mother's normal relation with her child. Creativity, as Webstser rightly indicates, is basically the process of *making*, of *bringing into being*.

THE CREATIVE PROCESS

Let us now inquire: What is the nature of the creative process? And let us seek our answers for this by trying to describe as accurately as possible what actually happens in artists and scientists in the moment of creative acting itself. I shall speak mostly about artists, because I know them, have worked with them, and to some extent practice art myself. This does not mean that I underestimate creativity in other activities; I assume that the following analysis of the nature of creativity will apply to scientists and technologists as well, and even to the man of the street in his creative moments.

THE ENCOUNTER

The first thing we notice in a creative act is that it is an encounter. The artist encounters the landscape he proposes to paint—looks at it, observes it from this angle and that, is, as we say, absorbed in it. Or, in the cases of abstract painters, the encounter may be with an idea, an inner vision which in turn may be led off by the brilliant colors on the artist's palette or the inviting rough whiteness of his canvas. The paint, the canvas, and the other materials then become a secondary part of this encounter; they are the language of it, the *media*, as we rightly put it. Or the scientist confronts his experiment, his laboratory task, in a similar situation of encounter.

The encounter may or may not involve voluntaristic effort, that is, what is called "will power." A healthy child's play, for example, also has the essential features of encounter, and we know it is one of the important prototypes of adult creativity. The essential point is not the presence or absence of voluntaristic effort, but the degree of absorption, the degree of intensity (which we shall deal with in detail below); there must be a specific quality of *engagement*.

Immediately, at this first point, we come upon one important distinction between pseudo, escapist creativity on one hand and that which is genuine on the other. Escapist creativity is precisely that which lacks encounter. This was illustrated vividly to me in working with a patient in psychoanalysis. This young man, a talented professional, had rich and varied creative potentialities, but he always stopped just short of actualizing them. He would suddenly get the idea and outline for an excellent story, would work it out in his mind to a full outline which could have then been written up without much further trouble, and would relish and enjoy the ecstasy of the experience. And then he would stop precisely there, writing down nothing at all. It was as though the experience of seeing himself as one who was able to write, as being just about to write, had within it what he was really seeking and brought its own reward, and hence he never actually created. This was a fairly baffling problem to him and to me. We had analyzed many aspects of it: his father had been a somewhat gifted writer but a failure; his mother had made much over the father's writings, but had shown only contempt for the father in other realms. The boy, an only child, had been pampered and overprotected by the mother and often given preference over the father by special food at meals, and so on. The patient was in clear competition with the father and faced a threat if he should succeed. All of this and more we had analyzed in some detail. A vital link of experience, however, was missing.

One day the patient came in to announce that he had made an exciting discovery. The evening before, while reading, he had gotten his customary sudden creative flow of ideas for a paper and had taken his usual pleasure in the fact; and at the same time he had a peculiar sexual feeling. And he then recalled for the first time that he had always had this sexual feeling at precisely this abortively creative moment. I shall not go into the complex analysis of the associations, which demonstrated that this sexual feeling was both a desire to be given comfort and sensual gratification of a passive sort, and a desire to be unconditionally admired by any given woman. I only wish to indicate that the upshot was clearly that his creative "bursts" of ideas were ways of getting admiration, gratification from his mother; that he needed to show mother and other women what a fine, gifted person he was. And once he had done that by getting the beautiful, lofty visions, he had achieved what he wanted. He was not really interested, in this context, in creating; creativity was in the service of something quite else. Now no matter how you may interpret the *causes* of this pattern, one central feature is clear: the *encounter was lacking*. Is not this the essence of escapist art? Everything is there but the encounter. And is not this the central feature of many kinds of exhibitionism appearing in artists, or what Rank calls the *artiste manqué?* We cannot make a valid distinction by saying one kind of art is neurotic and the other healthy; who is to judge that? We can only say that in exhibitionistic, escapist forms of creativity, there is no real encounter, no engagement with reality. That is not what the patient is after; he wants to be passively accepted and admired by mother. In these kinds of cases it is accurate to speak of *regression* in the negative sense. The only trouble is that we are dealing not with creativity but with something else.

The concept of encounter also enables us to make a clearer distinction between *talent* and *creativity*. In studies in this field it is important to know whether you are studying talent—such as originality, musical ability, and so forth; these capacities may well have their neurological correlates, and can be studied as "given" to a person. A man may have talent whether he uses it or not; talent can probably be measured in the person as such. But creativity can be seen only in the act. It is not, strictly speaking, proper to speak of a "creative person" but only of a *creative act*, the person creating. Sometimes, as in the case of Picasso, we have great talent and at the same time great encounter, and as a result great creativity. Sometimes we have great talent without fully realized creativity, as in the case of Jackson Pollack. I appreciate his work; but I think he will live because of the historical role cast upon him, not because of the intrinsic quality of his productions themselves. Sometimes also we have a highly creative person who seems not to have much talent. It was said of Thomas Wolfe that he was a "genius without talent." In my judgment, Wolfe is one of the highly creative figures of the American scene. But he was this precisely because he threw himself so completely into his material and the challenge of saying it; he was great because of the intensity of his encounter.

INTENSITY OF THE ENCOUNTER

This leads us to the second element in the creative act, namely, the *intensity* of the encounter. The words "absorption," "being caught up in," "wholly involved," and so on are used commonly to describe the state of the artist or scientist when creating, or even the child at play. By whatever name one calls it, genuine creativity is characterized by an intensity of awareness, a heightened consciousness. So we must now lengthen our definition to say, the creative act is encounter characterized by a high degree of consciousness. The artist, and you and I in moments of intensive encounter, experience quite clear neurological changes. These seem to be quickened heart beat, probably heightened blood pressure, increased intensity and narrowness of vision, with eyelids narrowed so that we can see more vividly the scene we are painting; and we become oblivious to things around us (as well as to the passage of time). We experience also a lessening of appetite: creative persons lose interest in eating at the moment and may work right through meal times without noticing it. Now, all of these correspond to a lowering of the functioning of the parasympathetic division of the autonomic nervous system (which has to do with ease, eating, nourishment) and an activation of the sympathetic nervous division. And lo and behold! we have the same picture which Cannon described as the "flight-fight" mechanism, the energizing of the organism for fighting or fleeing. This is the neurological correlate of what we find, in broad terms, in anxiety and fear. But the affect the artist or creative scientist feels is *not* anxiety or fear: it is *joy*. I use that word meaning precisely that—not happiness or pleasure. The artist at the moment of creating does not experience gratification or satisfaction or happiness (although he may well retrospectively when he has a cocktail or a pipe smoke in the evening afterwards); he experiences *joy*, joy defined as the affect that goes with heightened consciousness, the affect that accompanies the experience of actualizing one's own potentialities.

This intensity of awareness is not necessarily connected with conscious purpose or "willing." It may occur in reverie or on so-called unconscious levels or in dreams. An eminent professor at one of the universities in New York related this highly illustrative story. That this man is highly creative is clear; he received a Nobel prize for a new formula. He had sought this formula for some time without success. One night in his sleep he had a dream in which the formula was fully worked out. He woke up in great excitement and got up in the darkness to write it down. All he could find was a piece of paper handkerchief; on this he scribbled the formula. But in the morning, alas, he could not read his own scribbling. Each night thereafter on going to bed he concentrated his hopes upon dreaming the dream again. Fortunately, after some nights he did, and he then wrote the formula down for good. It was in actuality the formula he had sought.

We have all had similar experiences. Processes of forming, making, building go on even if we are not consciously aware of them at the time. William James once said that we learn to swim in the winter and to skate in the summer. Whether you wish to interpret these phenomena in terms of some formulation of the unconscious, or prefer to follow William James in connecting them with some neurological processes which continue even when we are not working on them, or prefer some other approach, as I do, it is still clear that creativity goes on with varying degrees of intensity on levels not directly under the control of conscious willing. Hence the heightened awareness we are speaking of does not all mean increased *self-consciousness*. It is rather correlated more with abandon, absorption, and involves a heightening of awareness in the whole personality.

But let it be said immediately that the unconscious insights, or the answers to problems that come in reverie, do not come hit and miss. They come *only in the areas to which the person is intensively committed in his conscious living*. In other words, the fact that inspiration comes from the subconscious or in dreams does not mean we can go off on a vacation or take it easy, waiting for the "subconscious to do it." These answers or creative impulses may indeed come in times of relaxation or in reverie or in other times when we alternate play with work; but what is entirely clear is that they come in those areas in which the person has worked laboriously and with dedication in his conscious experience. *Purpose* in the human being is a much more complex phenomenon than what used to be called will power; purpose involves all levels of experience. We cannot *will* to have insights, we

cannot *will* creativity; but we can will to give ourselves to the encounter with intensity of dedication and commitment. The deeper
aspects of awareness are activated to the extent that the person is
committed to the encounter.

We must also point out that this "intensity of encounter" is not
to be identified with what is called the Dionysiac aspect of creativity.
You will find this word used often in books on creative work. Coming
from the name of the Greek god Dionysus, the god of wine, the term
refers to the upsurge of vitality, the abandon which characterized ancient Dionysian, orgiastic revels. Nietzsche in his important book,
The Birth of Tragedy, cites the Dionysian principle of surging vitality
over against the Apollonian principle of form and rational order as
the two dialectical principles which are involved in creativity. This
dichotomy is assumed, following Nietzsche, by many students and
writers.

This aspect of intensity can be studied psychoanalytically easily
enough, but it is an error to identify Dionysiac "letting go" with the
intensity of which we speak. Every artist has tried at some time or
other to paint under the influence of alcohol. And what happens generally is what we would expect, and it happens in proportion to how
much alcohol is consumed: namely, that he *thinks* he is doing wonderful stuff, indeed much better than usual; but in actual fact, as he
notes next morning when, sober, he looks at the picture, he has actually performed less well than usual. Certainly Dionysiac periods of
abandon are good, particularly in our mechanical civilization where
creativity and the arts are all but starved into permanent death by
the routine of punching clocks and attending endless committee
meetings, by our intellectual assembly lines and the pressures to produce ever-greater quantities of papers and books, pressures which have
infested the academic world as well as the industrial. I am all for the
periods of "carnival" such as they still have in the Mediterranean
countries.

But the intensity which comes in the creative act itself should be
related to the encounter objectively and not released merely by something the artist "takes." Alcohol is a depressant, and possibly necessary to an industrial civilization; but when one needs it regularly to
free himself from inhibitions, the problem really is why the inhibitions exist in the first place? Hordes of persons now take benzedrene,

and the many derivatives, particularly in Hollywood and the business worlds of the large cities. The psychological studies of the upsurge of vitality and other effects that come with such drugs are exceedingly interesting, but one must sharply distinguish these from the intensity which goes with the encounter itself. We shall see below that the encounter is not something that occurs merely because we ourselves have subjectively changed; it represents a real relationship with the objective world.

The more important and profound aspect of the Dionysian principle is seen in the problem of *ecstasy*. It was in connection with Dionysian revels that Greek drama developed, a magnificent summit of creativity which achieved a sublime union of *form* and *order* with *passion* and *vitality*. Ecstasy is the technical term for the process in which this union occurs. The topic of ecstasy is one to which we should give real attention in psychology. I use the word of course not in its popular and cheapened sense of "hysteria," but in its historical etymological sense of "ex-stasis," that is meaning literally the capacity to "stand out from," to be freed from the usual split between subject and object which is an almost insurmountable barrier in most human activity. "Ecstasy" is the accurate term for the level of intensity of consciousness which occurs in the creative act. But again, ecstasy is not to be thought of merely as a Bacchic "letting go"; it involves acting as a total person, with subconscious and unconscious levels in personality acting in some form of unity with conscious levels. It is not, thus, *irrational*; it rather is suprarational. It brings intellectual, volitional, and emotional functions into play all together.

What I am saying may sound strange in the light of our traditional academic psychology. It *should* sound strange. Our traditional psychology has been founded on the dichotomy between subject and object which has been the central characteristic of Western thought for the past four centuries. Ludwig Binswanger calls this dichotomy "the cancer of all psychology and psychiatry up to now." It is not avoided by behaviorism or operationalism, which would define experience only in the objective terms, nor is it avoided by the isolation of the creative experience as a subjective phenomenon. Most psychology and modern thought still assumes this split without being aware of it. We have tended to set reason over against emotions and have tended to assume, as an outgrowth of this dichotomy, that we could observe something most accurately if our emotions were not involved. That is to say, we would be least biased if we had no emotional stake at all in the matter at hand. Now I think this is an error. There are now data in Rorschach protocols, for example, that indicate that people can observe more accurately precisely *when* they are emotionally involved; that is to say, reason works better when emotions are present, the person sees more acutely, sharply, accurately when his emotions are engaged. (I am not speaking here, of course, of "neurotic" emotions.) Indeed, I think it can be demonstrated that we cannot really see the object unless we have some emotional involvement with it. I commend this for further study.

The Dionysian and Apollonian must be united. It may well be that reason works best precisely in the state of ecstasy. The whole matter of Dionysian vitality rests on this question, *what manner of encounter releases the vitality?* What particular relation to landscape or inner vision or idea heightens the consciousness, brings forth the intensity?

Encounter as Interrelating with World

In analyzing the creative act we arrive finally at the question: What is this intense encounter *with?* An encounter is always a meeting between two poles; what is the objective pole of this dialectical relationship? I shall use a term which will sound too simple: It is the artist's or scientist's encounter with his *world.* I do not mean the usual connotations of "world"; certainly not environment, not the "sum total" of things around, nor do I refer at all to objects about a subject. All of our English connotations of "world" are emaciated from the cancer of Western thought, the subject-object split. I use world in the German sense of *Welt.* World is the pattern of meaningful relations in which the person exists and in the design of which he participates. It has objective reality, to be sure, but it is not simply that; world is interrelated to the existing person at every moment. A continual dialectical process goes on between world and self, and self and world; one implies the other, and neither can be defined if we omit the other. This is why you can never localize creativity as a *subjective* phenomenon; you can never study it in terms simply of what goes on within the person. The pole of world is an inseparable part of the creativity of the given individual. As mentioned above, we cannot speak of a "creative person"; we can only speak of a creative act. For what is occurring is always a process, a doing; specifically, a process interrelating the person and his world.

How the artist encounters his world is illustrated in the work of every genuinely creative painter. We had a beautiful and gripping illustration of this recently in New York in an exhibition of the early paintings of Mondriaan. From his first realistic work in 1904 and 1905 all the way to his later mathematical rectangles and squares in the 1930's, one could see his struggle to find the underlying forms of the objects, particularly trees, he was painting. He seems to have loved trees. The paintings around 1910, beginning somewhat like Cézanne, move further and further into the underlying meaning of tree—the roots rise organically from the ground, the branches curve and indeed bend into the trees and hills of the background in cubistic form, beautifully illustrative of what the underlying essence of "tree" is to most of us. Then we see Mondriaan struggling more and more deeply to find the "ground forms" of nature; now it is less "tree" and more the eternal geometric forms underlying all reality. And finally we see him pushing inexorably toward the squares and rectangles that are the one ultimate form of purely abstract art. Impersonal? To be sure; the individual self is lost. But is this not precisely a reflection of Mondriaan's world—the world of the decades of the 1920's and 1930's, the world in the period of emerging fascism, communism, conformism, atomic power, in which the individual not only feels lost but is lost, alienated from nature and others as well as himself?

It is absurd to think of the artist simply as "painting nature," as though he were only an anachronistic photographer of trees and lakes and mountains. Nature rather is for him a medium, one language by which he reveals his world. What any genuine painter does is to reveal the underlying psychological and spiritual condition of his relation to his world; and therefore, in the works of a great painter, we have a reflection of the emotional and spiritual condition of human beings in that period of history. If you wish to understand the real psychological temper of any historical period, you can do no better than to try to understand its art, for in the art the underlying spiritual meaning of the period is expressed directly in symbols. This is not at all because the artist is didactic or sets out to teach or to make propaganda; to the extent that he does, his power of expression is broken;

his direct relation to the inarticulate, or if you will, "unconscious," levels of the culture is broken. He has the power to reveal the underlying meaning of any period precisely because the essence of art is the powerful and alive encounter of the artist with his world.

Nowhere was this encounter demonstrated more vividly than in the famous retrospective exhibit of Picasso's works, presented in New York last spring and summer. Broader in temperament than Mondriaan, Picasso is a spokesman for his time *par excellence*. Even in his early works, around 1900, his vast talent was already visible. And in the stark, realistic paintings of peasants and poor people in the first decade of this century, his passionate relationship to human suffering was shown. You can then see the spiritual temper of each succeeding decade in his work. In the early 1920's we find Picasso painting classical Greek figures, particularly bathing by the sea; an aura of escapism hovers above these pictures in the exhibit. Was not this 1920's, this decade after the first World War, in reality a period of escapism in the Western world? Then, toward the end of the 1920's and in the early 1930's, these bathers by the sea became pieces of metal, mechanical, gray-blue curving steel. Beautiful indeed, but impersonal, unhuman. And here one is gripped in the exhibit with an ominous foreboding—the prediction of the beginning of the decades when man is to become impersonal, objectivated, a numbered unit in collectivism; it is the ominous prediction of the beginnings of man the robot. Then in 1937 comes the great painting "Guernica," with figures torn, separated, split from each other, against gray and black starkness. It was Picasso's specific reaction to the inhumanity of the bombing of the helpless Spanish town of Guernica by Mussolini's Fascist planes in the Spanish revolution; but it is much more than that. It is the most vivid portrayal imaginable of the atomistic, split-up, fragmentized state of contemporary man, and implies the conformism, emptiness, and despair which was to go along with this. And then, in the late 1930's and 1940's, Picasso's portraits become more and more machinelike—people turned literally into metal. Faces become distorted: it is as though no person, no individual, exists any more; and their places are taken by hideous witches. Pictures now are not *named*, but *numbered*. The early bright colors which are so delightful are now largely gone; in these rooms at the exhibit one feels as though darkness has settled at noon upon the earth. One gets the same stark and gripping feeling of modern man's loss of humanity as you get in the novels of Kafka. The first time I saw this exhibit, I was so overcome with the foreboding picture of man losing his face, his individuality, his humanity, and the prediction of the robot to come, that I could look no longer and had to hurry out of the room and onto the street again. To be sure, all the way through, Picasso preserves his own sanity by "playing" with paintings and sculptures of animals and his own children. But it is clear that the main stream is a portrayal of the modern condition of man which has been psychologically portrayed by Riesman, Mumford, Fromm, Tillich, and others. The whole is an unforgettable portrait of modern man in the process of losing his person and his humanity.

In this sense the genuine artist is so bound up with his age he cannot speak separated from it. In this sense, too, the historical situation conditions the creativity. For the consciousness which obtains in creativity is not the superficial level of objectified intellectualization, but an encounter with the world on a level which undercuts the subject-object split. "Creativity," to summarize our definition, "is the encounter of the intensively conscious human being with his world."

6

Toward a Theory of Creativity

CARL R. ROGERS

I maintain that there is a desperate social need for the creative behavior of creative individuals. It is this which justifies the setting forth of a tentative theory of creativity—the nature of the creative act, the conditions under which it occurs, and the manner in which it may constructively be fostered. Such a theory may serve as a stimulus and guide to research studies in this field.

THE SOCIAL NEED

Many of the serious criticisms of our culture and its trends may best be formulated in terms of a dearth of creativity. Let us state some of these very briefly:

In education we tend to turn out conformists, stereotypes, individuals whose education is "completed," rather than freely creative and original thinkers.

In our leisure-time activities, passive entertainment and regimented group action are overwhelmingly predominant, whereas creative activities are much less in evidence.

In the sciences, there is an ample supply of technicians, but the number who can creatively formulate fruitful hypotheses and theories is small indeed.

In industry, creation is reserved for the few—the manager, the de-

¹ Copyright, 1954, by the International Society for General Semantics. Reprinted from ETC.: A Review of General Semantics, Summer 1954, 11 (4); 249–260, by permission of the author and publisher.

signer, the head of the research department—whereas for the many life is devoid of original or creative endeavor.

In individual and family life the same picture holds true. In the clothes we wear, the food we eat, the books we read, and the ideas we hold, there is a strong tendency toward conformity, toward stereotypy. To be original or different is felt to be "dangerous."

Why be concerned over this? If, as a people, we enjoy conformity rather than creativity, shall we not be permitted this choice? In my estimation such a choice would be entirely reasonable were it not for one great shadow which hangs over all of us. In a time when knowledge, constructive and destructive, is advancing by the most incredible leaps and bounds into a fantastic atomic age, genuinely creative adaptation seems to represent the only possibility that man can keep abreast of the kaleidoscopic change in his world. With scientific discovery and invention proceeding, we are told, at a geometric rate of progression, a generally passive and culture-bound people cannot cope with the multiplying issues and problems. Unless individuals, groups, and nations can imagine, construct, and creatively revise new ways of relating to these complex changes, the lights will go out. Unless man can make new and original adaptations to his environment as rapidly as his science can change the environment, our culture will perish. Not only individual maladjustment and group tensions but international annihilation will be the price we pay for a lack of creativity.

Consequently it would seem to me that investigations of the process of creativity, the conditions under which this process occurs, and the ways in which it may be facilitated, are of the utmost importance.

It is in the hope of suggesting a conceptual structure under which such investigations might go forward, that the following sections are offered.

THE CREATIVE PROCESS

There are various ways of defining creativity. In order to make more clear the meaning of what is to follow, let me present the elements which, for me, are a part of the creative process, and then attempt a definition.

In the first place, for me as scientist, there must be something observable, some product of creation. Though my fantasies may be extremely novel, they cannot usefully be defined as creative unless they eventuate in some observable product—unless they are symbolized in words, or written in a poem, or translated into a work of art, or fashioned into an invention.

These products must be novel constructions. This novelty grows out of the unique qualities of the individual in his interaction with the materials of experience. Creativity always has the stamp of the individual upon its product, but the product is not the individual, nor his materials, but partakes of the relationship between the two.

Creativity is not, in my judgment, restricted to some particular content. I am assuming that there is no fundamental difference in the creative process as it is evidenced in painting a picture, composing a symphony, devising new instruments of killing, developing a scientific theory, discovering new procedures in human relationships, or creating new formings of one's own personality as in psychotherapy. (Indeed it is my experience in this last field, rather than in one of the arts, that has given me special interest in creativity and its facilitation. Intimate knowledge of the way in which the individual remolds himself in the therapeutic relationship, with originality and effective skill, gives one confidence in the creative potential of all individuals.)

My definition, then, of the creative process is that it is the emergence in action of a novel relational product, growing out of the uniqueness of the individual on the one hand, and the materials, events, people, or circumstances of his life on the other.

Let me append some negative footnotes on this definition. It makes no distinction between "good" and "bad" creativity. One man may be discovering a way of relieving pain, whereas another is devising a new and more subtle form of torture for political prisoners. Both these actions seem to me creative, even though their social value is very different. Although I shall comment on these social valuations later, I have avoided putting them in my definition because they are so fluctuating. Galileo and Copernicus made creative discoveries which in their own day were evaluated as blasphemous and wicked, and in our day as basic and constructive. We do not want to cloud our definition with terms which rest in subjectivity.

Another way of looking at this same issue is to note that to be regarded historically as representing creativity, the product must be acceptable to some group at some point of time. This fact is not helpful to our definition, however, both because of the fluctuating valuations already mentioned and because many creative products have undoubtedly never been socially noticed, have disappeared without ever having been evaluated. So this concept of group acceptance is also omitted from our definition.

In addition, it should be pointed out that our definition makes no distinction regarding the degree of creativity, since this too is a value judgment extremely variable in nature. The action of the child inventing a new game with his playmates; Einstein formulating a theory of relativity; the housewife devising a new sauce for the meat; a young author writing his first novel; all of these are, in terms of our definition, creative, and there is no attempt to set them in some order of more or less creative.

THE MOTIVATION FOR CREATIVITY

The mainspring of creativity appears to be the same tendency which we discover so deeply as the curative force in psychotherapy—man's tendency to actualize himself, to become his potentialities. By this I mean the directional trend which is evident in all organic and human life—the urge to expand, extend, develop, mature—the tendency to express and activate all the capacities of the organism, to the extent that such activation enhances the organism or the self. This tendency may become deeply buried under layer after layer of encrusted psychological defenses; it may be hidden behind elaborate façades which deny its existence; it is my belief however, based on my experience, that it exists in every individual and awaits only the proper conditions to be released and expressed. It is this tendency which is the primary motivation for creativity as the organism forms new relationships to the environment in its endeavor most fully to be itself.

Let us now attempt to deal directly with this puzzling issue of the social value of a creative act. Presumably few of us are interested in facilitating creativity which is socially destructive. We do not wish, knowingly, to lend our efforts to developing individuals whose creative genius works itself out in new and better ways of robbing, exploiting, torturing, killing other individuals; or developing forms of political organization or art forms which lead humanity into paths of physical or psychological self-destruction. Yet how is it possible to make the necessary discriminations such that we may encourage a constructive creativity and not a destructive?

The distinction cannot be made by examining the product. The very essence of the creative is its novelty, and hence we have no standard by which to judge it. Indeed history points up the fact that the more original the product, and the more far-reaching its implications, the more likely it is to be judged by contemporaries as evil. The genuinely significant creation, whether an idea, or a work of art, or a scientific discovery, is most likely to be seen at first as erroneous, bad, or foolish. Later it may be seen as obvious, something self-evident to all. Only still later does it receive its final evaluation as a creative contribution. It seems clear that no contemporary mortal can satisfactorily evaluate a creative product at the time that it is formed, and this statement is increasingly true the greater the novelty of the creation.

Nor is it of any help to examine the purposes of the individual participating in the creative process. Many, perhaps most, of the creations and discoveries which have proved to have great social value, have been motivated by purposes having more to do with personal interests than with social value, while on the other hand history records a somewhat sorry outcome for many of those creations (various Utopias, Prohibition, etc.) which had as their avowed purpose the achievement of the social good. No, we must face the fact that the individual creates primarily because it is satisfying to him, because this behavior is felt to be self-actualizing, and we get nowhere by trying to differentiate "good" and "bad" purposes in the creative process.

Must we then give over any attempt to discriminate between creativity which is potentially constructive, and that which is potentially destructive? I do not believe this pessimistic conclusion is justified. It is here that recent clinical findings from the field of psychotherapy give us hope. It has been found that when the individual is "open" to all of his experience (a phrase which will be defined more fully), then his behavior will be creative, and his creativity may be trusted to be essentially constructive.

The differentiation may be put very briefly as follows. To the extent that the individual is denying to awareness (or repressing, if you prefer that term) large areas of his experience, then his creative formings may be pathological or socially evil, or both. To the degree that the individual is open to all aspects of his experience, and has available to his awareness all the varied sensings and perceivings which are going on within his organism, then the novel products of his interaction with his environment will tend to be constructive both for himself and others. To illustrate, an individual with paranoid tendencies may creatively develop a most novel theory of the relationship between himself and his environment, seeing evidence for his theory in all sorts of minute clues. His theory has little social value, perhaps because there is an enormous range of experience which this individual cannot permit in his awareness. Socrates, on the other hand, although also regarded as "crazy" by his contemporaries, developed novel ideas which have proven to be socially constructive. Very possibly this was because he was notably nondefensive and open to his experience.

The reasoning behind this will perhaps become more clear in the remaining sections of this paper. Primarily however it is based upon the discovery in psychotherapy:

. . . that if we can add to the sensory and visceral experiencing which is characteristic of the whole animal kingdom the gift of a free and undistorted awareness of which only the human animal seems fully capable, we have an organism which is aware of the demands of the culture as it is of its own physiological demands for food or sex; which is just as aware of its desire for friendly relationships as it is of its desire to aggrandize itself; which is just as aware of its delicate and sensitive tenderness toward others as it is of its hostilities toward others. When man's unique capacity of awareness is thus functioning freely and fully, we find that we have, not an animal whom we must fear, not a beast who must be controlled, but an organism able to achieve, through the remarkable integrative capacity of its central nervous system, a balanced, realistic, self-enhancing, other-enhancing behavior as a resultant of all these elements of awareness. To put it another way, when man is less than fully man—when he denies to awareness various aspects of his experience—then indeed we have all too often reason to fear him and his behavior, as the present world situation testifies. But when he is most fully man, when he is his complete organism, when awareness of experience, that peculiarly human attribute, is most fully operating, then he is to be trusted, then his behavior is constructive. It is not always conventional. It will not always be conforming. It will be individualized. But it will also be socialized (Rogers, 1953a).

THE INNER CONDITIONS OF CONSTRUCTIVE CREATIVITY

What are the conditions within the individual which are most closely associated with a potentially constructive creative act? I see these as possibilities.

A. *Openness to experience: extensionality.* This is the opposite of psychological defensiveness, when to protect the organization of the self certain experiences are prevented from coming into awareness except in distorted fashion. In a person who is open to experience each stimulus is freely relayed through the nervous system, without being distorted by any process of defensiveness. Whether the stimulus originates in the environment, in the impact of form, color, or sound, on the sensory nerves, or whether it originates in the viscera, or as a memory trace in the central nervous system, it is available to awareness. This means that instead of perceiving in predetermined categories (trees are green; college education is good; modern art is silly) the individual is aware of this existential moment as *it* is, thus being alive to many experiences which fall outside the usual categories (*this* tree is lavender; *this* college education is damaging; *this* modern sculpture has a powerful effect on me).

This last suggests another way of describing openness to experience. It means lack of rigidity and permeability of boundaries in concepts, beliefs, perceptions, and hypotheses. It means a tolerance for ambiguity where ambiguity exists. It means the ability to receive much conflicting information without forcing closure upon the situation. It means what the general semanticist calls the "extensional orientation."

This complete openness of awareness to what exists at this moment is, I believe, an important condition of constructive creativity. In an equally intense but more narrowly limited fashion it is no doubt present in all creativity. The deeply maladjusted artist who cannot recognize or be aware of the sources of unhappiness in himself may nevertheless be sharply and sensitively aware of form and color in his experience. The tyrant (whether on a petty or grand scale) who cannot face the weaknesses in himself may nevertheless be completely alive to and aware of the chinks in the psychological armor of those with whom he deals. Because there is the openness to one phase of experience, creativity is possible; because the openness is *only* to one phase of experience, the product of this creativity may be potentially destructive of social values. The more the individual has available to himself a sensitive awareness of all phases of his experience, the more sure we can be that his creativity will be personally and socially constructive.

B. *An internal locus of evaluation.* Perhaps the most fundamental condition of creativity is that the source or locus of evaluative judgment is internal. The value of his product is, for the creative person, established not by the praise or criticism of others, but by himself. Have I created something satisfying to *me?* Does it express a part of me—my feeling or my thought, my pain or my ecstasy? These are the only questions which really matter to the creative person, or to any person when he is being creative.

This does not mean that he is oblivious to, or unwilling to be aware of, the judgments of others. It is simply that the basis of evaluation lies within himself, in his own organismic reaction to and appraisal of his product. If to the person it has the "feel" of being "me in action," of being an actualization of potentialities in himself which heretofore have not existed and are now emerging into existence, then it is satisfying and creative, and no outside evaluation can change that fundamental fact.

C. *The ability to toy with elements and concepts.* Though this is probably less important than A or B, it seems to be a condition of creativity. Associated with the openness and lack of rigidity described under A is the ability to play spontaneously with ideas, colors, shapes, relationships—to juggle elements into impossible juxtapositions, to shape wild hypotheses, to make the given problematic, to express the ridiculous, to translate from one form to another, to transform into improbable equivalents. It is from this spontaneous toying and exploration that there arises the hunch, the creative seeing of life in a new and significant way. It is as though out of the wasteful spawning of thousands of possibilities there emerges one or two evolutionary forms with the qualities which give them a more permanent value.

The Creative Act and Its Concomitants

When these three conditions obtain, constructive creativity will occur. But we cannot expect an accurate description of the creative act, for by its very nature it is indescribable. This is the unknown which we must recognize as unknowable until it occurs. This is the improbable that becomes probable. Only in a very general way can we say that a creative act is the natural behavior of an organism which has a tendency to arise when that organism is open to all of its inner and outer experiencing, and when it is free to try out in flexible fashion all manner of relationships. Out of this multitude of half-formed possibilities the organism, like a great computing machine, selects this one which most effectively meets an inner need, or that one which forms a more effective relationship with the environment, or this other one which discovers a more simple and satisfying order in which life may be perceived.

There is one quality of the creative act which may, however, be described. In almost all the products of creation we note a selectivity, or emphasis, an evidence of discipline, an attempt to bring out the essence. The artist paints surfaces or textures in simplified form, ignoring the minute variations which exist in reality. The scientist formulates a basic law of relationships, brushing aside all the particular events or circumstances which might conceal its naked beauty. The writer selects those words and phrases which give unity to his expression. We may say that this is the influence of the specific person, of the "I." Reality exists in a multiplicity of confusing facts, but "I" bring a structure to my relationship to reality; I have "my" way of perceiving reality, and it is this (unconsciously?) disciplined personal selectivity or abstraction which gives to creative products their esthetic quality.

Although this is as far as we can go in describing any aspect of the creative act, there are certain of its concomitants in the individual which may be mentioned. The first is what we may call the Eureka feeling—"This is it!" "I have discovered!" "This is what I wanted to express!"

Another concomitant is the anxiety of separateness.[2] I do not believe that many significantly creative products are formed without the feeling, "I am alone. No one has ever done just this before. I have ventured into territory where no one has been. Perhaps I am foolish, or wrong, or lost, or abnormal."

Still another experience which usually accompanies creativity is the

[2] For this and the idea in the following paragraph I am specifically indebted to my student and colleague, Mr. Robert Lipgar.

desire to communicate. It is doubtful whether a human being can create, without wishing to share his creation. It is the only way he can assuage the anxiety of separateness and assure himself that he belongs to the group. He may confide his theories only to his private diary. He may put his discoveries in some cryptic code. He may conceal his poems in a locked drawer. He may put away his paintings in a closet. Yet he desires to communicate with a group which will understand him, even if he must imagine such a group. He does not create in order to communicate, but once having created he desires to share this new aspect of himself-in-relation-to-his-environment with others.

CONDITIONS FOSTERING CONSTRUCTIVE CREATIVITY

Thus far I have tried to describe the nature of creativity, to indicate that quality of individual experience which increases the likelihood that creativity will be constructive, to set forth the necessary conditions for the creative act and to state some of its concomitants. But if we are to make progress in meeting the social need which was presented initially, we must know whether constructive creativity can be fostered, and if so, how.

From the very nature of the inner conditions of creativity it is clear that they cannot be forced, but must be permitted to emerge. The farmer cannot make the germ develop and sprout from the seed; he can only supply the nurturing conditions which will permit the seed to develop its own potentialities. So it is with creativity. How can we establish the external conditions which will foster and nourish the internal conditions described above? My experience in psychotherapy leads me to believe that by setting up conditions of psychological safety and freedom, we maximize the likelihood of an emergence of constructive creativity. Let me spell out these conditions in some detail, labeling them as X and Y.

X. *Psychological Safety.* This may be established by three associated processes:

1. *Accepting the individual as of unconditional worth.* Whenever a teacher, parent, therapist, or other person with a facilitating function feels basically that this individual is of worth in his own right and in his own unfolding, no matter what his present condition or behavior, he is fostering creativity. This attitude can probably be genuine

only when the teacher, parent, etc., senses the potentialities of the individual and thus is able to have an unconditional faith in him, no matter what his present state.

The effect on the individual as he apprehends this attitude is to sense a climate of safety. He gradually learns that he can be whatever he is, without sham or façade, since he seems to be regarded as of worth no matter what he does. Hence he has less need of rigidity, can discover what it means to be himself, can try to actualize himself in new and spontaneous ways. He is, in other words, moving toward creativity.

2. *Providing a climate in which external evaluation is absent.* When we cease to form judgments of the other individual from our own locus of evaluation, we are fostering creativity. For the individual to find himself in an atmosphere where he is not being evaluated, not being measured by some external standard, is enormously freeing. Evaluation is always a threat, always creates a need for defensiveness, always means that some portion of experience must be denied to awareness. If this product is evaluated as good by external standards, then I must not admit my own dislike of it. If what I am doing is bad by external standards, then I must not be aware of the fact that it seems to be me, to be part of myself. But if judgments based on external standards are not being made then I can be more open to my experience, can recognize my own likings and dislikings, the nature of the materials and of my reaction to them, more sharply and more sensitively. I can begin to recognize the locus of evaluation within myself. Hence I am moving toward creativity.

To allay some possible doubts and fears in the reader, it should be pointed out that to cease evaluating another is not to cease having reactions. It may, as a matter of fact, free one to react. "I don't like your idea" (or painting, or invention, or writing), is not an evaluation, but a reaction. It is subtly but sharply different from a judgment which says, "What you are doing is bad (or good), and this quality is assigned to you from some external source." The first statement permits the individual to maintain his own locus of evaluation. It holds the possibility that I am unable to appreciate something which is actually very good. The second statement, whether it praises or condemns, tends to put the person at the mercy of outside forces. He is being told that he cannot simply ask himself whether this product is a valid expression of himself; he must be concerned with what others think. He is being led away from creativity.

3. *Understanding empathically.* It is this which provides the ultimate in psychological safety, when added to the other two. If I say that I "accept" you, but know nothing of you, this is a shallow acceptance indeed, and you realize that it may change if I actually come to know you. But if I understand you, empathically, see you and what you are feeling and doing from your point of view, enter your private world and see it as it appears to you—and still accept you—then this is safety indeed. In this climate you can permit your real self to emerge, and to express itself in varied and novel formings as it relates itself to the world. This is a basic fostering of creativity.

Y. *Psychological freedom.* When a teacher, parent, therapist, or other facilitating person permits the individual a complete freedom of symbolic expression, creativity is fostered. This permissiveness gives the individual complete freedom to think, to feel, to be, whatever is most inward within himself. It fosters the openness, and the playful and spontaneous juggling of percepts, concepts, and meanings, which is a part of creativity.

Note that it is complete freedom of *symbolic* expression which is described. To express in behavior all feelings, impulses, and formings may not in all instances be freeing. Behavior may in some instances be limited by society, and this is as it should be. But symbolic expression need not be limited. Thus, to destroy a hated object (whether one's mother or a rococo building) by destroying a symbol of it, is freeing. To attack it in reality may create guilt and narrow the psychological freedom which is experienced. (I feel unsure of this paragraph, but it is the best formulation I can give at the moment which seems to square with my experience.)

The permissiveness which is being described is not softness or indulgence or encouragement. It is permission to be free, which also means that one is responsible. The individual is as free to be afraid of a new venture as to be eager for it; free to bear the consequences of his mistakes as well as of his achievements. It is this type of freedom responsibly to be oneself which fosters the development of a secure locus of evaluation within oneself, and hence tends to bring about the inner conditions of constructive creativity.

PUTTING THE THEORY TO WORK

There is but one excuse for attempting to discover conceptual order and stating it in a theory; that is to develop hypotheses from the theory which may be tested. By such testing profitable directions for action may be found, and the theory itself may be corrected, modified, and extended. Thus if this theory which I have tentatively formulated is worthwhile, it should be possible to develop from it hypotheses which might be objectively tested in classes in the arts; in education outside of the arts; in leadership training groups whether in industry or the military services; in problem-solving groups of any sort. Let me suggest a few of the general hypotheses which might be given more specific and operational form for any of the above groups. They would apply whether one was concerned with the development of creative artists or creative leaders; with originality of design or creative methods of problem-solving.

Hypotheses regarding inner conditions:

1. Individuals who exhibit a measurably greater degree of conditions A, B, and C (openness, internal locus of evaluation, ability to toy with materials) will, over any given period of time spontaneously form more products judged to be novel and creative, than a matched group who exhibit a lesser degree of A, B, and C.

2. The products of the first group will not only be more numerous, but will be judged to be more significant in their novelty. (Such a hypothesis could be given operational definition in art classes, problem-solving groups, or leadership training groups, for example.)

3. Condition A (openness to experience) can be predicted from conditions B or C, which are more easily measurable. (It is not at all certain that this hypothesis would be upheld, but it would be worth careful investigation. If conditions A, B, and C are highly intercorrelated, then they could jointly be predicted from the one which proved most easily measurable. Thus we might gain clues as to how we might less laboriously select graduate students, for example, with a high creative potential.)

Hypotheses regarding fostering constructive creativity:

4. Given two matched groups, the one in which the leader establishes a measurably greater degree of conditions X1, X2, X3, and Y (psychological safety and freedom) will spontaneously form a greater

number of creative products, and these products will be judged to be more significantly novel.

5. Conditions X1, X2, X3, and Y are not of equal importance in fostering creativity. By comparing different groups in which one or another of these conditions is emphasized or minimized it may be possible to determine which of these conditions is most effective in facilitating creativity.

6. A group in which conditions X1, X2, X3, and Y are established should, according to our theory, have more effective and harmonious interpersonal relationships than a matched group in which these conditions are present to a lesser degree. (The reasoning is that if creativity is all of a piece, then a group in which the fostering conditions are established should be more constructively creative in social relationships.)

7. The extent to which different groups in our culture provide the fostering conditions (X and Y) could be measured. In this way one could determine whether creativity is now being fostered to a greater degree by the family group, classes in schools and colleges, bull sessions, social clubs and groups, interest groups, military groups, industrial groups. (One wonders how college classes would show up in such a comparison.)

Conclusion

I have endeavored to present an orderly way of thinking about the creative process, in order that some of these ideas might be put to a rigorous and objective test. My justification for formulating this theory and my reason for hoping that such research may be carried out is that the present development of the physical sciences is making an imperative demand upon us as individuals and as a culture for creative behavior in adapting ourselves to our new world if we are to survive.

7

Creativity in Self-Actualizing People

ABRAHAM H. MASLOW

I FIRST had to change my ideas about creativity about fifteen years ago, when I began a study of persons who were positively healthy, highly evolved, and matured, self-actualizing. These ideas have been evolving ever since and will, I suppose, continue to change. This is, therefore, a report of progress. Side by side with it has gone a change in my conception of what psychology is and should be.

I early had to give up my stereotyped notion that health, genius, talent, and productivity were synonymous. A large proportion of my subjects, although healthy and creative in a special sense that I am going to describe, were *not* productive in the ordinary sense, nor did they have great talent or genius, nor were they poets, composers, inventors, artists, or creative intellectuals. It was obvious that some of the greatest talents of mankind were certainly not psychologically healthy people—Wagner, for example, or Van Gogh or Dégas or Byron. Some were and some were not, it was clear. I early had to come to the conclusion that great talent was not only more or less independent of goodness or health of character but also that we know little about it. For instance, there is some evidence that great musical talent and mathematical talent are more inherited than acquired (Scheinfeld, 1950). It seemed clear then that health and special talent were separate variables, maybe only slightly correlated, maybe not. At this time, we may as well admit that psychology knows little about special talent of the genius type. I shall say nothing more about it, confining myself instead to that more widespread kind of creativeness which is the universal heritage of every human being that is born, and which co-varies with psychological health (Moustakas, 1956). Furthermore, I soon discovered that I had, like most other people, been thinking of creativeness in terms of products, and secondly, I had unconsciously confined creativeness to certain conventional areas only of human endeavor. That is, I unconsciously assumed that any painter was leading a creative life, any poet, any composer. Theorists, artists, scientists, inventors, writers could be creative. Nobody else could be. You were in or you were out, all or none, as if creativeness were the sole prerogative of certain professionals.

But these expectations were broken up by various persons among my subjects. For instance, one woman, uneducated, poor, a full-time housewife and mother, did none of these conventionally creative things and yet was a marvelous cook, mother, wife, and homemaker. With little money, her home was somehow always beautiful. She was a perfect hostess. Her meals were banquets. Her taste in linens, silver, glass, crockery, and furniture was impeccable. She was in all these areas original, novel, ingenious, unexpected, inventive. I just had to call her creative. I learned from her and others like her to think that a first-rate soup is more creative than a second-rate painting, and that generally, cooking or parenthood or making a home could be creative whereas poetry need not be; it could be uncreative.

Another of my subjects devoted herself to what had best be called social service in the broadest sense, bandaging up wounds, helping the downtrodden, not only in a personal way but in an organizational way as well. One of her "creations" is an organization which helps many more people than she could individually.

Another was a psychiatrist, a "pure" clinician who never wrote anything or created any theories or researches but who delighted in his everyday job of helping people to create themselves. This man approached each patient as if he were the only one in the world, without jargon, expectations, or presuppositions, with innocence and naïveté and yet with great wisdom, in a Taoistic fashion. Each patient was a unique human being and therefore a completely new problem to be understood and solved in a completely novel way. His great success even with very difficult cases validated his "creative" (rather than stereotyped or orthodox) way of doing things. From another man I learned that constructing a business organization could be a creative activity. From a young athlete, I learned that a perfect tackle could be as aesthetic a product as a sonnet and could be approached in the same creative spirit. In other words, I learned to apply the word "creative" (and also the word "aesthetic") not only to products but also to people in a characterological way, and to activities, processes, and attitudes. And furthermore, I had come to apply the word "creative" to many products other than the standard and conventionally accepted poems, theories, novels, experiments, or paintings to which I had hitherto restricted the word.

CHARACTERISTICS OF SELF-ACTUALIZING PERSONS

The consequence was that I found it necessary to distinguish "special talent creativeness" from "self-actualizing creativeness" which sprang much more directly from the personality, which showed itself widely in the ordinary affairs of life, and which showed itself not only in great and obvious products but also in many other ways, in a certain kind of humor, a tendency to do *anything* creatively; e.g., teaching. Frequently, it appeared that an essential aspect of self-actualizing creativeness was a special kind of perceptiveness which is exemplified by the child in the fable who saw that the king had no clothes on; this, too, contradicts the notion of creativity as products. These people can see the fresh, the raw, the concrete, the ideographic, as well as the generic, the abstract, the rubricized, the categorized, and the classified. Consequently, they live far more in the real world of nature than in the verbalized world of concepts, abstractions, expectations, beliefs, and stereotypes that most people confuse with the real world (Maslow, 1954, Chaps. 12, 14). This is well expressed in Rogers's (1956) phrase "openness to experience."

All my subjects were relatively more spontaneous and expressive (Maslow, 1954, Chaps. 11, 12). They were able to be more "natural" and less controlled and inhibited in their behavior, which seemed to be able to flow out more easily and freely and with less blocking and self-criticism. This ability to express ideas and impulses without strangulation and without fear of ridicule from others turned out to be an essential aspect of self-actualizing creativeness. Rogers (1956) has used the excellent phrase "fully functioning person" to describe this aspect of health.

Another observation was that self-actualizing creativeness was in many respects like the creativeness of all happy and secure children. It was spontaneous, effortless, innocent, easy, a kind of freedom from stereotypes and clichés. Again it seemed to be made up largely of "innocent" freedom of perception and "innocent," uninhibited spontaneity and expressiveness. Almost any child can perceive more freely, without a priori expectations about what ought to be there or what must be there or what has always been there. And almost any child can compose a song or a poem or a dance or a painting or a play or a game on the spur of the moment, without planning or previous intent.

It was in this childlike sense that my subjects were creative. Or to avoid misunderstanding, since my subjects were after all not children (they were all people in their fifties or sixties), let us say that they had either retained or regained at least these two main aspects of childlikeness; namely, they were nonrubricizing and "open to experience," and they were easily spontaneous and expressive. These characteristics were, however, different in quality from what is found in children. If children are naïve, then my subjects had attained a "second naïveté" as Santayana called it. Their innocence of perception and expressiveness was combined with sophisticated minds.

In any case, this all sounds as if we are dealing with a fundamental characteristic, inherent in human nature, a potentiality given to all or most human beings at birth, which most often is lost or buried or inhibited as the person gets enculturated.

My subjects were different from the average person in another characteristic that makes creativity more likely. Self-actualizing people are relatively unfrightened by the unknown, the mysterious, the puzzling, and often are positively attracted by it; i.e., selectively pick it out to puzzle over, to meditate on, and to be absorbed with. I quote from my description:

They do not neglect the unknown, or deny it, or run away from it, or try to make believe it is really known, nor do they organize, dichotomize, or rubricize it prematurely. They do not cling to the familiar, nor is their quest for the truth a catastrophic need for certainty, safety, definiteness, and order, such as we see in an exaggerated form in Goldstein's brain injured or in the compulsive-obsessive neurotic. They can be, when the total objective situation calls for it, comfortably disorderly, sloppy, anarchic, chaotic, vague, doubtful, uncertain, indefinite, approximate, inexact, or inaccurate (all, at certain moments in science, art, or life in general, quite desirable).

Thus it comes about that doubt, tentativeness, uncertainty, with the consequent necessity for abeyance of decision, which is for most a torture, can be for some a pleasantly stimulating challenge, a high spot in life rather than a low (Maslow, 1954, p. 206).

One observation I made has puzzled me for many years but it begins to fall into place now. It was what I described as the resolution of dichotomies in self-actualizing people. Briefly stated, I found that I had to see differently many oppositions and polarities that psychologists had taken for granted as straight line continua. For instance, to take the first dichotomy, I could not decide whether my subjects were selfish or unselfish. Observe how spontaneously we fall into an either-or here. The more of one, the less of the other is the implication of the style in which I put the question. But I was forced by sheer pressure of fact to give up this Aristotelian style of logic. My subjects were unselfish in one sense and selfish in another sense. And the two fused together, not like incompatibles, but rather in a sensible, dynamic unity or synthesis much like what Fromm (1956) has described in his paper on self-love; i.e., on healthy selfishness. My subjects had put opposites together in such a way as to make me realize that to regard selfishness and unselfishness as contradictory and mutually exclusive is itself characteristic of a lower level of personality development. So also in my subjects were many other dichotomies resolved into unities, cognition versus conation (heart versus head, wish versus fact) became cognition "structured with" conation as instinct and reason came to the same conclusions. Duty became pleasure and pleasure merged with duty. The distinction between work and play became shadowy. How could selfish hedonism be opposed to altruism, when altruism became selfishly pleasurable? These most mature of all people were also strongly childlike. These same people, the strongest egos ever described and the most definitely individual, were also precisely the ones who could be most easily ego-less, self-transcending, and problem centered (Maslow, 1954, pp. 232–234).

But this is precisely what the great artist does. He is able to put together clashing colors, forms that fight each other, dissonances of all kinds, into a unity. And this is also what the great theorist does when he puts puzzling and inconsistent facts together so that we can see that they really belong together. And so also for the great states- man, the great therapist, the great philosopher, the great parent, the great lover, the great inventor. They are all integrators, able to put separates and even opposites together into unity.

We speak here of the ability to integrate and of the play back and forth between integration within the person, and his ability to inte- grate whatever it is he is doing in the world. To the extent that crea- tiveness is constructive, synthesizing, unifying, and integrative, to that extent does it depend in part on the inner integration of the person.

In trying to figure out why all this was so, it seemed to me that much boiled down to the relative absence of fear in my subjects. They were certainly less enculturated; that is, they seemed to be less afraid of what other people would say or demand or laugh at. It was found that they had less need of other people and therefore, depending on them less, could be less afraid of them and less hostile against them. Perhaps more important, however, was their lack of fear of their own insides, of their own impulses, emotions, thoughts. They were more self-accepting than the average. It was this approval and acceptance of their deeper selves that made it possible to perceive bravely the real nature of the world and also made their behavior more spontaneous (less controlled, less inhibited, less planned, less "willed" and de- signed). They were less afraid of their own thoughts even when they were "nutty" or silly or crazy. They were less afraid of being laughed at or of being disapproved of. They could let themselves be flooded by emotion. By contrast, average and neurotic people walled off, through fear, much that lay within themselves. They controlled, they inhibited, they repressed and they suppressed. They disapproved of their deeper selves and expected that others did, too.

What I am saying in effect is that the creativity of my subjects seemed to be an epiphenomenon of their greater wholeness and inte- gration, which is what self-acceptance implies. The civil war within the average person between the forces of the inner depths and the forces of defense and control seems to have been resolved in my sub- jects and they are less split. As a consequence, more of themselves is available for use, for enjoyment, and for creative purposes. They waste less of their time and energy protecting themselves against themselv

THE "PEAK-EXPERIENCE"

Another later investigation on "peak-experiences" supported and enriched these conclusions (Maslow, 1959). What I did was to question many persons (not only healthy ones) about the most wonderful, most ecstatic experiences of their lives. This had started out as an attempt to make a generalized, all-inclusive theory of the changes of cognition which had been described in the various specific literatures on the creative experience, the esthetic experience, the love experience, the insight experience, the orgasmic experience, the mystic experience. The generalized word I used for all these happenings was "peak-experience." It was my impression that each of these experiences changed the person and his perception of the world in similar or parallel ways. And I was impressed by the fact that these changes often seemed to parallel my already-described self-actualization, or at least a transient unifying of the splits within the person.

So it turned out. But here, too, some comfortable beliefs had to be given up. For one thing, I had to respect constitutional differences of the Sheldonian sort more than I had, as Morris (1956) had also discovered. Different kinds of people get their peak-experiences from different kinds of happenings. But no matter where they get them from, the subjective experience is described in about the same way. And I assure you that it was a startling thing for me to hear a woman describing her feelings as she gave birth to a child in the same words used by Bucke (1923) to describe the "cosmic consciousness" or by Huxley to describe the "mystic experience" in all cultures and eras or by Ghiselin to describe the creative process or by Suzuki to describe the Zen *satori* experience. It opened up for me also the possibility of different kinds of creativeness, as well as of health.

The main finding relevant to our present topic, however, was that an essential aspect of the peak-experience is integration within the person and therefore between the person and the world. In these states of being, the person becomes unified; for the time being, the splits, polarities, and dissociations within him tend to be resolved; the civil war within is neither won nor lost but transcended. In such a state, the person becomes far more open to experience and far more spontaneous and fully functioning, essential characteristics as we have already seen, of self-actualizing creativeness.

One aspect of the peak-experience is a complete, though momentary, loss of fear, anxiety, inhibition, defense, and control, a giving up of renunciation, delay, and restraint. The fear of disintegration and dissolution, the fear of being overwhelmed by the "instincts," the fear of death and of insanity, the fear of giving in to unbridled pleasure and emotion, all tend to disappear or go into abeyance for the time being. This, too, implies a greater openness of perception since fear distorts.

It may be thought of as pure gratification, pure expression, pure elation. But since it is "in the world," it represents a kind of fusion of the Freudian "pleasure principle" and "reality principle" (Maslow, 1959).

Observe that these fears are all of our own depths. It is as if in the peak-experience we accepted and embraced our deeper selves instead of controlling and fearing them.

For one thing, not only the world but also he himself becomes more a unity, more integrated, and self-consistent. This is another way of saying that he becomes more completely himself, idiosyncratic, unique. And since he is so, he can be more easily expressive and spontaneous without effort. All his powers then come together in their most efficient integration and coordination, organized and coordinated much more perfectly than usual. Everything then can be done with unusual ease and lack of effort. Inhibition, doubt, control, self-criticism diminish toward a zero point and he becomes the spontaneous, coordinated, efficient organism, functioning like an animal without conflict or split, without hesitation or doubt, in a great flow of power that is so peculiarly effortless, that it may become like play, masterful, virtuoso-like. In such a moment, his powers are at their height and he may be startled (afterwards) by his unsuspected skill, confidence, creativeness, perceptiveness and virtuosity of performance. It is all so easy that it can be enjoyed and laughed with. Things can be dared that would be impossible at other times.

To put it simply, he becomes more whole and unified, more unique and idiosyncratic, more alive and spontaneous, more perfectly expressive and uninhibited, more effortless and powerful, more daring and courageous (leaving fears and doubts behind), more ego-transcending and self-forgetful (Maslow, 1959).

And since almost everyone I questioned could remember such experiences, I had to come to the tentative conclusion that many, perhaps most, people are capable of temporary states of integration, even of self-actualization, and therefore of self-actualizing creativeness.

(Of course, I must be tentative in view of my casual and inadequate sampling.)

PRIMARY, SECONDARY, AND INTEGRATED CREATIVENESS

Classical Freudian theory is of little use for our purposes and as a matter of fact is partially contradicted by our data. It is (or was) essentially an id psychology, an investigation of the instinctive impulses and their vicissitudes, and the basic Freudian dialectic is seen to be ultimately between impulses and defenses against them. But far more crucial than repressed impulses for understanding the sources of creativity (as well as the sources of play, love, enthusiasm, humor, imagination, and fantasy) are the so-called primary processes which are essentially cognitive rather than conative. As soon as we turn our attention to this aspect of human depth-psychology, at once we find much agreement between the psychoanalytic ego-psychology (Kris, 1952; Milner, 1957; Ehrenzweig, 1953), the Jungian psychology, and the American self-and-growth psychology.

The normal adjustment of the average, commonsense, well-adjusted man implies a continued successful rejection of much of the depths of human nature, both conative and cognitive. To adjust well to the world of reality means a splitting of the person. It means that the person turns his back on much in himself because it is dangerous. But it is now clear that by so doing he loses a great deal, too, for these depths are also the source of all his joys, his ability to play, to love, to laugh, and, most important for us, to be creative. By protecting himself against the hell within himself, he also cuts himself off from the heaven within. In the extreme instance, we have the obsessional person, flat, tight, rigid, frozen, controlled, cautious, who can not laugh or play or love or be silly or trusting or childish. His imagination, his intuitions, his softness, his emotionality tend to be strangulated or distorted.

The goals of psychoanalysis as a therapy are ultimately integrative. The effort is to heal this basic split by insight, so that what has been repressed becomes conscious or preconscious. But here again we can make modifications as a consequence of studying the depth sources of creativeness. Our relation to our primary processes is not in all respects the same as our relation to unacceptable wishes. The most important difference that I can see is that our primary processes are not as dangerous as the forbidden impulses. To a large extent they are not repressed or censored but rather are forgotten as Schachtel (1947) has shown, or else turned away from, suppressed (rather than repressed) as we have to adjust to a harsh reality which demands a purposeful and pragmatic striving rather than revery, poetry, play. Or to say it in another way, in a rich society there must be far less resistance to primary thought processes. I expect that education processes, which are known to do rather little for relieving repression of "instinct," can do much to accept and integrate the primary processes into conscious and preconscious life. Education in art, poetry, dancing, can in principle do much in this direction. So also can education in dynamic psychology; for instance, Deutsch and Murphy's (1955) *Clinical Interview*, which speaks in primary process language, can be seen as a kind of poetry. Milner's (1957) extraordinary book *On Not Being Able to Paint* makes my point perfectly.

The kind of creativeness I have been trying to sketch out is best exemplified by the improvisation, as in jazz or in childlike paintings, rather than by the work of art designated as "great." In the first place, the great work needs great talent which, as I found, turned out to be irrelevant for my concern. In the second place, the great work needs not only the flash, the inspiration, the peak-experience, it also needs hard work, long training, unrelenting criticism, perfectionistic standards. In other words, succeeding upon the spontaneous is the deliberate; succeeding upon total acceptance comes criticism; succeeding upon intuition comes rigorous thought; succeeding upon daring comes caution; succeeding upon fantasy and imagination comes reality testing. Now come the questions, "Is it true?" "Will it be understood by the others?" "Is its structure sound?" "Does it stand the test of logic?" "How will it do in the world?" "Can I prove it?"

Now come the comparisons, the judgments, the evaluations, the cold, calculating, morning-after thoughts, the selections and the rejections.

If I may say it so, the secondary processes now take over from the primary, the Apollonian from the Dionysian, the "masculine" from the "feminine." The voluntary regression into our depths is now terminated, the necessary passivity and receptivity of inspiration or of peak-experience must now give way to activity, control, and hard work. A peak-experience happens *to* a person; but the person *makes* the great product. It could be described as a masculine phase succeeding upon a feminine one.

Strictly speaking, I have investigated this first phase only, that which comes easily and without effort as a spontaneous expression of an integrated person, or of a transient unifying within the person. It can come only if a person's depths are available to him, only if he is not afraid of his primary thought processes.

I shall call "primary creativity" that which proceeds from and uses the primary process much more than the secondary processes. The creativity which is based mostly on the secondary thought processes, I shall call "secondary" creativity. This latter type includes a large proportion of production-in-the-world, the bridges, the houses, the new automobiles, even many scientific experiments and much literary work which are essentially the consolidation and exploitation of other people's ideas. It parallels the difference between the commando and the military police behind the lines, the pioneer and the settler. That creativity which uses *both* types of process easily and well in good fusion or in good succession, I shall call "integrated creativity." It is from this kind that comes the great work of art or philosophy or science.

CONCLUSION

All of these developments can, I think, be summarized as an increased stress on the role of integration (or self-consistency, unity, wholeness) in the theory of creativeness. Resolving a dichotomy into a higher, more inclusive unity amounts to healing a split in the person and making him more unified. Since the splits I have been talking about are within the person, they amount to a kind of civil war, a setting of one part of the person against another part. In any case, so far as self-actualizing creativeness is concerned, it seems to come more immediately from fusion of primary and secondary processes rather than from working through repressive control of forbidden impulses and wishes. It is, of course, probable that defenses arising out of fears of these forbidden impulses also push down primary processes in a kind of total, undiscriminating, panicky war on all the depths. But it seems that such lack of discrimination is not in principle necessary.

To summarize, self-actualizing creativeness stresses first the personality rather than its achievements, considering these achievements to be epiphenomena emitted by the personality and therefore secondary to it. It stresses characterological qualities like boldness, courage, freedom, spontaneity, perspicuity, integration, self-acceptance, which make possible the kind of generalized creativeness I have been talking about, which expresses itself in the creative life or the creative attitude or the creative person. I have also stressed the expressive or Being quality of self-actualizing creativeness rather than its problem-solving or product-making quality. Self-actualizing creativeness is "emitted," like radioactivity, and hits all of life, regardless of problems, just as a cheerful person "emits" cheerfulness without purpose or design or even consciousness. It is emitted like sunshine; it spreads all over the place; it makes some things grow (which are growable) and is wasted on rocks and other ungrowable things.

As I come to the end I am quite aware that I have been trying to break up widely accepted concepts of creativity without being able to offer in exchange a nice, clearly defined, clean-cut substitute concept. Self-actualizing creativeness is hard to define because sometimes it seems to be synonymous with health itself. And since self-actualization or health must ultimately be defined as the coming to pass of the fullest humanness, or as the "Being" of the person, it is as if self-actualizing creativity were almost synonymous with, or a *sine qua non* aspect of, or a defining characteristic of, essential humanness.

There are, however, at least two important practical consequences of this change of direction in thinking. It definitely discourages the either-or, all-or-none approach to creativity which is now so widespread, and which amounts to a dichotomous separation of sheep from goats, creative from noncreative, those who are from those who are not. Instead it tends to see more or less creativity in every person, if only as a suppressed potential, and asks the questions, "Why was it lost?" "How much is left?" "How much can be recovered?"

In addition, I think this change in concept may help to resolve the dilemma of the "lack" of creativeness in the female, for offhand there seems to be no gender difference in creativeness. If, as I think, there are constitutionally determined sex self-actualizing differences in interest in production of publications, paintings, symphonies, etc. (women probably are as *able* to do these things but they are not as *interested* in doing them), then creativity of the conventional "pro-

duction" type may be synonymous with a masculine type of productiveness. The old dilemma may then be translated as "Why do
women have female interests and not male ones?" Stated so, it resolves itself and disappears.

8

Vicissitudes of Creativity

HENRY A. MURRAY

T HE word "vicissitudes" was the wanton response to a stressful situation occasioned by a long distance telephone call demanding the immediate deliverance of a title for the talk I was to give five months later. Why vicissitudes? I thought, as I hung up the receiver. I discovered that in my head "vicissitudes" meant fortunes and misfortunes with a very heavy accent on misfortunes, and that on the telephone it had meant "What a *misfortune* to be pressed to create a title in a few seconds!"

Since "vicissitudes" was already on its way to public print, it necessarily became an irrevocable ruling member of my household, a ruler, however, who never succeeded in carrying out his functions. On the one hand, he was unable to curb the flow of errant ideas and, on the other, he failed to kindle any enthusiasm for what he meant to me— *misfortunes* of creativity. Our world, I thought, is soaking in misfortunes; must we number creativity among them?

It was the big *Oxford English Dictionary* which, at long last, shifted the acid-base equilibrium of my cortex by permitting a reversal of the initial meaning of the title, and giving me instead: "the *fortunate* change of creativity."

I mention this to illustrate a long-known, fundamental characteristic of the creative process, namely, that it is autonomous and rebellious far more often than it is submissive to the conscious will. To be imperatively directed by another person or by oneself to invent something fresh and valuable that is pertinent to a fixed topic may be enough to paralyze or half-paralyze this process, or, if not this, to cause it to run away on some other course like a scared doe or defiant child. Furthermore—and this is another of its widely acknowledged characteristics—the creative process never flies like an arrow or a bullet to a target, but proceeds toward an unknown destination by countless digressions and irrelevancies, decompositions and altered recompositions, many of which take place outside the reach of consciousness during periods of incubation. Consequently, the creative process takes time, its own time, maybe a lifetime, and very often death arrives before the fulfillment of its hope.

Obviously, I am giving the word "creative"—at least for the time being—a broad meaning, broad enough to include certain happenings in my own head as well as in the head of each and every one. But here the grievous fact I am confessing is that during the last season, before this essay was due, these processes failed to work for me on schedule, and left me a few days before deadline with a book of roving cerebrations without boundaries instead of a capsule of neatly articulated sentences. As a consequence of the defection of these energies, in the very act of writing about the fortunes of creativity I shall be illustrating one of its misfortunes, and thereby do justice to both faces of "vicissitudes."

Although Whitehead would have no truck with the dictum that necessity is the mother of invention, it happened, in this instance, that out of the womb of my embarrassing necessity there emerged a plan which seemed to have a higher probability than any orthodox procedure. The plan is to communicate the substance of the first paragraphs of each of the early chapters of this renegade book and let every reader finish it in any way *his* creativities dictate.

TITLE: THE FORTUNATE CHANGE OF CREATIVITY

PREFACE

What fortunate change? Well, the recent fortunate change in the direction of creativities in the heads of social scientists, manifested first in their turning to creative processes in human nature as foci for systematic studies, and second in their turning to the generation of concepts and propositions adequate to the formulation of processes of this class as foci for their thoughts.

We are through—or should be through—with the analysis of everything into its elementary components without subsequent synthesis. Behind us are the various tried forms of elementalism and reductionism, endeavors to explain human transactions largely in terms of discrete sensations, of conditioned reflexes, of traits, of infantile complexes, or in physiological or animal-learning terms. Gestalt psychology, first applied to perceptual events, and organismic psychology, derived from the observation of biological phenomena, have been expanded and elaborated, in conjunction with field theory, to correct the deficiencies of elementalism, and today we have systems theory and propositions pertaining to the continuation and restoration of the steady state of systems. Ahead of those who are game for it lies the inviting possibility of explaining irreversible formations and transformations—compositions and decompositions—of systems and subsystems.

The high positive cathexis which the word "creativity" has been acquiring in diverse spheres of activity, as Boring (1950) noted, the multiplicity of scientific investigations of this phenomenon, recently completed or now in progress in this country—the studies, for example, of Barron (1955, 1958), Guilford (1950, 1956a, 1957b), Roe (1946, 1953b), Rogers (1953b), Meer and Stein (1955), Stein (1958), Wilson (1958), Wilson, Guilford, et al. (1954), and others too numerous to be mentioned here—the many well-attended conferences and symposia on this subject—such as the Ohio Conference in 1953 (Barkan and Mooney, 1953) and these Michigan State University Symposia—which have been held within the last few years and not earlier—these, it seems to me, are evidences of the incipience of a change, mutation, or vicissitude in the evolution of the human spirit which is in league with the possibility of a better world. It marks, as I view it, a little vital turning point, initiated as always by a statistically insignificant minority, which, if our species is vouchsafed a future, will be apperceived in retrospect as a movement of historic import.

Since we are living in an era when even the slightest sign of presumption or dogmatism is obnoxious, I am prompted at the outset to acknowledge much ignorance of the subject-matter of this symposium. Although I have conscientiously attended to it for thirty years— as it occurs in lower organisms, in literature, in science, and in interpersonal relations—I have no statistical findings to report, and most of what I have to say is either self-evident, well known, speculative, or hypothetical. But if presumption and authoritarianism are the Scylla of our time, the Charybdis is intellectual timidity—hemming and hedging, surrounding every cautious forward step one takes with an array of qualifications and apologies as well as a smoke-screen of jokes and banter. I shall try to steer a course between these two: the hybris of Scylla and the cowardice of Charybdis.

CHAPTER 1. DEFINITION OF CREATION

The word "creation" usually points either to a compositional process which results in something new, or to the *resultant* of this process, a new composition, regardless of its value, destiny, or consequences. But, in conformity with the accepted orientation of these Symposia, "creation," in many contexts of the present discourse, will refer to *the occurrence of a composition which is both new and valuable.* "New" will mean that the entity is marked by more than a certain degree of novelty, or originality, relative to sameness, or replication; and "valuable" will mean *either* intrinsically or extrinsically valuable as such to one or more persons, or generative of valuable compositions in the future (whether or not it is valuable as such). To suit the purposes of research, these very general statements must be reduced to more concrete operational terms by the definition of suitable criteria of novelty and of value, the construction of scales based on these criteria, the selection of cutting-points, and, finally, statements respecting the statuses, degrees of pertinent knowledge, dispositions, and abilities of the judges. The last, because a necessary, integral part of the definition of an evaluated entity is a sufficient characterization of its evaluators.

As a rule, psychologists who decide to investigate creative processes or the personalities of creative persons will choose a panel of acknowledged experts (if there are any in the given field of activity) to serve as judges, eliminate the sources of compositions about which the judges disagree, and select for study those whose works are placed above the arbitrarily selected cutting-point. But in doing this, psychologists are or should be fully aware of the high probability that some subjects who have been ranked below the set level will at some future date be accorded a high status and vice versa.

Up to quite recent times it was customary to think of creativity as something wholly mysterious and miraculous, an epiphenomenal power that in a few rare geniuses was "added on" to the normal aggregate of human potentialities. Indeed, it was not until the late eighteenth century that the word creation could be applied without irreverence to anything but the works of God. Following Plato and Aristotle, dramatists and poets had been regarded as imitators or reflectors whose function it was to hold a mirror up to nature or, if not this, to serve as mouthpieces of the gods, of the moral order, or of the one God of Christianity. And even after it became permissible to speak of the "creations" of romantic poets, the word was rarely free of overtones suggestive of divine gifts or powers. Coleridge's self-image in *Xanadu* is a peculiarly fine example of this then-current apperception:

> And all should cry, Beware! Beware!
> His flashing eyes, his floating hair!
> Weave a circle round him thrice,
> And close your eyes in holy dread,
> For he on honey-dew hath fed,
> And drunk the milk of Paradise.

Today, however, the referents of this imagery (leaving opium aside) have been turned outside in: the creative endowments and powers that were formerly attributed to one transcendent, celestial Person and Place outside the order of nature are now known to be immanent in nature, especially in human nature, to constitute, in fact, one of the givens at the hidden, unconscious "core" of nature. And instead of creativity being considered a very rare capacity in man, many of us acknowledge that it is manifested in some way and to some extent by almost everybody.

In stating this proposition, I have, of course, been influenced by Whitehead, who, as you know, adumbrated a theoretical system of systems in which creativity is a metaphysical ultimate. His conception is that of a procession of overlapping and interdependent events, or *actual concrete occasions*, in space-time. Each concrete occasion is a temporally bounded concrescence (organization, composition) of prehensions (appropriating or vectorial processes), the duration of each occasion being the time required for the composition of the prehended elements into a single unit. A fine, microanalysis would yield a sequence of occasions, or actual entities, each of which—with a duration, say, of a fraction of a second—would perish at the instant of its composition and be immediately succeeded by another actual occasion. A grosser, macroanalysis would take a whole act, or endeavor, as the "really real thing" (Whitehead), the direction and quality of which has imposed itself on its constituent parts.

The moving picture, here, is that of a sequence of discrete corpuscles of actuality, bound together, as it were, by a vectorial force or continuity of aim. Translated to the mind, this would be illustrated by the composition of an image which is immediately decomposed, only to be followed by the composition of another image, or with the formation of a word which dies as another word succeeds it, and so forth. Our senses being less acute than certain delicate instruments, we are scarcely aware of these individual "drops" of mental life and are more prone to choose metaphors of fluid continuity, such as the "stream" of consciousness or the "flow" of thought. One might say that a "wave theory" is closer to our immediate experience than a "corpuscular theory." The latter, however, may prove more serviceable in the end.

Now, according to Whitehead, every actual concrescence is unique in some respects, and hence, strictly speaking, a creation, since an infinitesimal variation is sufficient to justify the adjective "unique." Thus the actual world is said to have the character of a temporal passage into novelty. If we accept this, then every coherent series of actual occasions, short or long—a sentence, a paragraph, a ten-minute conversation, or a ten-year correspondence between two people—is even more of a creation, since each of these is a unique temporal integration of unique components, a creation of creations. Personally, I am content with this, but would prefer—at least for the duration of this discourse—to substitute "composition" for "creation," and reserve the latter term for valuable compositions with a high degree of novelty relative to sameness.

I have taken time to present this short, rough approximation of Whitehead's conception of actual occurrences in order to remind you that one of the most enlightened geniuses living at the time of the great metamorphosis of basic science was committed to the notion that creativity is of the very essence of reality.

One more comment: the word "create" will not be used as a synonym of "incite" or "cause." It will certainly not refer to a process which terminates in a state of greater disunion than previously existed. It might be said that somebody "created a disturbance," "created havoc," etc., but this has the exact opposite meaning. Although *decomposition* is, for us, a necessary variable, since it quite regularly precedes the process of creation, the two words are antonyms, like anabolism and katabolism, not synonyms. Living as we do in an era when the release of every spontaneous impulse in childhood and in adolescence is often correlated with creativity, it is sometimes difficult to distinguish these opposites, to tell the difference between a lot of noise and a symphonic composition, between excretion and secretion.

Won't you carry on from here?

CHAPTER 2. BASIC REQUIREMENTS, LEVELS, AND CHRONOLOGY
OF CREATION

As basic requirements of creation at all levels I would propose the following: a *sufficient concentration* within a given region of *different mobile or motile entities* with *mutual affinity*, entities which have *never been combined*. Then, as a fifth requirement, *sufficient circulation* of these entities, which means a *sufficient source of energy*. Finally, there must be the possibility of *favorable conditions for combination*. Granted these seven factors, the *mutual attraction*, *approximation*, and *association* of two or more entities—in other words, *creation*—is certain to occur.

And here is where *chance* comes in. I say "chance" because it is not ordinarily possible to predict precisely which heretofore uncombined entities will come within each other's sphere of influence at precisely what place and what instant, and—at *that* particular point in space-time—what conditions favorable or unfavorable, will prevail.

Numerous other special factors are, of course, involved at each conventional level of scientific analysis and formulation—physical, chemical, biological, psychological, sociological, culturological—but I believe that the ones which I have named can be illustrated by analogies at all levels.

If we look back in time as far as the astronomers' fairy tales will carry us—after the hypothetical Big Bang which sent the matter in the universe flying in all directions—we come upon the simplest variety of creative energy—mutual attraction, or gravitational force—starting its big job of forming thousands of stellar constellations of which our solar system is but one late product. According to the terminology I am using, the great dispersion of matter subsequent to the Big Bang would be an example of *decomposition* of an existing state, the persistence of which momentum accounts for the apparent expansion of the universe. Hesiod, as quoted in Plato's *Symposium*, pictured it in somewhat different terms. He said: first Chaos came (that is to say, the Big Bang), then Love (that is to say, the force of gravitation) and with it the broad-bosomed Earth (that is to say, the maternal environment for further creativities).

Now, if we give ear to the speculations of those most deserving of our ear, some two million years ago the watery surface of this broad-bosomed earth provided favorable conditions for the circulation, mutual attraction, and combination of chemical substances at successive levels of complexity, each of which was a heretofore unexampled configuration of matter with an unexampled set of properties. There are now a few plausible hypotheses and even some experimental evidence relative to the composition of the simplest organic compounds leading up to the creation of macroproteins—similar in some respects to viruses and genes. Later, we may surmise, the most rudimentary forms of metabolic life came into being, marked by recurrent compositions, decompositions, recompositions. Then, supposedly, unicellular organisms made their debut, followed in due course by multicellular organisms, their developments being initiated by countless new genetic combinations and mutations. Finally, as consequence of new, genetically derived properties and capacities, we can imagine societies of higher organisms evolving down the centuries until the arrival of our own species—families and clans of primordial men and women. The emergence of human morphology is correlated, we now believe, with the emergence of the capacity to form concepts, to verbalize and compose a language, to envisage future possibilities, and, in view of these, to plan cooperative endeavors. Here then was the incipience of the human imagination: the potentiality for insanity, on the one hand, and, on the other, potentialities for the composition of myths, religions, philosophies, effective forms of government, works of art, scientific theories, et cet.

Although this is "old hat" to everyone, I have given my hop, skip, and jump version of the evolutionary fable first of all to illustrate in a rough way creativity everywhere *immanent* in nature at different *levels* and to suggest in this connection that chemistry and genetics provide better models than physics has to offer for students of consequential compositions. Secondly, it seemed advisable to emphasize the chronology of creation, the fact that it proceeds in a slow, step-wise fashion—usually from the smaller and simpler to the larger and more complex—that A must occur before B is possible, and B before C, and C before D; and that it may take a million years, a thousand years, a hundred years of trials and mistakes and eventually of surviving transformations before C becomes D. For example, before American democracy was constituted, numerous pilot experiments had been undertaken, such as the city-states of Greece, including Aristotle's commentary, and finally certain creative processes in the mind of Locke and in the mind of Rousseau had to reach completion and be published. Also, let us note that not yet—although spurred to the endeavor by centuries of senseless persecutions, animosity, and slaughter—have the creative processes in any head arrived at a form of world government or form of world religion which is sufficiently inviting and persuasive to triumph over the egotisms and prides of individual nations and religions.

Thirdly, I wanted to point out that although what Darwin called "accidental variations" are dependent on chance encounters among different genes, the crucial determinant is something else, namely the inherent capacity of genes—as well as of numberless other entities—to participate in the composition of new and valued generating entities. And so, as I pointed out earlier, when we study creative processes we are focusing not on some sort of epiphenomenon that occurs only in the minds of a few "born" geniuses, but on processes that carry on, like coral insects, secretly and unobtrusively on all levels.

Fourthly, I thought that the story of evolution would serve as preparation for my avowal that the metabolic cycle of anabolism-katabolism or composition-decomposition is the theme song or model of most of the thought-stuff I am offering. Katabolic processes in every cell of the body are the homefires at the "core" of animal nature which provide the necessary energy for anabolic growth and other functions, and it can be said that all the covert and overt activities that comprise the total nutritional cycle of intakes and outputs are devoted, directly or indirectly, to keeping these millions of cellular homefires burning. Viewed in relation to the covert physiological and biochemical sequences of the nutritional cycle, the overt sequences—the food-acquiring activities of the organism, which are the most real of real things to the animal psychologist—are relatively superficial and constitute but one of several, different, temporally-bound functions involved in the transposition of nutritive substances from the external environment to the interior of each cell. Food in the mouth—which terminates the span of concern of most animal psychologists—is of no benefit to the animal *per se*: it is simply the first of a succession of reinforcements, or achievements, which are required before the incorporated stuff can fulfill its destined role. The point I am making here is that most of the behavior which we, as positivists, are expected to observe consists of movements in space—either translocations of the motile organism itself or transpositions of objects by the organism—and these perceptible movements are all basically dependent on events that are not perceptible directly, namely, the compositions and decompositions that occur when entities reach their destination. In short, I am arguing for a deeper and more valid realism than that of the devout behaviorist who believes that the external things about which there is least disagreement among observers constitute the best basis for the construction of a theoretical system.

But now to return to my elected model for central processes on all levels, the metabolic cycle of anabolism-katabolism. The details are, of course, far too complicated to be mentioned here. For present purposes, all I need is a rough definition of three relationships: *one*, when anabolism exceeds katabolism, as it does at the moment of conception and during the entire period of growth; *two*, when anabolism and katabolism are about equal, as they are during the more or less homeostatic period of maturity; and *three*, when katabolism exceeds anabolism, as it does near and after the end of life. Generalizing this, and adding another factor in order to include parallel phenomena on other levels, societal and cultural, the *first* relationship will be called the phase of *composition* or creation; the *second*, the phase of *recomposition* or conservation; and the *third*, the phase of *decomposition* or destruction. Different kinds of composition and of decomposition should be distinguished, and it should be noted that biological senescence leading on to death—as well as senescence of other sorts—is chiefly characterized not by decomposition, but by *induration* (that is, hardening or fixation) of structure, typical of the last part of the conserving phase. But, after making important distinctions of this sort as well as the necessary modifications at each level, system of systems theory, so far as I can see, is capable of formulating these phases in an illuminating and experimentally fruitful manner.

Here you may be reminded of the ancient Hindu trinity of Brahma, the creator, Vishnu, the conservator, and Siva, the destroyer. Personally, I am all in favor of this mode of speech. It makes me think of a statement of a famous physiologist to the effect that when the physiologist, the psychologist, and the poet begin to talk corresponding languages we shall be on our way to a genuine understanding of human nature. Since some of us enthusiasts for system of systems theory are so ready to go down to physics for our analogies, why should we not cover the whole scale and occasionally reach up to a suitable mythology?

Would you like to carry on from here?

CHAPTER 3. CREATION AT THE MENTAL LEVEL

This, I take it, is the topic of these Symposia—new, valuable, mental compositions, whether they are imaginations of better mechanical designs, better scientific theories, better governmental legislation, better or variant forms of art, better or variant systems of personality, or better or variant patterns of interpersonal relations.

As always, we have to consider the requirements, levels, and chronology of creation, and here with attention to features special to the mind. For example, among the requirements, as I said above, is a *sufficient concentration of relevant combinable entities* never previously combined. These are both inside the mind (*representors* in the preconscious and in the unconscious), and outside the mind (objects and events to be observed in the environment as well as products of the mental processes of other people, spoken or written). That is to say, a person must have a great fund of pertinent images and imagents (imagined events), concepts and postulates acquired over the years. In this case, as you know, these are not free to move hither and thither like chemicals dissolved in a homogeneous fluid, but are located in differentiated and bounded mental places. And this brings me to the next requirement, *circulation of the heretofore-uncombined entities*, because if the entities acquired in the past remain in the places where they first settled—as they often do in the rigid minds of walking encyclopedias of written knowledge—novel combinations will be less probable. To get heretofore uncombined entities within each other's sphere of influence there must be, first of all, a good deal of more or less passionate *psychic energy*, occasionally approaching hypomania— what Socrates called "divine madness"—to stir things up. Then, there must be sufficient *permeability* (flexibility) of boundaries, boundaries between categories as well as boundaries between different spheres of interest and—most important for certain classes of creation—sufficient permeability of the boundary between conscious and unconscious psychic processes. Here I am thinking of a kind of playful, happily irresponsible, or drunken state of mind. Too much permeability is insanity, too little is ultraconventional rationality. A third and overlapping factor is represented by Siva—destruction preliminary to creation: there must be periodic, if not almost incessant, decompositions—de-differentiations and disintegrations—of what has already been composed—composed in the minds of others but *more especially* in our own minds. A person must have a certain gust for temporary chaos.

The next requirement is too complicated to be summarized here, namely *favorable conditions for combination*, inside and outside the mind—freedom from impertinent intrusions, for example. It is here, largely, that chance plays the role of fate. Pasteur spoke of "chance and the prepared mind," Charles Pierce of "chance, love, and logic," Darwin of "accident." It is the wonder of a rare event: two heretofore-unconnected entities come together in space-time at just the moment when the psyche is prepared to appreciate the significance of that particular combination. It is a perfectly natural event, but if we insist that our laws of nature are necessarily statistical, then this event is necessarily illegal.

At the mental level there are a number of other variables to be considered, most of which might well be classified as components, or intrinsic determinants, of the total creative enterprise. My own practice has been to point to these with symbols of two, three, or four letters (as in chemistry), which can be semantically combined in any number of ways with their relative potencies expressed as ratios. For example, Go is the above-mentioned basic, explosive energy factor which circulates the entities, Co is the combinational process and its energy (Brahma), Va is the evaluating process, together with the standards and cutting-points employed (the scientific, aesthetic, moral, or strategic superego); and, usually in its service though sometimes autonomous, are Ca, the disposition to incorporate whatever comes to mind or whatever is seen or read, and Na, the disposition to reject and exclude entities which are superfluous, irrelevant, indigestible, or obnoxious. Ra is the retaining and recomposing process (Vishnu) which conserves and continues the better compositions. Ru is the analyzing, decomposing, and eliminating process (Siva) which reduces entities to their elements preparatory to a new synthetic trial, or which ruthlessly deletes previously incorporated elements. Se is the disposition, prompted largely by insatiable curiosity, to search either within or without the mind (in the service of Ca) for suitable entities to be incorporated and then to be properly placed, or categorized, in mental space by Ro, the process of allocating things and thereby putting the intellect in order, Se and Ca, I should say, are almost invariably combined with Nev, the relish for novelty, since without novelty there can be no creation.

A number of other variables require definition; but space is short, and I shall stop after mentioning one more, the target of the whole endeavor, Hola, which is usually an indefinite mental vision—a vague hypothesis, idea, plot of a play, conception of a way of life—which must be made definite, worked out in detail, decomposed, corrected, and reintegrated, tried and validated, represented in words or in music, or enacted in real life. Hola is either of this character or in the nature of a question or problem for which there is no accepted answer or solution. In any case, one of the distinguishing marks of a culturally creative person is the presence of a strong RaHola, that is, a continuing, hopeful commitment and allegiance to a selected aim. Once, when Freud was reminded that almost all of his ideas—the idea of unconscious processes, for instance—could be found in the works of earlier authors, he answered with his usual delicious wit: "Ah, yes. But those were mere flirtations. Mine was a responsible marriage." So much for some of the major requirements and intrinsic determinants of creation at the mental level.

In some of all this, the ego, the "I" of consciousness, feels subjectively as if its role were quite important. And yet it knows full well that its power to produce the basic psychic energy of *Go* is practically nil and its influence on the compositional processes of *Co* is very slight. And now, I should like to explain that a sentence I composed at the very start of this essay—"How misfortunate to be pressed to create a title in a few seconds"—was a meaningless *façon de parler* forced on me by an acquired semantic habit which, as Whorf (1956) has indicated, makes one feel that a verb requires some noun in front of it. If there is an act, must there not be an actor, obvious or concealed? Do not the words "create a title" cry out for the designation of the agent? But if two entities—two chemicals, two people, two ideals—with mutual affinity unite for the first time in known history and remain united, can we point to a creator of this unequivocal creation? I think not. What we have here are two *participants* in a creative process, both of which are about equally responsible for, and equally necessary to, the unique outcome. In short, as I see it, the psyche is a *region* where creations may or may not flourish, and if two people are involved, there are two regions and their intercommunicating processes to be considered. The powers of the self-conscious *I* (in the language of William James)—*I* the activator, *I*, the knower, *I*, the judge—are definitely limited. At best, its role is to *preside* over an interior transaction which may or may not come out with something that is worth seizing. The "*I*" can never command or force a veritable creation. If it were capable of this, all the world's problems could be solved as fast as thought by those who had sufficient knowledge; and any number of effective policies, valid theories, comedies, and symphonies could be manufactured to order and time.

Sudden and spectacular creations, like dreams and visions, often seem to come from without rather than from within the mind, which in some measure accounts for the fact that in the past they were invariably attributed to gods or devils. Better to treat them in this way, it seems to me, than to look down on them from an inflated scientific superego. Constantly at work in our minds, these energies, like the divinities of mythology, are beyond our jurisdiction, respond, when ready, only to our supplications, and are responsible for the greatest wonders. Why should we not honor them?

Would you like to carry on from here?

CHAPTER 4. DYADIC CREATIONS

Otto Rank (1932), whose mind was a hive of generative ideas, prophesied that a "new type of humanity" would become possible when men with creative power could "give up artistic expression in favor of the formation of personality" and in return for this renunciation they would enjoy a "greater happiness." This philosophy is already flourishing in our midst, with one of the contributors to these Symposia, Abraham Maslow, as its most ardent and devoted advocate.

I take it for granted that those readers who have met Professor Maslow's persuasive presentation would prefer not to peruse some futile attempt on my part to paint his lily; and so I have decided to say a few words about dyadic, rather than monadic, creativity. This means that we shall be dealing with two interdependent regions of imagination operating as a single system. Also, both members of the dyad will be endeavoring to translate their imaginations into actual, overt reciprocations and collaborations. It will be like two people singing a duet and making up the music as they go along.

In this type of creation, the basic entities to be composed into a mutually enjoyable and beneficent concatenation of activities will consist of potentially complementary or cooperative dispositions and capacities. Successful complementations can be partially formulated in terms of different sorts of zestful and capable transmissions resulting in appreciative receptions. The person who functions as the transmittor in one proceeding may function as the receptor in the next, in which case one may speak of reciprocation, or reversal of complementations. There are numerous different classes and modes of functional transmission, such as transmission of affection, of gifts, of information, of suggestions for action, and so forth. If one person repeatedly fulfills the same transmissive function, he or she may be designated by a suitable name: donor, stimulator, narrator, interpreter, orientor (of talk or movement), critic, entertainer, etc. Such face-to-face interactions, where the aim is mutual stimulation and enjoyment, are often hardly distinguishable from cooperations. These occur when both members of the dyad, together or separately, endeavor to achieve a common aim or, through division of labor, to accomplish a different part of some required task. So much as an outline of one possible mode of grossly formulating dyads.

Now, when we study creations in other fields—say in science or in art—we choose as subjects talented people whose vocational goals are superordinate; and so here, if we want to obtain comparable intensities of dedication (*GoHola*), we would be well advised to select man-woman erotic dyads, in or out of marriage. As Shakespeare said: "Love's a mighty Lord, and to his Service, no such joy on earth." Today a marriage is more likely to be superordinate than a friendship. Furthermore, the sexual instinct, we now realize, is involved in many of the greatest accomplishments of the imagination. As Nietzsche—originator of the concept of sublimation—pointed out, "the degree and quality of man's sexuality" may "reach up to the utmost pinnacle of his mind" (Morgan, 1941). But, he explained, as the urge "becomes more intellectual it gets a new name, a new charm and new evaluation." In short, if we include the sexual instinct, we shall be dealing with whole personalities whose "depths" will be engaged in the dyadic enterprise, and, consequently, there will be less chance of getting caught in that "booby trap" of American psychology, superficiality.

Over the last few years a few of us at the Harvard Psychological Clinic have been engaged in intensive studies of short stressful dyadic discussions as recorded by a moving picture camera with sound track and, as you might expect, have found marked differences, both in degrees of achievement relative to the assigned task and in the smoothness and deftness with which each participant deals with the competing alter. In a trying situation, a few subjects are capable both of getting along with their rival and of getting ahead with the job. I have been calling this capacity *impromptu, short-span, strategic creativity*. Although there are no figures to support me as yet, I have gained a strong impression that those who exhibit this kind of ability do occasionally, but more often do not possess potentialities for "deeper," more significant, and lasting creativities. Some of them might be described as "slick operators" with cool heads who have substituted craft for the ideal and who, by means of an artificial smile and a few cute maneuvers that evade all touchy issues, succeed in arriving at genial pseudo agreements before the other person is fully aware of what has happened. The point I am aiming at is that we psychologists can disqualify ourselves as fruitful investigators of dyadic creativity if we take repeatedly pseudo-harmonious interactions as our chief criterion for the evaluation of creativities in friendship or in marriage.

What is the significance of Riesman's "lonely crowd" if not a lot of friendliness without friendship, a lot of people whose social life is played out on the surface, with no exchanges of nourishing, gutty thoughts or feelings.

Let me illustrate the difference by referring to a particular marriage. It happens that once upon a time I was a psychotherapist of a class not simply labeled—a deviant Freudian, let us say—and among a number of cases in my files there was one that came to mind as made to order for this moment. It was that of a man on the verge of divorce who had fallen in love with a woman in a similar predicament. She had already undergone a psychoanalysis and, as one outcome of her pilgrim's progress through the maze of the unconscious, was determined not to fail another time but to make a *real thing* out of her marriage with my patient. Since, in due course, a reciprocal resolve took stout root in the man's psyche, the situation was that of two ardent lovers—hereafter to be known as Adam and Eve—both of them coming out of a dead marriage and both of them already in possession of a working version of creativity and prepared to give it leeway.

Already we know enough to suggest the operation of a compound determinant of creativity which might be compacted into three words: vision, passion, and the superordination of the vision. Passion is the emotional energy factor (Go) in a dyadic form. The superordinate vision is the *Hola* factor with the addition of a cognitive component, namely, some previous knowledge, gained from psychoanalysis, of modes of creative transformation. Without extraordinary love neither Eve nor Adam would have felt impelled to attach enough energy to this goal, and, without the vision of creativity, both lovers, Adam with his romantic images and projections and Eve with hers—like Tristan and Isolde after partaking of the magic passion-potion—might well have felt that a perfect union had already been fatefully created and that they were on a wave of the future that would never let them down.

Another possible predeterminant was the existence of an unhealed narcissistic wound in each of them occasioned by the failure of a previous attempt at marriage. It brings to mind that pair in Eden and the basic mythic theme of the Fortunate Fall, about which Weisinger

(1953) has written with such distinction. By contemporary standards it was cruel of Jehovah to deny Adam and Eve a second chance after their failure to keep the rules of Paradise. Presumably, they had learned a searing moral lesson and thereafter, in the fear of God, might well have proved invariably obedient denizens of that region. But this is no moment to deplore primordial injustices. Our present focus is a new Adam and a new Eve, both of whom were happily granted a second chance.

Although they moved to another place as a happier station for their conjoined life, Adam was now and again prompted to return to Cambridge, avowedly to consult me about the vicissitudes of his marriage. Actually, the greater part of our time together was spent in my listening to his account of a to-me unique dyadic enterprise, and so, thanks to his zest for communication, I was enabled to keep abreast of the progress of this relationship and recently, with Adam's collaboration, to attempt a few tentative formulations. But since space is running short, I shall mention but one more major determinant—the lively circulation and expression of combinable entities—which, in my opinion, was the outstanding feature of Adam's and Eve's mode of dyadic creativity. I offer it as the exact opposite of the ideal of invariably courteous and hence necessarily superficial interactions.

By unappreciable transitions—Adam cannot remember any originating incident—he and Eve found themselves engaged now and again in unpremeditated, serious yet playful, dramatic outbursts of feeling, wild imagination, and vehement interaction, in which one of them—sometimes Adam, sometimes Eve—gave vent to whatever was pressing for expression. Walpurgis was the name they gave to episodes of this insurgent nature. Usually it was Eros that·supplied the energy, with some sort of intoxicant—which they called Soma after the Hindu Dionysius—liquidating the boundary of consciousness. But besides Eros, there were compelling needs for dominance, clamoring egotisms and assertions of omniscience, anger and resentment, not to speak of feelings of helplessness and inferiority, complemented by nurturance and encouragement. And so—layer after layer, one might say—each of these two psyches, through numberless repetitions, discharged its residual as well as its emergent and beneficent dispositions, until nearly every form of sexuality and nearly every possible complementation of dyadic roles had been dramatically enacted. All this within the frame of their conception of the necessary digressions and progressive spiral-ings of the creative process, and all within the compass of an ever-mounting trust in the solidarity of their love, evidenced in the Wal-purgis episodes by an apparently limitless mutual tolerance of novelty and emotional extravagance.

Adam admits that faith in the virtue of those unruly hours came largely from psychoanalysis, although, of course, their dyadic form was not an asymmetrical verbal relationship with a lenient father or mother figure but a symmetrical acting-out with both of them wholly engaged on all levels. Although they knew nothing of psychodrama, Moreno's conceptions, it seems to me, provide a better model than psychoanalysis, particularly in view of Adam's insistence that neither he nor Eve ever checked or diminished the gustful process of eruption and expression by attributing its genesis to some banal infantile im-pulsion. Of course, Walpurgis, for them, was more real, more urgent, than psychodrama, although only very rarely was it carried to the wounding point, and then always immediately shut off and the wound healed. Just recently—recollecting in tranquility these past ecstasies and their consequences—Adam emphasized several benefits which I shall summarize in my own words: one, the exultant catharsis of con-ventionally forbidden needs—such as most of us experience only empathically and vicariously in witnessing a drama (as Aristotle ex-plained); two, the eventual riddance from one's personality of un-wanted states and urges; three, the incorporation of new and joyous modes of interaction which might otherwise have been excluded; four, the expansion and deepening of an intimate experiential conscious-ness of self, of alter, and of self and alter as a system, and hence a greater increment of wisdom than a psychoanalysis can provide; and, finally, five, the ultimate demise of all pressures to put forth in social life the irrationalities of infancy and adolescence.

To balance the wildness of all this, one last determinant should be listed, namely an above-normal capacity to evaluate with fine discrimi-nation—in terms of some enlightened standard (Va)—the worth and relevance of what has been brought forth, coupled with the disposi-tion to reject (Na) what is unacceptable in those scales and to accept and incorporate (Ca) whatever is fitting and propitious.

The hypothesis that is suggested by the history of this particular dyad is that periodic, complete emotional expression within the compass of an envisaged creative enterprise—not unlike the orgiastic Dionysian rites of early Greek religion in which all participated—is a highly enjoyable and effective manner of eliminating maleficent (socially harmful, deviant, criminal, neurotic, and psychotic) tendencies as well as of bringing into play beneficent modes of thought and action which might otherwise have been blocked out. In sharp contrast to this is both the traditional Christian doctrine of repression of primitive impulsions and the psychoanalytic notion of the replacement of the id by the ego (rationality), which results so often in a half-gelded, cautious, guarded, conformist, uncreative, and dogmatic way of coping with the world.

Would you carry on from here?

CHAPTER 5. CENTRAL-SUPERORDINATE-CULTURAL CREATIONS

The integrative imaginations which preceded, accompanied, and followed the dyadic activities I have just described could be taken as parts of one variety of central-superordinate-cultural creation, or mythology of life. Creations of this class are called central because they spring from central (that is, basic, nuclear, deep, potent) human needs which generate visions or revelations of possible fulfillment and of ways to this fulfillment. They are called "superordinate" because the generated visions are accorded the highest place among the valued aims of an individual or group; and they are called "cultural" because their composition is encouraged by the implicit or explicit hope or certainty that the envisaged aims and ways will eventually be adopted by other people.

I am assuming that the germ of a central-superordinate creation originates in the unconscious of one person or of a few persons, most often out of suffering and estrangement engendered by the existing state of things. If this suffering is shared by other people and the curative vision is engagingly represented in words or enacted in deeds, it will sooner or later be assimilated by a small minority and get started on a long voyage of transmission through many other minds, some of which may have greater creative capacities than the originating one. In any case, over the ensuing years the initial vision is likely to be greatly altered—elaborated, revised, refined, systematized. When fully developed, creations of this class are long-range, over-all mythologies, philosophies, or ideologies which consist, for the most part, of representations of sacred objects, better means or better aims, a better society, a better world (here or elsewhere), better states or ways of life, better persons, or better interpersonal relations, as well as of enemies that stand in the path to these desired ends and of ways to be avoided. The emphasis may be on any one of these: reformation or transformation of one's own society, creation of a new society in a new place, conversion or transformation of the world, of other persons, or of the self, to be brought about by God or by concerted human effort. In all events, it is a matter of cardinal importance to all concerned, since a change in any one of these spheres of thought and action affects all others.

Most powerful of this class of creations in the Western world has been the Judaeo-Christian religion and second to this, in potency as well as time, has been its virtual antithesis, the mythology of freedom, of rebellion, independence, and self-sufficiency. Since the imagery of Judaeo-Christianity is evidently derived from the earliest father-son relations in a conservative patriarchal family, it might be said to belong to the phase of spiritual childhood. The newborn infant, being utterly helpless and ineffective, is wholly dependent on his parents and hence a petitioner for everything that he needs. From the point of view of this lowly, ignorant, impotent, and fallible creature, the father stands forth as the exact opposite: high, omniscient, omnipotent, and infallible. Also, the father is the only male who has a fixed design for the boy's life and whose commandments must be obeyed if he is to deserve the support, guidance, and affection that he then requires as well as the elevated status (as his father's right-hand man) that is conditionally promised him at the end of his period of probation.

In contrast to all this, the imagery of the mythology of freedom is clearly derivable from that period in a boy's life when he has achieved some measure of self-sufficiency and is in a better position to defy successfully the authority of a relatively weaker father. Now, instead of a guarded, bounded homestead, there is unbounded locomotion and exploration; instead of dependence, there is independence; instead of docile submission, there is protest, rebellion, secession, and emancipation; instead of waiting to be given benefits, there is search, seizure, and appropriation; instead of an even-handed, paternalistic distribution of goods and privileges, there is strenuous, aggressive competition; and instead of dreaming of being lifted to some better world in heaven, there is travel and migration in hopes of finding one on earth. This I shall call the phase of spiritual adolescence.

Under the best conditions in the phase of spiritual childhood—as in the Western thirteenth century, let us say—there is relative homogeneity, unity, order, conservation, and homeostasis on the ideational, cultural level: Vishnu is predominant. But in the phase of spiritual adolescence—reaching its first peak, say, at the time of the French Revolution—everything is different: authority is denied, decomposed, reduced; there may be deicide and regicide, justified by the glorification of uncorrupted human nature, human reason, and the *vox populi,* the fraternal peer group; or there may be greater insistence on freedom of personal thought, speech, and decision, the idealization of individuality, resulting in ever-greater heterogeneity, division, disunity, disorder. The time comes when "the center cannot hold, things fall apart": Siva is predominant. This is the era of egocentrism, competitions of egocentrism, nihilism, and teen-age terrorisms, largely due to the fact that the spiritually adolescent parents have not given their offspring the needed experience and steady discipline of the phase of spiritual childhood at its best. In short, adolescents are not prepared for the responsibilities of individuality and temperate rebellion and in a state of chaos become susceptible to the dictatorial leadership and machinations of a Moloch, who brings them back as physiological adults to a secularized phase of spiritual childhood under the cloud of an inflexible and infallible doctrine.

Today, however, there are evidences, here and there, that people are approaching, with more knowledge and more insight than has been heretofore available, the phase of spiritual manhood and womanhood, the era of Brahma, with its mythology of creativity, fundamentally derived from that period of life when a man and woman participate in the formation of a dyad, of a home, of offspring, and of a new family culture. This spiritual phase, this symbolism, might be exemplified, it seems to me, on all levels: an embracement and reunion of the opposites: man and nature, male and female, conscious and unconscious, superego and id, reason and passion, rational and irrational, science and art, enjoyable means and enjoyable ends, upper class and lower class, West and East. Instead of dependence or independence, we may see fruitful interdependence; instead of passive reception or greedy acquisition of great quantities of things, we may see construction, whenever feasible, of what is necessary and what is aesthetically symbolic; instead of vainly hoping for an impossible world or voyaging in search of one, we may be engaging in more enlightened endeavors to transform the place and the society in which we live; in short, instead of thesis and antithesis, we may achieve synthesis at the center: creation for creation—let us say, *creativism*—rather than creation for a giant suicidal murder. It is in view of this barely possible ideal that I have subtitled this essay: *the fortunate change of creativity.*

I hope you will go on happily from here.

9

Creativity as Personality Development

HAROLD H. ANDERSON

———

THE thought of creativity brings to mind in many persons the "Mona Lisa" by Leonardo da Vinci; the poems of Milton; the "Thinker" of Rodin; the lightning rod, bifocal lenses, and the Franklin stove of Benjamin Franklin; the telegraph of Morse; the telephone of Alexander Graham Bell; the electric light and phonograph of Edison. Creativity in these instances is associated with a painting, a sculpture, a sonnet, an invention, a product that can be seen, studied, enjoyed.

There is another kind of creativity, which we may call psychological or social invention, whose product is not an object as such. This is creativity not with objects but with persons: creativity in human relations. Creativity in human relations requires intelligence, sharp perceptions, subtle sensitivities, respect for the individual person, and a personal boldness to explain one's point of view and to stand for one's convictions. Creativity in human relations requires individual integrity and an ability to work with others. Historical examples are found in social and political attempts to deal with differences. Magna Charta, the Bill of Rights, the Emancipation Proclamation, constitutions, by-laws and their amendments, codes of law, and city ordinances are examples of social invention. There are other interpersonal examples of social creativity such as arranging car pools, keeping on good terms with one's neighbors, courting, making love, and child rearing.

Creativity in human relationships is a positive view of human behavior that admits the uniqueness and dignity of man. The creativity with which we shall be concerned here is a form or manner of relating to others which admits of one's own uniqueness and dignity and at the same time respects a uniqueness and dignity in others. This relating we call positive, harmonious, and creative in contrast to another kind of relating which we shall call negative, conflicting, and restricting. In a negative relating one denies the right to uniqueness in others and does not respect the dignity of the human being.

The relationships which we have just mentioned are not simple, neither are they absolutes; that is, they are not all-or-none. Whether positive or negative they are relative and are found in degrees. The degrees to which one respects the dignity of others depend upon many factors: one's native endowment, that is, whether one is bright or dull; one's age or stage of maturity in development, whether one is an infant, a child, or a man; the range of one's opportunity for experiences; the validity of one's perceptions; and many other factors from the environment, including the degree to which one is himself respected as an individual and the degree of security or insecurity under which one's experiences have taken place.

The degree to which one admits of one's own uniqueness and dignity is also affected by these many variables and probably by others not identified nor even suspected. Psychologists have different words for referring to this process of self-regarding. They may call it ego development or ego strength, individuality or individuation, personal integrity or integerness. They may call it spontaneity, self-realization, self-expression, self-respect, self-actualization, or self-producing.

In this connection I quote from Kierkegaard (taken from Rank, 1932):

The individual becomes conscious of himself as being this particular individual with particular gifts, tendencies, impulses, passions, under the influence of a particular environment, as a particular product of his milieu. He who becomes thus conscious of himself assumes all this as part of his own responsibility. At the moment of choice he is thus in complete isolation, for he withdraws from his surroundings and yet he is in complete continuity, for he chooses himself as product; and this choice is a free choice, so that we might even say when he chooses himself as product, that he is producing himself.

In order to discuss the topic of creativity as personality development, let us take an example from biology and examine the stuff out of which we are made. Your life and mine have been procreated by the union of a spermatozoon and an unfertilized egg. Physiologists tell us that this union and what happens immediately thereafter is a complex process. There are no doubt many things which we do not understand about this process and perhaps many other things going on which we cannot even see.

The unfertilized egg is living in an environment in which there is a spermatozoon. Each is said to be an individual organism. Each is different from the other in structure and in function. Each constitutes a part of the environment of the other. It can be said that the presence of the egg makes a difference in the behavior of the spermatozoon and that the presence of the spermatozoon makes a difference in the behavior of the egg. I shall use this biological example of a spermatozoon and an egg to explain two of the terms in my title, namely, *creativity* and *development*. I shall then use this example to illustrate certain parallels in the third term in my title: *personality* development. I shall do this by stating several propositions. From there I shall continue the discussion with results of research and further theoretical formulations.

CREATIVITY AND DEVELOPMENT

Differentiation and *integration* are the two generally accepted criteria for growth. There are certain other statements, however, that can be made about the union of a spermatozoon and an egg and of what happens thereafter. But all these statements seem merely restatements or elaborations of what is included under the terms differentiation and integration. Let us now examine six somewhat overlapping propositions.

1. With the spermatozoon and the egg there is the *confronting of differences*. There is an interaction, or an activity-between. It is not sufficient to think, as we used to, that this confronting or activity-between represents a stimulus-response relating. Stimulus and response are terms that are too static, too slow, and too oversimplified to designate what is happening. By confronting we mean a process of relating in which the behavior or the presence of one organism makes a difference in the behavior of the other. Confronting requires an-

other quality: it must represent a certain integrity, integerness, or individuality in each organism. There is not only the fact of difference but an *acting* differently. The egg behaves, *acts* like an egg, and the spermatozoon behaves, *acts* like a spermatozoon. Each is biologically free to be "itself." In the hypothesis that growth occurs only through the confronting and the free interplay of differences there is necessarily not only a concept of the integrity of differences, but also of action-between consistent with this biological integerness.

2. *Confronting* of differences is not necessarily *conflict* of differences. Conflict of differences as we shall use the term implies an outside attack against the biological integrity of one organism by another, from which we derive our psychological concepts of defense, rigidity, disunity, disorganization, and disintegration. There is nothing in the behavior or the relating of the spermatozoon and the egg that resembles conflict. In contrast with conflict, which represents one-way communication, growth, in a very real biological sense, is a process of *two-way communication* between individual cells or organisms. Growth is the confronting and free interplay of differences.

3. Growth is *integration*. The spermatozoon becomes one with the egg and the egg becomes one with the spermatozoon. It can be said that they integrate their differences. They are finding a common biological purpose. They are *working with* each other. They are not *working against* each other. There is a uniting, a unity, or an integration, a oneness of behaving, a harmony in behaving. Integration is essentially harmonious behavior. I use all these words because it is difficult to communicate what really seems to be happening. And I choose these words because we find them throughout the biological and psychological literature.

There is a common purpose among differences implied in the biologists' discovery that the individual acts as a whole. There is an expenditure of energy by the parts in such a way that the changing needs of the entire body tend to be satisfied. Integration of differences is, by definition, the emergence of an original, the creation of something different. In this sense growth is a process of creativity.

4. Growth is a *yielding*, a *giving up*. The fertilization of the egg by the spermatozoon represents an abandoning by each of its own particular structure and its own particular function. The spermatozoon gives up its structure and its function as a spermatozoon. And

the egg abandons its structure and its function as an unfertilized egg for a new structure and new function that are in process of emerging. Growth is a noncoerced abandoning. It is a giving up of oneself as he is at the moment for a new self that is in process of emerging.

5. Growth is a process of *differentiating*. This one-celled fertilized egg multiplies. It multiplies fairly rapidly. Each of the new cells that is produced is supposed to have through the chromosomes an "identical" heredity. This process is not just sub-division, nor are the cells identical. Biologists tell us that the cells become differentiated. The cells take on specialized functions and specialized structures, and we call them by different names. Some are called nerve cells; some bone cells; others muscle cells; still others gland cells. Why is it that man boasts that he is the highest form of biological life? It is because in man the cells have become more highly specialized; that is, more highly differentiated than the cells of any other species. It is also because in man the cells have achieved a higher level of organization or integration, or harmony in behaving, as in Proposition 3.

In cell division, or cell multiplication, the new cells are different from the original cells. The children, so to speak, are different from the parents, and are different from each other. Differentiation is by definition the emergence of originals, the creation of differences. Again growth is creativity.

6. Growth, moreover, is *positive*; it has direction. That growth is a positive process is implied in each of the preceding propositions. Growth is a continuing process of differentiating, of self-producing, moving on to more and more complexity; it is integrating and harmonious, not disintegrating nor disharmonious; it is confronting, not conflicting; it represents free interplay of differences, spontaneous abandoning, yielding of present structures and functions. Disintegration, disharmony, conflict, rigidity, inflexibility, unyieldingness, force, coercion are, from the standpoint of growth, negative concepts. To the extent that these terms have meaning for a biological organism that organism is in a lower state of growth than it would be without such meaning.

In the six propositions above we find not only that we started with differences, that is, with originals, but we have been dealing with the producing of originals, with the flow of originality. Growth creates differences. Creativity is a characteristic of development; it is a quality of protoplasm. There is creativity in everyone.

Personality Development

Now let us examine the six propositions from the standpoint of psychology and consider the meaning of personality.

1. The *psychological confronting of differences takes place between persons or groups of persons.* Instead of cells as units in our illustration we now have individual human beings as units. We advanced the proposition that growth, that is, differentiation and integration, occurs through the confronting of differences and the free interplay of differences. This is another way of stating a proposition of social learning. If all persons were alike we could not learn from each other.

2. Confronting of differences is not necessarily *conflict* of differences. Confronting may occur in the positive or creative relationship as in the high level communication between scientists in search of truth. Or, confronting may occur at a lower level of relating in the negative or conflicting relationship where power, threat, status, or defense are involved.

The ideal of confronting is that it be an expression of what the person himself thinks, feels, believes, desires. A lie, to use an extreme example, is a misrepresentation; it is what a scientist would call invalid behavior. It expresses something that is not what it purports to be. A lie is a defense mechanism. When one lies he does not present himself to another; he does not confront. He does not want to be understood as he really is. He hides himself from another. Under certain circumstances one may choose to lie or to keep silent when he has an opportunity to speak, but to that extent there is something less than the confronting of differences. To the extent that confronting is related to creativity or personality development it must have present the personal qualities of honesty and integrity. To the extent that behavior is defensive or falls short of honesty and personal integrity it falls short of valid interplay.

It follows that creativity is unrelated to neurotic behavior, or that it is impaired to the extent of the neurosis. A neurotic person, to the extent of his neurosis, is unable to confront, to reveal his true self to those about him. Some parts of his desires have been driven into the unconscious where they are unavailable even to himself. In psychoanalytic theory neurosis is represented by the extent of the gap between the conscious and the unconscious. A goal of psychotherapy is to reduce the gap between the conscious and the unconscious. Creativity when it occurs in a neurotic person may represent an attempt at a break-through from an inhibiting neurosis. It represents an attempt to be oneself, to be honest in a non-threatening or less-threatening medium.

3. Our third point on *integration* of differences will be discussed below in connection with social learning.

4. In a psychological sense the proposition that growth is a progressive *yielding* or a *giving up*, must include in some fashion a psychology of learning. For learning, too, is an abandoning of ideas one has at the moment for new ideas that are in process of emerging.

In the discussion of his paper on "Scientific Creativity" (Chapter 1), Eyring said that if one wanted to become a creative chemist one should certainly learn all he could about chemistry. He should then decide to refuse to believe any of it. From then on he would be free to select on the basis of his own thinking the relevant ideas and reject the irrelevant.

All about us we see terrific resistance to new ideas and to change. The human failure to give up habits of thinking and stereotypes in values is one of the most mystifying problems encountered in all disciplines.

Conant (1947) has given us an example of an outstanding failure by chemists to give up the contradictory, the inconsistent, and the irrelevant, and of the problem presented for creativity and learning by this failure to yield. The modern theory of combustion was propounded by Lavoisier who, before he was beheaded in 1794, discovered how to make nitrogen and oxygen separately. The original cue to the modern interpretation of combustion had been published 150 years earlier by Jean Rey. For 150 years chemists held to the erroneous theory of the "fire principle" or the phlogiston theory. Yet the phlogiston theory was so wrong that it could not be adapted to the new data and had finally to be rejected. Conant interpreted this example, dramatic in retrospect, as illustrating a tendency for an old, inadequate theory long intrenched in the minds of scientists to become a barrier to the acceptance of a better theory. A failure to think for oneself, to define for oneself the erroneous, and to abandon the irrelevant seems to illustrate a problem specially pertinent to the psychology of learning and to creativity.

Conant's example raises the old problem of throwing out the baby with the bath: how to differentiate the relevant. We have always been told that the chief error has been to throw out the baby. I submit that it is a more common error in civilization not to throw out anything. Since childhood we have each heard so often, "Don't! . . . Don't! . . . Don't! . . ." that we have become afraid to throw out even the dirty water for fear that, somehow, out might go the baby. For fear of doing "something wrong" we often do not do anything. We have been told so many times in childhood what is right and what is wrong, what is good behavior and what is bad behavior, and in college what is phlogiston, that long before graduate school we have learned to depend on someone else to tell us what is relevant. In the Ph.D. preliminary examinations professors usually examine on what to them is relevant. They examine the candidate on what the professors think is the baby, or in Conant's example on what is phlogiston. An occasional graduate student feels way down deep in his unconscious soul that about half of the preliminary examination is undifferentiated dirty water.

5. The fifth proposition that growth is a process of *differentiation* is consistently accepted by psychologists as a psychological principle applying to personality and to learning. By the process of differentiation the person moves from general experiences to particular interpretations—learns to see similarities and differences and to discriminate between his perceptions. In so doing he not only becomes more unique but demonstrates a process of becoming from day to day more unique and from moment to moment more individualized, more himself.

6. Personality development is a *positive, constructive process.* There is nothing in the phenomena of differentiation and integration and of the emergence of originals that can be meaningfully described in terms of domination, submission, aggression, frustration, hostility, mastery, rigidity, compensation, conflict, or even sublimation. These are negative terms which are used to refer to behavior under interpersonal conflict or psychological "stress." Operationally defined, differentiation and integration are proceeding at their maximum under the existing conditions of the organism, of its environment, and of

the nature of the interplay between them. Rigidity, submission, mastery, aggression, conflict, hostility, pathology, and disease are terms used to designate conditions, relations, and processes that are low in differentiation, low in integration, or in which the growth processes are abnormally obstructed or retarded.

The emphasis which psychologists have given to mental disease and to these other associated concepts constitutes a negative approach to the understanding of personality. The very concept of *defense mechanisms* implies some answer not only to the negative question, "Defense against what?" but also to the positive question, "Defense for what?" Defense mechanisms are called into play when trouble arises, when "something is the matter," when the environment has interfered with the positive creative growth processes of differentiation and integration. Defense mechanisms are used when the person needs to protect his spontaneity, his autonomy, his own differentiating processes, his integrity, his biological and psychological processes of growing.

Fromm (1947) refers to growth and productiveness as the "primary potentials" of man and to defense mechanisms and destructiveness as a secondary "potentiality" that comes into manifest existence only in case of abnormal, pathogenic conditions. Similar views have been strongly emphasized by Goldstein (1939), Sullivan (1947), Horney (1937, 1945), and others.

Personality Development as Social Learning

There is one important difference between biological creativity and psychological creativity: that is, the role of learning. In the biological interacting of cells within the organism the processes of differentiation and integration seem both to be inborn. Evolution, if considered on a biological time scale, might be regarded as "biological learning." The biological organism has a built-in program of creativity that has in some way become established over millions of years.

Psychologically the human infant has a built-in program for self-differentiation, for being himself, for self-actualizing. He does not have a similar built-in system for achieving harmony with others. Though he may have an inborn need for social integration, he can achieve it only through social interacting and social learning. Spontaneity is innate; harmony must be learned. Harmony is achieved through *activity with* others, through the *interweaving* of goals and desires. Harmony is achieved through the discovery of common purposes with others and with the invention of means for attaining them. This is the meaning of socially integrative behavior.

Learning in the interacting of persons is an activity-between. The infant cannot be separated from his environment, nor can he be considered separate from it. The infant is within the environment and the environment is within the infant. The English language (Whorf, 1956) which developed upon a structure of subject-object relationships is inadequate to describe or symbolize the process of integration or the process of social learning. The meaning of this dynamic activity-between has been referred to in different ways, such as transacting, mutuality, or as responding to a relating. From Murphy's (1947) biosocial viewpoint, "personality is an interaction of organism and culture, and the situation is consequently part of the personality . . . the interpersonal relations depend on the individuals, but . . . the individuals also depend on the relations."

Rotter (1954) gives as his first basic postulate for a "Social Learning Theory of Personality. . . . The unit of investigation for the study of personality is the interaction of the individual and his meaningful environment."

Not only the individual *and* his environment but the *process of interacting* must be understood. This process of interacting is social learning.

There have been many attempts to define personality. What is it about this person in process of reacting with others that one thinks of as his personality? My working definition is that personality is one's rate of psychological growth in social situations. Personality cannot develop in a vacuum nor in an ivory tower. It does not even develop well in an orphanage nor in many children's hospitals. Personality is the rate of psychological differentiating or self-actualizing and at the same time the rate with which one develops harmony in interacting with others. It is the rate at which now, at this moment, in this situation, a person who is becoming more and more an individual is at the same time seeking and finding an increasing personal unity with those about him. Personality defined in this way is one's rate of social creativity. It follows that when one attempts to "measure" personality, what one actually measures is the process of inter-acting or the lack of it.

OPTIMUM GROWTH AND A PROPITIOUS ENVIRONMENT

Social creativity cannot be forced or coerced; it can only be facilitated or restricted. What then is the role of the human environment as a facilitator and as a restrictor? One needs to consider more than space permits here the meaning of optimum personality growth and the characteristics of a propitious environment.

Growth, learning, creativity, like everything else a psychologist discusses, exist in degrees. Although the units of measurement or of comparison are often crude or even nonexistent, growth, learning, and creativity may be considered as faster or slower or as more or less. Theoretically, there are limits beyond which a given individual cannot go. Practically speaking, however, it is difficult to say when anyone achieves this highest limit or that anyone ever achieves it. In other words, a person is growing at his optimum rate, or he is growing at something less than his optimum. It is helpful to postulate a concept of optimum growth, which necessitates also a concept of propitious environment (Anderson and Anderson, 1954a).

One child is differentiating at a more rapid rate than another of the same age. One mother permits or assists her child to emancipate (differentiate) himself from her faster than another mother. The units of comparison are coarse and crude, but the comparisons are possible and useful. The question may well be raised whether child training or the impact of culture on the infant seems to have mainly a deadening or stultifying effect on originality, creativity, and optimum psychological development? Man is not only a product of his environment; in a very real sense man is also a victim of his environment.

The concepts of optimum growth and propitious environment are quite acceptable in other biological sciences and can be useful to psychologists.

CIRCULAR BEHAVIOR

Follett (1924), in her book *Creative Experience*, was the first, according to my knowledge, to have extended the concept of circular behavior as a psychological term to the interaction of human beings.

SOCIALLY INTEGRATIVE BEHAVIOR—THE CREATIVE GROWTH CIRCLE

Socially integrative behavior expresses high degrees of the two essential qualities of growth which I have discussed as differentiation and integration. Through the confront of differences and the free interplay of differences shown in open-minded discussion, Follett observed the solutions to problems which she, as mediator of labor disputes, thought could not have been devised without the participation of all parties in the dispute. Problem solving in social conflict, for Follett, was not a psychology of adjustment, but a psychology of invention. Creative experience was the outcome of a circular process in interacting, the product of the interweaving of experiences, of the activity-between, the working together. The emergence of originals represented an integration of differences. The free interacting of minds in disagreement was creative. Follett maintained as early as 1924 that the interacting was not a sequence of stimulus-response behaviors, but a process; the response was not just to a stimulus, but to a relating. Circular behavior was creative, inventive; it was a growth circle. This appears to be the essence of a dynamic psychology. This is circular behavior in the direction of growth, social invention, creativity.

The socially propitious human environment as it concerns human interacting is a mutually accepting circular phenomenon. If one human being tends to make a propitious environment for another, the other tends to make a propitious environment for the one. If one tends to work with another, the other tends to work with the one. If one tends to listen to another, tries to understand him, to learn from him, the other tends to listen to the one, to try to understand him, to learn from him. This kind of propitious, accepting, nonthreatening, nonconflictual relating constitutes a growth circle in human interacting. Socially integrative behavior increases two-way communication, increases understanding.

It is in this positive accepting, nonthreatening relating with one's environment that are found the positive emotions mentioned by poets and psychologists. Delight, joy, enthusiasm, ecstasy are associated with experiences of spontaneity and harmony, with action, communication, production, achievement.

The hypothesis of the growth circle is: Socially integrative behavior in one person tends to induce socially integrative behavior in others.

DOMINATION—THE VICIOUS CIRCLE

There is another kind of circular behavior in persons who cannot integrate their activities in a creative direction. This behavior is domination, the depriving by one person of the opportunity for spontaneous activity by another. Domination is, as Follett stated, the use of *power over* others instead of, as in integration, the use of *power with* others.

Domination is found in schoolrooms, families, and factories. It has been a conspicuous part of international diplomacy of all time. In the psychology of human behavior all uses of force, coercion, domination, shame, blame, guilt have one effect: the stifling of the creative process, the annihilation of originality. This is the environmental degrading of the quality of behavior. No matter what social justification there may be for momentary use of domination, without more than domination the effect is the same.

The anticipated reaction to domination is resistance. Aggression meets aggression; that is, domination incites resistance as long as it is "safe" to resist. Within this range domination sets up a vicious circle of interacting. If, however, domination is so great that it is not safe to resist, domination will produce ambiguous, vacillating, unstructured, confused relating. A further increase of domination will produce conformity, submission, a cessation of confronting.

In this relating of interpersonal conflict are found the negative emotions mentioned by psychologists. Anger, fear, jealousy, rage are found in the vicious circle of human relating. In such emotions as bewilderment, grief, despair the degree of spontaneity is too low to show the circular reactions of resistance.

The hypothesis of the vicious circle is: Domination in one person tends to incite domination (resistance) in others.

RESEARCH ON SOCIALLY INTEGRATIVE AND DOMINATIVE BEHAVIOR

A number of years ago I began a series of research studies to establish measures of the dynamics of relating and to test the hypotheses of circular behavior. The first study concerned the interactions of preschool children. It was designed to determine whether socially integrative behavior and dominative behavior, as such, could be reliably observed and recorded in the form of quantitative data (Anderson,

1937a, 1937b). The data were recorded items of actual behavior of preschool children in a free play situation in an experimental playroom. Two of the groups of children lived in an orphanage where a research experimental nursery school had been established. Half of the children attended nursery school and constituted a nursery school group. The other half, individually matched with the others, did not attend nursery school and constituted a control group of non-nursery school children. The orphanage children were below average in intelligence and came from generally low socioeconomic levels.

Analysis of the data revealed high internal consistency and supported three hypotheses: (1) integrative behavior in one child induced integrative behavior in the companion; (2) domination incited domination; and (3) integration and domination were psychologically different. Two years later a similar study with a contrasting group of kindergarten children of superior intelligence coming from high socioeconomic backgrounds again yielded consistent evidence for the hypotheses of the growth circle and of the vicious circle of dynamic relating (Anderson, 1939).

Research was then carried into the schools to see whether the teacher's contacts with the children—these so-called intangibles in human relating—could be reliably observed and recorded. To illustrate the kinds of situation in schools from which our records were made I want to cite two examples (Anderson, 1940).

The first example is from a second grade. It illustrates a teacher's encouragement of social participation and of spontaneity and shows a teacher *working with* the children in a common purpose. The second example is from a kindergarten where the teacher was working essentially *against* the children, where the teacher was depriving the children of opportunities for creative experience at the child's level of competence. The first example illustrates a facilitator of creativity; the second example represents a restrictor of creativity in the child.

EXAMPLE OF ENVIRONMENTAL FACILITATING

In a second grade during singing period one of the children asked for the song about the organ-grinder and the monkey. Another child volunteered the page number. After the children had sung it, the teacher asked, "I wonder if you would like to play it (act it)?" There was general agreement. The boy who had asked for the song was asked to choose the organ-grinders. He designated three, who in turn chose their monkeys. Two monkeys had been chosen. James was hesitating, although several hands indicated that he could have a monkey.

"Why don't you choose, James?" the teacher asked.

James looked over the room again and said, "I want a little person and I want somebody who wants to be a monkey." A hand shot up from a little girl who fitted the specifications which James, by himself, had formulated, and she became the third monkey.

After the children had sung the song while the organ-grinders and their monkeys performed at the front of the room, a child asked, "Don't they go down the street?"

"The organ man decides that," the teacher replied. The organ-grinders and the monkeys and the other children together seemed to decide it. The monkeys and organ-grinders moved slowly down the aisles and the children began to reach with ostensible gestures into imaginary purses for imaginary pennies to drop into imaginary cups. They sang the song again and the teacher, adding her imaginary pennies, remarked, "Well, I hope you enjoyed their song, and that the monkeys received lots of pennies."

The importance of this example lies in the freedom of the children and encouragement by the teacher to think for themselves and to participate. This teacher had many opportunities to make decisions for the children, but she allowed the children to volunteer and she turned problems back to the children for their decision and action.

Not every choice that a child makes is a critical experience, nor is every product of the child's originality a gem. What is important is the process of choosing and the process of producing. Through action comes a confidence by which a child knows that he is free to choose and free to produce his own contribution without threat, censor, or guilt from the environment.

EXAMPLE OF ENVIRONMENTAL RESTRICTING

The teacher in this kindergarten was a conscientious, mild-mannered person. The children, however, had little autonomy in their activities. Materials were "prepared" for them, distributed with precise directions as to how they were to be used. In extremely small details the children were not permitted to experiment in developing ideas of their own nor to depart from the teacher's plan.

A group of kindergarten children were making May baskets. Terry had folded his basket on the lines which had been drawn on the material the night before by the teacher. He had pasted the flaps as he had been instructed and had the handle fastened in place. The teacher had cut out of other paper a handful of diamond-shaped pieces which she had distributed four to a child. She had explained to the children that these were to serve as decorations to be pasted horizontally on the basket. As she walked about the room she noticed Terry pasting his diamond decoration vertically.

"Oh, oh, Terry," she said, "the decorations are to be pasted on lying down and not standing up."

"But I want to paste mine this way," said Terry.

"Well, that isn't the way they are supposed to go. Here now, just paste it this way." And she turned the diamond horizontally and pasted it before Terry seemed to know what had happened. She remained while Terry at her instruction pasted two more shapes horizontally. Then she turned away leaving Terry to paste the fourth.

At the end of the period Terry had only three decorations on his basket. When the teacher inquired about the baskets, Terry, pointing to the undecorated side of his basket, said that he did not want one there.

"Oh, but every basket should have four. Here is one your color. We'll just paste it on quickly." And with Terry speechless and transfixed, she pasted it on quickly.

Mary Lou had observed that at her table several handles did not stick. "I guess I don't want a handle," she remarked to the boy seated next to her. She cut up the handle of her basket and pasted the pieces as decorations all over the basket. The teacher's remark to this *fait accompli* was, "Oh, you've spoiled yours, Mary Lou; yours is all messy and doesn't have a handle."

Terry and Mary Lou were children who appeared to show a measure of originality and spontaneity. Their behavior showed that they had ideas that differed from the expressed ideas of the "oldest and wisest" member of the group. Their behavior satisfies the criteria of being "experimentally minded," and of "thinking for oneself"—important aspects of growth, basic ingredients of creativity, and basic objectives of education. Terry's spontaneous idea was nipped in the bud. Mary

Lou's idea was translated into action which was subsequently disapproved.

In this room can children have ideas different from those of the teacher; if so, in what circumstances and how often? In this room where does creativity begin? Where can creativity in the child flourish? Must the product, even the first draft, the first sketch, meet the approval, the predetermined stereotypes, the "values," the standards of the experts? Must each early effort at creativity in the child be summarily judged until the child does only those things which his parents and teachers have already thought of and approved? Who has the right, who is qualified to judge any child's creative effort? These were questions for which there were no answers.

Our research problem was to devise methods for recording teacher-child interaction. We then had the problem of showing whether the behavior of the teacher would make a difference on the one hand in the spontaneity, problem solving, social contributions, of the children and on the other hand in their resistance, nervous habits, and conformity. If through domination the teacher found herself in conflict with the children and the domination incited resistance, would the teacher in some way be able to cut the vicious circle? Theoretically the socially integrative behavior by an accepting teacher is a means of cutting the vicious circle in the school room. Would the observational methods show the operation of the growth circle in the teacher's relations with the children? The research objective was to develop quantitative measures of the activity and social interplay of children and of the facilitating and restricting behavior of the teachers.

In a sequence of observational studies in schools, kindergarten teachers used twice as many dominative restrictive contacts as integrative (facilitative) contacts with individual children (Anderson, 1939). Teachers also revealed a wide range of frequencies of contacts with individual children, showing that the children lived in different psychological environments in the same schoolroom. H. M. Brewer and Anderson (1945) found that the kindergarten teachers were meeting aggression with aggression and were systematically inciting resistance instead of cutting the vicious circle in a socially creative, integrative way.

J. E. Brewer (1946) made records of the behavior of teachers and children in two second-grade rooms in the same school building. One teacher was found to be consistently more integrative (facilitative, democratic) and less dominative; the other was consistently more dominative (dictatorial, restrictive). The differences were large and statistically significant. Children with the more integrative teacher showed significantly higher frequencies of behavior in several categories representing socially creative behavior in children: spontaneity, initiative, and social contributions to others. The data confirmed the hypothesis that *integration in the teacher induces integrative behavior in the child*. Moreover, children with the more dominating teacher showed significantly higher frequencies of nonconforming behavior, directly supporting the hypothesis that *domination incites resistance*. The behavior of the children also supported the further hypothesis that severe domination produces not resistance but submission and atrophy.

Reed (1946) observed Brewer's two rooms of children one year later in the third grade with new teachers and the same two second-grade teachers one year later with new groups of children. She found that while teacher personalities were relatively constant, there was much more flexibility and responsiveness in the children. Reed also found the operation of the facilitating growth circle and of the restricting vicious circle. The more integrative teacher was cutting the vicious circle; the more dominating teacher was not.

Anderson and J. E. Brewer (1946) made consecutive studies from fall to winter in two third grades. In *group contacts* there was no evidence that after five months either teacher was reducing conflict in the room by "cutting the vicious circle" of domination. The report for teachers' *contacts with individual children* was different: one teacher was cutting the vicious circle; the other teacher was not.

Another type of approach bearing on circular behavior is found in the studies of induced "social climates" reported by Lewin and Lippitt (1938), and summarized by Lippitt and White (1943). The "democratic climate" was the productive relation of socially integrative behavior which in the group was circular and self-renewing. There was mutual acceptance and a working with each other, "working together for common goals." In the *laissez-faire* climate there was a considerable amount of domination, interpreted as a source of "group disruption," a "vicious circle of frustration-aggression-frustration. . . ."

Circular behavior is reported by other persons in studies of attitudes, symbolism, fantasy, and ratings of behavior. These studies have been reviewed elsewhere by Anderson and Anderson (1954a).

SOCIAL DEVELOPMENT VERSUS SOCIALIZATION

I cannot discuss creativity as personality development without a word of contrast between Social Development and Socialization. In Anderson and Anderson (1954a) the following definition of social development was presented in a chapter on that subject:

The perception and reciprocal communication to others of one's needs and desires, the reciprocal interpretation to others of one's judgments and values, and in meeting human needs the mutual discovery of common purposes among differences at the level of action without coercion, threat, or guilt—this is a crude statement of psychological growth; this is social development. Anything less than this represents, by that much less, a lower level of social development; anything more represents, by that much more, a higher level of social development.

This definition of social development comprises a positive process. It is applicable to all levels of development and competence and at all ages. It includes the six propositions concerning growth which we have mentioned above. It admits of self-respect, self-production, and respect for the individuality and dignity of others. It requires two-way communication and excludes the negative relationships of cultural domination as in the use of force, threat, and guilt. According to this definition social controls are meaningfully, that is, mutually and voluntarily determined. In this kind of relationship there is no limit to one's creativity or social development. The limit is infinity in social evolution.

The term "Socialization" (Child, 1954), defined in a chapter of the same title and quoted here, designates a quite different relationship and the outcome is quite different:

"Socialization" is used here as a broad term for the whole process by which an individual, born with behavioral potentialities of enormously wide range, is led to develop actual behavior which is confined within a much narrower range—the range of what is customary and acceptable for him according to the standards of his group.

Socialization as thus defined includes both positive and negative forms of relating. It can be achieved without regard for the individual's needs and without respect for the dignity of the person. It may have no relation to the individual's growth. It often represents one-way communication, and is usually achieved by various punitive devices: by the use of commands, threats, force, guilt, and punishment. In the socializing process the limit of the child's differentiation or creativity is what the culture has already discovered and found acceptable. The child's social development cannot by this definition of socialization rise above the culture. The emergence of originals in the areas of socialization as different from the standards of the group is not permitted.

From the point of view of personality growth the contrasting aim of *social development* is to achieve for the child the socially integrative relation; that is, the maximum of spontaneity with the maximum of harmony. Obviously, much of the actual *socializing* process is a throttling of the child's spontaneity and a stifling of his creativity.

In all cultures the child is required to achieve some acceptable measure of harmony with those about him. There is great variability in the areas of activity in which harmony is required and great variability also in the means by which different cultures attempt to develop acceptable behavior in the child. Research is needed on both problems of variability. It is not at all clear that the high degrees of throttling and stifling are necessary for the degree of harmony achieved.

Harmony is a creative use of energy, the interrelating of spontaneities. We have long confused conformity with harmony. In the process of socializing the child we have been mainly concerned with conformity. Conformity is a degradation of the quality of behavior, the uncreative stifling of spontaneity. However justified conformity may be in a given situation, it is not harmony; it is not creative; it is not growth.

Murray and Kluckhohn (1948), writing about the socialization process, stated that an organism can be oversocialized. Allport (1955) made a similar comment: "It is a limitation of current theories of socialization that they do in fact deal only with the mirror-like character of the so-called super-ego, that they tend to define socialization exclusively in terms of conformity, and not also in terms of creative becoming."

Social or cultural domination means the arbitrary deprivation of experience in another person through the use of power over another.

Power over another can be expressed in the outward use of force and threats or in the subtler, insidious symbolic forms of control as in disapproval, ridicule, sarcasm, even praise and blame.

Terry and Mary Lou in the example above were being "socialized"; they were being taught to behave according to standards which the "culture" would determine and approve. They were in reality being deprived of opportunities for spontaneity, autonomy, personal differentiation, artistic originality, experimental trials in manipulating their material environments. They were being deprived of the right to be themselves. With some motivation unknown to the observers and probably unknown to the teacher herself, the teacher was forbidding Terry and Mary Lou to be creative.

BRAINWASHING

A modern term for the deprivation of sensory, emotional, and cognitive experience, for the arbitrary selectivity by one person of what another may see, do, feel, or think is *brainwashing*. One might think that brainwashing is a psychological technique of recent Chinese origin; that is not so. Brainwashing of children has been a technique of child training in the Western cultures for centuries. As growth is made up of small activities, increments, experiences, so the cultural deprivation of experience, the so-called socializing, the polite cultural brainwashing of children is made up of small incidents, small obstructions, small deflections. Like lead poisoning in the blood stream, cultural brainwashing of children at home and at school is not sudden, dramatic, or easily detected. But after months and years, if the child has not revolted, the spirit becomes heavy, the motivation is sluggish, and activity lacks direction, meaning, or purpose. The spark of creativity becomes stifled. Out of such deprivations of spontaneous experience, do children become uncreative, unimaginative, self-conscious, self-protecting conformists?

THE OPEN SYSTEM VERSUS THE CLOSED SYSTEM

Practically everything which I have discussed may be viewed from another perspective, that of an *open system* of human relating versus a *closed system*. Throughout our discussion different pairs of concepts or polarities have been used: positive and negative approaches; growth circle and vicious circle; harmony and conflict; accepting and rejecting; a propitious environment and an unpropitious environment; environmental facilitators of creativity and environmental restrictors of creativity. Each of these polarities points on the one hand in the direction of openness in human relating or on the other hand in the direction of a closed system of relating.

The relation between an openness and a closedness can be represented on a vertical continuum (Anderson and Anderson, 1954a). The scale from top to bottom would be a kind of barometer of psychological atmospheric pressure or a measure of environmental domination of the individual person at a given moment of time. At the top is the open, socially integrative, propitious environment of rarefied air where acceptance is high and the pressure of environmental attack is negligible. The terminus of the open relation would be infinity at the top of this continuum. No matter in how propitious an environment one found himself, it could theoretically always be improved.

The terminus of the closed relating is a finite point at the bottom of the scale. As one approaches the bottom the environmental pressure on the person is heavy indeed. The very bottom of this continuum represents 100 per cent of human environmental domination, the complete use of power over the person, complete psychological rejection, complete intolerance of the person, a completeness found only in murder and capital punishment.

The scale, although having several discriminable units, has two major divisions: an upper part and a lower part which comprise the positive and negative polarities. In the upper part the relating is characterized by an essential harmony with those in one's environment. Persons are task-oriented and self-abandoning, relatively unconcerned about their personal status and security. There is high confronting without personal conflict. Power is used *with* others and not *against* others.

The lower part of the scale, however, denotes a relating in conflict in which those in the environment try to use power over the person, to think for him, to make decisions for him, and to require conformity in his behavior. Persons in this kind of human environment are not task-oriented. They are personally threatened; their first attention is to personal security, protection, and defense. As a consequence their perceptions become more highly selective, restrictive, even distorted, and under severe pressure delusional. Communication becomes wary, even deceptive. Confronting may disappear, as in conformity and submissiveness. Such confronting as is manifest tends to be hostile and aggressive.

It is not just "acceptance" or the "permissive" atmosphere of an open system that produces creativity. There must, in addition, be stimulation, intense, invigorating stimulation through the confronting and free interplay of differences. It is only partly true to say that one can be as creative as the environment permits. In addition to spontaneity there must be interaction with one's environment: social learning, social invention, and a progressive and developing wholeness, harmony, integration. Creativity as personality development is not only a product of openness in human relating; it is a further opening to higher levels of harmony in the universe.

10

Traits of Creativity

J. P. GUILFORD

W HEN some time ago this author presented hypotheses concerning the component talents contributing to creativity (Guilford, 1950), he was subsequently amazed at the evidence of widespread interest in the subject. Incidentally, the interest seemed to be stronger from outside the field of psychology than from within its boundaries. There is undoubtedly in this country, and possibly also in others, an undercurrent of need felt for increased creative performance and a desire to know more about the nature of creativity itself. Boring (1950) has suggested that an unusually strong interest in the subject is an aspect of our *Zeitgeist*. The present Symposium is one expression of it.

REASONS FOR THE INTEREST IN CREATIVITY

If we ask ourselves the reasons for this element in our *Zeitgeist*, speculation leads to several suggestive conclusions. The most urgent reason is that we are in a mortal struggle for the survival of our way of life in the world. The military aspect of this struggle, with its race to develop new weapons and new strategies, has called for a stepped-up rate of invention. Having reached a state of stalemate with respect to military preparedness, we encounter challenges on all intellectual fronts, scientific and cultural as well as economic and political. Again and again, we have been shaken out of our lethargy and our complacency by new developments.

Other reasons probably arise from states of boredom. There is likely to be a period of relative boredom following a great war. Boredom has also been a creeping disease in modern industry, where men and women need to perform less and less like human beings. Their work no longer calls upon them, as formerly, for decisions and for constructive thinking. The advances in automation have not helped this situation. There is also boredom arising from increased leisure time. Fortunately, satiation with any condition usually leads to corrective measures. The best solution would seem to be to direct leisure-time activities into channels of creative effort, giving individuals a taste of the rewards that can come from such efforts.

The coming of the age of space is another force contributing to the upsurge in interest in creativity. It stirs the imagination and it calls for readjustments at an accelerated rate. Many of the adjustments that we are forced to make are to the accelerated technological advances, but many are also due to the social implications of those advances. In a world grown small so far as travel and communication are concerned and a world in which the exploding population competes ever more strongly for its resources, adjustments in the political and personal-relations areas call increasingly for imaginative solutions. From any aspect from which we may view the scene, the needs for creativity are enormous.

A PSYCHOLOGICAL APPROACH TO CREATIVITY

These needs have found psychology ill prepared. Some years ago, a professor of journalism came to the author asking what psychologists knew about creative thinking. He had a strong desire to develop talents for creative writing among his students. With considerable regret and chagrin, it was necessary to tell him that there was almost nothing that psychologists knew about the subject.

In large part this deficiency on the part of psychology may be attributed to the general adoption of its stimulus-response model. There is no questioning of the advances that psychology has made with this conceptual model. But when we come to the higher thought processes, particularly to problems of creative thinking, the limitations of the model become very apparent. In approaching these problems it becomes more important than elsewhere to develop concepts pertaining to what goes on within the organism. We are forced to draw inferences regarding these events from what we can observe in terms of stimuli and responses, but we can no longer describe those events adequately in terms of stimulus-response concepts, or even in terms of intervening-variable concepts of the Hullian types.

The prevailing, alternative approach is through an emphasis upon trait concepts. Traits are properties of individuals, and they are fruitfully investigated by an approach that emphasizes individual differences. A trait is any distinguishable, relatively enduring way in which one individual differs from another. The psychologist's interest, of course, is heavily weighted in the direction of behavior traits. Wherever we can point out a trait variable along which individuals differ systematically, it may be concluded that this variable pertains to some property that individuals possess in common but to different degrees. But the property may also apply to a way of functioning and hence it may provide a concept for describing the way in which the individual operates.

The most defensible way of discovering dependable trait concepts of this kind at present is that of factor analysis. Factor analysis starts with information regarding the concomitant variations of performances. To say that the interest is confined to performances would be incorrect, for the performances whose intercorrelations are investigated are obtained under experimental control of the situations that help to instigate them. By varying the kind of test both qualitatively and quantitatively we can arrive at more accurate interpretation of factors and delineation of their properties. Information regarding factors may often thus be used as information regarding basic psychological functions.

It is the purpose of this chapter, first, to give a very brief survey of the known primary traits that are believed to be related to creativity. Primary traits are found by factor analysis. The survey will include both aptitude and nonaptitude traits, among the latter being traits of temperament and of motivation. Second, the paper will point out what seems to be the place of the aptitudes for creativity within the general framework of intellect. In doing so, some predictions will be made concerning undiscovered aptitudes for creative thinking. Third, some relationships of the factors of creativity to evaluations of creative performance other than those in the aptitude-test category will be mentioned, to indicate that the factors of creativity do have some support from other sources, including evaluations of everyday life performances.

PRIMARY TRAITS RELATED TO CREATIVITY

The status of our information regarding the primary traits of creativity can perhaps be most meaningfully presented on the background of some hypotheses that were adopted for investigation in 1950.[1]

APTITUDE FOR CREATIVE THINKING

In 1950 (Guilford, 1950) it was predicted that we should find a factor characterized as an ability to see problems; a generalized sensitivity to problems. Such a trait was found, and it is best indicated by tests asking examinees to state defects or deficiencies in common implements or in social institutions or to state problems created by common objects or actions. The factor has more recently been identified logically as belonging in the general category of evaluative abilities (Guilford, 1957a). The reason is that the act involved is essentially a judgment that things are not all right; that goals have not been reached; or that not everything to be desired has been achieved. Such a decision would play no constructive part in productive thinking, but without this step productive thinking would not get started.

It was hypothesized that fluency of thinking would be an important aspect of creativity. This is a quantitative aspect that has to do with fertility of ideas. Our results in the Aptitudes Project have verified and extended information concerning four fluency factors (Wilson, Guilford, et al., 1954).

There is the factor of *word fluency*, first reported by Thurstone (1938). This is an ability to produce words each containing a specified letter or combination of letters. It is not easy to see where this ability would have much importance in creative work in everyday life, but Drevdahl (1956) has found it to be related in both science and arts students.

A factor of *associational fluency* is indicated best in a test that requires the examinee to produce as many synonyms as he can for a given word in limited time. In contrast to word fluency, where only

---

[1] Much of the information to be mentioned in succeeding pages comes from the project on Aptitudes of High-Level Personnel at the University of Southern California, under contract N6onr-23810 with the Office of Naval Research.

letter requirements are to be observed, associational fluency involves a requirement of meaning for the words given. One would expect such an ability to be important to the average writer who wants to find a word to satisfy a particular meaning he has in mind and a quick running over of words in that area is an advantage. We are testing this hypothesis in a study of theme writing in freshman English.

A factor of expressional fluency is best measured by a test calling for the production of phrases or sentences. The need for rapid juxtaposition of words to meet the requirements of sentence structure seems to be the unique characteristic of tests of this ability. Whether the same ability pertains to oral speech we do not know, but there is some reasonable presumption of at least a moderate correlation between corresponding performances in writing and in oral speech. Although in writing one does not ordinarily work under pressure of time, the facility for framing sentences must be an important asset. In oral speech it should be of even greater importance, particularly for oratorical talents. It can be said that the possession of a high degree of expressional fluency, as measured by written tests, can apparently lead observers to the conclusion that the expressionally fluent person has a high degree of creativity. In one study, not yet published, ratings of men in several different traits of creativity tended to be correlated positively with scores for the factor of expressional fluency.

A trait of probably much wider usefulness is fluency in the production of ideas, or the factor of ideational fluency. This is the ability to produce ideas to fulfill certain requirements in limited time. A test of this factor may ask examinees to name objects that are hard, white, and edible or to give various uses for a common brick, or to write appropriate titles for a given story plot. In scoring for this factor, sheer quantity is the important consideration; quality need not be considered so long as responses are appropriate.

There are certain stages in most problem-solving where there must be a searching for answers. The problem as structured or defined provides the specifications for the solutions that are sought. Unless the specifications point to a unique solution, some searching and testing of alternative solutions is likely to occur. The scanning process is more likely to arrive at suitable solutions if it can elicit a greater number of possibilities. Thus ideational fluency probably plays an important role in problem-solving, and many problems require novel solutions, which means creative thinking.

In 1950 it was hypothesized that creative thinkers are flexible thinkers. They readily desert old ways of thinking and strike out in new directions. A factor of flexibility of thinking was therefore predicted. We found two abilities, both of which seem to fit into this general category (Wilson, Guilford, et al., 1954).

One of these factors has been called *spontaneous flexibility*. It is defined as the ability or disposition to produce a great variety of ideas, with freedom from inertia or from perseveration. In tests of this factor, the examinee shows his freedom to roam about in his thinking even when it is not necessary for him to do so. In naming uses of a common brick, he jumps readily from one category of response to another—the brick used as building material, as a weight, as a missile, or as a source of red powder, and so on. Rigid thinkers, on the other hand, tend to stay within one or two categories of response. Another example of spontaneously flexible thinkers in dealing with concrete material are those who see rapid fluctuations in ambiguous figures, such as the Necker outline cube or the staircase figure.

The other type of flexibility of thinking is called *adaptive flexibility* for the reason that it facilitates the solution of problems. This is shown best in a type of problem that requires a most unusual type of solution. The problem may appear to be soluble by means of more familiar or conventional methods, but these methods will not work. One task that calls for this kind of solution is based upon the familiar game involving matchsticks. The examinee is given a set of contiguous squares, each side formed by a match, and is told that he is to take away a certain number of matches, leaving a certain number of squares. He is not told that the squares must be all of the same size, but if he adopts this obvious assumption he cannot solve one or more problems, for the only satisfactory end result is a number of squares that differ in size. Persistence in wrong but inviting directions of thinking means low status on the factor of adaptive flexibility.

In the area of creativity one should certainly expect to find a trait of originality. It is indicated by the scores of some tests in which the keyed responses are weighted in proportion to their infrequency of occurrence in the population of examinees. Unusualness of responses, in a statistical sense, is one principle of measurement of *originality*.

The factor is also indicated by tests in which items call for remote associations or relationships; remote either in time or in a logical sense. If we ask examinees to list all the consequences they can think of in the event that a new discovery makes eating unnecessary, the number of remote consequences they give indicates originality, whereas the number of obvious consequences indicates ideational fluency. This means that it takes a quality criterion to indicate the extent of originality of which a person is characteristically capable.

A third way of indicating degree of originality in taking tests is the number of responses an examinee can give that are judged as being clever. The titles given for short-story plots, for example, can be rated as clever or not clever. The number of not-clever responses indicates ideational fluency whereas the number of clever responses indicates originality.

There is a growing suspicion that what we have called originality is actually a case of adaptive flexibility when dealing with verbally meaningful material, parallel to the factor of adaptive flexibility as now known, which pertains to tasks dealing with nonverbal material. In either case one must get away from the obvious, the ordinary, or the conventional in order to make a good score.

In 1950 a factor of redefinition was hypothesized, which called for an ability to give up old interpretations of familiar objects in order to use them or their parts in some new way. Factor analysis has well supported such a dimension of individual differences (Wilson, Guilford, et al., 1954). Which of the following objects, or their parts, could best be adapted to making a needle: pencil, radish, shoe, fish, or carnation? The keyed (correct) response is "fish," since a bone from a typical fish seems to be most readily adaptable for the purpose of making a needle. Improvising, in general, probably reflects the ability of *redefinition*. It has been suggested that a low status on this factor means the condition of "functional fixity" or "functional fixedness," which has been gaining in use to describe failure to solve problems in which improvising must occur, such as making a pendulum out of a string and pliers.

Another factor, which was predicted and found in a study of planning abilities (Berger, Guilford, and Christensen, 1957) and which needs further verification and analysis, may be mentioned. This is a factor called *elaboration*. It was indicated by a test in which the examinee is given one or two simple lines and told to construct on this foundation a more complex object. The score is the amount of elaboration demonstrated. It is also indicated by a test in which the bare outline of a plan is given, the examinee to list all the minor steps needed to make the plan work. It is possible that two abilities are involved, one pertaining to elaboration of figural material and one pertaining to elaboration of meaningful material. If so, the two abilities are probably positively correlated.

Not all of our early expectations in the way of factors have been supported with results. We predicted a unitary ability to analyze and also a unitary ability to synthesize, in thinking. Both hypotheses were apparently given ample opportunity to be verified if they were true, but the results did not come out that way. This is one example showing that we do not always get out of a factor analysis what we put into it. The result will no doubt seem contrary to common sense, for in our thinking we do analyze and we do synthesize.

The result does not refute the existence of these two kinds of operations. What it does indicate is that individuals do not differ systematically from one another with respect to a general ability to analyze in connection with many kinds of tasks nor do they differ systematically in a general ability to synthesize. In this sense, analysis and synthesis are like problem-solving. Factor analysis has not detected a unitary ability to solve problems. A number of unitary abilities undoubtedly play roles in solving problems, but the combinations of them and their respective weights depend upon the kind of problem. A similar conclusion may be drawn with regard to analyzing and synthesizing.

NONAPTITUDE TRAITS RELATED TO CREATIVITY

There are many, no doubt, who would look for the chief secrets of creative performance outside the modality of aptitudes. There is no denying that traits of motivation and of temperament should be expected to have significant determining effects upon whether or not an individual exhibits creative performance. These modalities of personality are definitely to be investigated in this connection. There has been little rigorously obtained information regarding the roles of such traits in creative performance, however. In her studies of leading artists and of leading scientists in several fields, Anne Roe found only one trait that stood out in common among individuals. This was a willingness to work hard and to work long hours (Roe, 1946, 1953a). This is a trait that may contribute to achievement and eminence in any field, however. There is no indication that it has a unique relation to creativity. The trait also merely means a very high level of general motivation, of whose sources we are uncertain. We are thus left with the problem, and the need for more analytical studies is strongly indicated.

In the Aptitudes Project our attention has recently been given to questions of nonaptitude traits that might contribute to creative thinking. Already mentioned is the conclusion that spontaneous flexibility in thinking appears to be a freedom from perseveration, which is one form of rigidity, and that adaptive flexibility appears to be a freedom from persistence in using previously learned, futile methods of solution, another form of rigidity. This raises the question as to whether the flexibility-rigidity factors in thinking should be classified in the modality of aptitudes or in the modality of temperament traits or whether in these instances we have traits with both temperamental and aptitudinal aspects, depending upon how one looks at them.

We have speculated regarding whether originality is perhaps an attitude of unconventionality, which predisposes an individual not to perform in the usual or the popular manner, preferring idiosyncratic ways of behaving. Our research only touches upon this question. As for the fluency factors, there have been a number of hypotheses mentioned in the literature regarding possible relationships between fluency of thinking and certain traits of motivation and temperament (Guilford, Christensen, et al., 1957).

Another reason for attention to these problems is the fact that factor analysis had previously indicated at least three primary traits of interest in different kinds of thinking, including interest in *reflective thinking, rigorous thinking,* and *autistic thinking.* Would these interests be found related to thinking performances of various kinds? There had also been found a pair of primary interests in aesthetic activities, one an interest called *aesthetic appreciation* and the other *aesthetic expression.* These interest variables might well be related to creative performance in the arts and possibly more generally in creative performance.

A recent factor-analytical investigation of thinking interests explored some hypotheses of still other possible variables (Guilford,

Christensen, *et al.*, 1957). With the use of self-inventory scores, which had been the basis for the discovery of the interest variables just mentioned, we found indications of some of the expected variables. One factor could be identified as *tolerance of ambiguity*. This is a willingness to accept some uncertainty in conclusions and decisions and a tendency to avoid thinking in terms of rigid categories. Another factor was identified as an interest in or liking for *convergent thinking*. Convergent thinking, which will be more fully explained in the next section, involves thinking toward one right answer, or toward a relatively uniquely determined answer. A companion factor was defined as an interest in or liking for *divergent thinking*, a type of thinking in which considerable searching about is done and a number of answers will do. Still another factor was found but it could not be very definitely identified. It could be an interest in originality or in creativity in general, or it could possibly be identified with either aesthetic expression or aesthetic appreciation.

In order to examine the possibilities that any or all of these factors have any bearing upon creative output, we correlated scores for these variables with scores for performance on tests of fluency, flexibility, and originality. It was possible, also, to correlate scores for a number of other inventory variables, involving other traits, with the same aptitude-test scores. Some of the more pertinent results will be very briefly mentioned. The conclusions are based upon statistically significant correlations, but the coefficients were all below .30.

From the results we may conclude that individuals who do well in tests of associational fluency tend to have a stronger need for adventure and they are more tolerant of ambiguity. This kind of result is interesting because to make a good score for associational fluency one must extend his list of synonyms to those that are only tenuously related to the given word. Individuals who are high on scores for ideational fluency are inclined to be more impulsive, more ascendant, and more confident and to have a stronger appreciation of creativity. Individuals who show more than ordinary signs of nervousness and depression are likely to be slightly lower on tasks requiring ideational fluency, but they show no handicaps on other types of fluency tests. The population in which the study was made probably included none who reached the pathological level in those temperamental traits. Those who score higher in tests of expressional fluency are inclined to be more impulsive, to appreciate aesthetic expression, and to like reflective thinking.

Measures of originality show relationships to a number of nonaptitude traits, but none very strong, so far as our results go. The original person tends to be more confident and tolerant of ambiguity and to like reflective and divergent thinking and aesthetic expression. The unoriginal person is inclined to be more meticulous and to feel a need for discipline. There is no indication that the original person is necessarily less inclined toward cultural conformity, which includes moral aspects. The hypothesis that originality rests upon an attitude of unconventionality is not supported. These results do not mean that for particular individuals there may not be such an association, but they do mean that in a general population the association is no more common than the lack of association.

The relations of the two flexibility factors to traits of rigidity were mentioned above. There were no other relationships found for the flexibility factors except some indication that persons high on spontaneous flexibility are likely to have a strong need for variety. The flexible person of this type rather obviously shows variety of directions in his work on tests.

The fact that all of these relationships were studied in the context of psychological testing should be emphasized. With motivation generally at a high pitch in taking tests, examinees have less room for showing very strong relationships between performance on those tests and any of the nonaptitude traits. Performances in daily life might well be found more strongly related to many of these traits of motivation and temperament.

CREATIVITY AND THE STRUCTURE OF INTELLECT

There has always been considerable interest in the relation between creativity and intelligence, particularly the extent to which the latter can account for the former. Unfortunately, "intelligence" has never been uniquely defined. Furthermore, accumulating evidence indicates that intelligence is a multidimensional affair, with many components having been discovered by factor analysis. Our next question is whether the abilities that seem to be components of creative talent can be regarded as components of intelligence. If so, have they any significant status among the intellectual abilities?

PRINCIPLES OF THE STRUCTURE OF INTELLECT

After considering all the known factors that could be regarded as belonging in the intellectual category, including the abilities of fluency, flexibility, and originality as well as sensitivity to problems, the author proposed a system of those factors and called it a "structure of intellect" (Guilford, 1956b, 1957a). The principles of that system will be very briefly reviewed here and some important, general revisions will be suggested toward a comprehensive theory of intellect. The creative-thinking abilities find logical places within the system.

There are some forty-seven known factors of intellect. An examination of their properties has suggested that they can be put into a three-way classification, demonstrating three principles by which they can be organized. First, the recognized dimensions of intellect can be grouped in three categories according to the kind of material or content of thought. One kind of material may be called *figural*, for it is in the form of perceived elements or objects with their various properties. Visual objects such as lines and forms have properties of shape, size, color, texture, gradations, and so on. Auditory elements are in the form of rhythms, melodies, and speech sounds. There are also tactual and kinesthetic materials, but the factor-analytical exploration of tests involving such materials has been practically non-existent. We might say that the abilities pertaining to the use of figural material constitute a general category of *concrete intelligence*.

Second, we have material that can be called conceptual or *semantic*. It consists of meanings, in verbalized form. The best-recognized tests of intelligence have been composed of verbal material and word meanings have been somehow involved.

Third, our aptitudes research has forced us to recognize a class of abilities to deal with what we have called *symbolic* material. Examples of such materials are numbers, syllables, words (word structures, not meanings), and all kinds of code material. Such elements have no natural meanings. Convention attaches uses and meanings to them arbitrarily. The alphabet and the number system provide convenient properties that make possible their uses in a multitude of ways. Aptitudes for mathematics and for languages probably rest heavily upon the symbolic abilities. The abilities pertaining to either semantic or symbolic materials would qualify for the commonly recognized category of "abstract intelligence," but since they form two distinct classes, it is best to speak of the categories of *semantic intelligence* and *symbolic intelligence*, respectively.

The second major principle of classification is according to the kind of operations that are performed upon the materials of thought. There are five recognized general kinds of operations, all five kinds apparently applying to each of the three kinds of materials. One class of abilities has to do with the achievement of cognitions of various kinds. These factors may be called discovery abilities, but they also pertain to rediscovering and recognition of elements and of things derived from them. We recognize figural objects, symbolic objects, and meanings. The recognition of word meanings is the essence of the factor of *verbal comprehension*, the dominating component in all verbal-intelligence tests.

Another group of aptitude factors is made up of memory abilities. There seems to be a different memory ability parallel to each cognition ability, insofar as the memory abilities are known. Two other groups have to do with the production of other information from given information by means of thinking processes. One of these groups has been identified as *convergent thinking* and the other as *divergent thinking*. Convergent thinking proceeds toward a restricted answer or solution. If asked, "What is the opposite of high?" you would probably respond with "Low." This is an example of convergent thinking. If asked, "What is two times five plus four?" you would have no other alternative than to say, "Fourteen." But if you were asked to give a number of words that mean about the same as "low," you could produce several different responses, all satisfying the requirement, such as "depressed," "cheap," "degraded," and the like, and you would be correct. In this example we have an instance of divergent thinking.

The fifth class of intellectual abilities pertains to making evaluations of information and of conclusions or other responses derived from given information. We may question our cognitions and things we recall as well as our solutions to problems and we arrive at decisions as to whether they are correct, suitable, or adequate, and so on. Such abilities come in the category of *evaluation*.

When we apply certain operations to certain kinds of materials, we come out with products of various kinds. The third major way of classifying intellectual abilities is according to the product involved. The product may be a unit of thought, such as a figure, a symbolic structure, or a concept. The product may be a class of units or it may be a relation between units. It may be a pattern, a system, or a gestalt of some kind, composed of units. Or it may be an implication, as when we make a prediction from the information that is available. Each of these kinds of product—units, classes, relations, systems, and implications—has its own primary abilities. Although it is not certain that all five classes of products apply to all kinds of material combined with all kinds of operations, there is enough similarity recognized at this stage to justify the prediction that when more is known we shall be able to apply the same product categories throughout. We may have to add a sixth category that has to do with changes or transformations, since such a product now applies in connection with some kinds of operations. Thus it appears that each primary, intellectual ability represents a kind of crossroad or intersection of a certain kind of operation, applied to a certain kind of material, yielding a certain kind of product.

A Comprehensive Theory of Intellect

If we apply common categories of materials, operations, and products throughout the range of intellectual abilities, we can represent the structure of intellect in the form of a three-dimensional diagram (see Figure 1). Figure 1 is a geometric model presented to represent a comprehensive theory of human intellect.

Shown in Figure 1 is provision for a fourth kind of material, namely, *behavioral*. There are no factor-analytical results that would justify such a category of intelligence, but there is enough information from other sources to justify the addition of such a class of factors in theory. Some thirty years ago, Thorndike proposed that there is a social intelligence distinct from abstract intelligence and from mechanical intelligence (Thorndike, et al., 1927). Today there is new interest in the explorations of "empathy," which probably falls within the same category.

The implications of a behavioral category in the structure of intellect are very interesting. It was pointed out earlier that there is a concrete intelligence, a symbolic intelligence, and a semantic intelligence, all of which are now supported by known factors. Since there

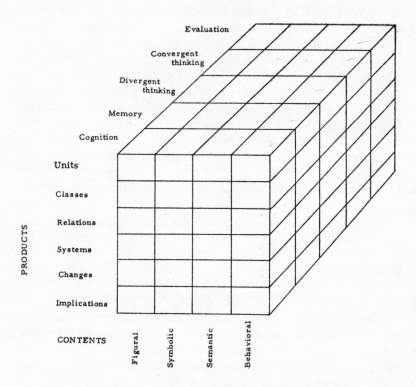

Theoretical model for the complete "structure of intellect."

FIGURE 1

are so many parallels among these three areas of intellect, it is reasonable to suggest that the same operations and products apply in the area of social intelligence or empathy. This would mean that we should look for abilities involving cognition of behavioral units, also of classes, relations, systems, and implications. There would be parallel memory abilities where behavioral matters are concerned, also parallel abilities to think productively regarding behavioral matters, and abilities to evaluate the results of any of these operations. It would seem reasonable to hypothesize that all such kinds of operations and products apply in the area of social or behavioral events. As a possible variation, we should also consider the possibility that there are different abilities in connection with one's own behavior and with the behavior of other persons.[2]

THE PLACE OF APTITUDES CONTRIBUTING TO CREATIVE PERFORMANCES

To return to the abilities more clearly related to creativity, it is apparent that the traits of fluency, flexibility, and originality come in the general category of divergent thinking. The factor known as sensitivity to problems, however, has been placed in the category of evaluation and the factor of redefinition in the category of convergent thinking, as stated earlier. It is probably true that other abilities outside the divergent-thinking category also make their contributions to productive thinking. We might arbitrarily define creative thinking as divergent thinking, but it would be incorrect to say that divergent thinking accounts for all the intellectual components of creative production.

There are a number of divergent-thinking abilities predicted by the system in the structure of intellect but not yet discovered, particularly in the figural and symbolic columns. Presumably these would have more to do with creative thinking in the arts (Guilford, 1957b) and in mathematics, whereas the known divergent-thinking abilities, being mostly in the verbal column, have more to do with creative thinking in the humanities, the sciences, and in everyday affairs. Divergent-thinking abilities in the behavioral column should be useful in contributing to better human relations, whether between persons or on the political or industrial scenes or in international affairs.

VALIDITY AND PROBLEMS OF TRAINING

SOME INFORMATION ON VALIDITY

Our work in the Aptitudes Project has been devoted almost entirely to basic research, with the belief that what we need most at this time is more intimate and thorough understanding of the nature of intellect and its components. We have not been without concern and interest with regard to the general applicability of our factorial concepts and we are frequently challenged in this regard. We, as well as others, have made a number of studies that bear on the question

[2] I am indebted to Philip R. Merrifield for this suggestion.

of the significance of the primary traits of creative aptitude from other than the factor-analytical point of view.

The information on validity is scattered and much of it was obtained incidental to studies with broader objectives. The construct validity of our tests of originality was well demonstrated by a study reported by Barron (1955). A hundred Air Force officers were assessed during a three-day period of observation and among other things were rated for degree of originality. A total score from tests of originality correlated .55 with the average ratings. Drevdahl (1956) found that a score for originality correlated .33 with instructor's ratings of originality of students in the arts and in the sciences.

One should not expect a great deal of predictive validity for test scores representing the factor of originality in connection with course grades. Hill (1955) found an average correlation of − .02 for an originality test in connection with grades in several small classes in upper-division and graduate mathematics courses. Recently we have found an average correlation of .27 between a test of originality and average grades in science and mathematics for two groups of engineering students of about a hundred each.

There is little evidence, as yet, that the factors of verbal fluency have general predictability for academic or technical performances. A score for expressional fluency correlated .25 with grades in a course in astronomy, for some unknown reason (Guilford, 1956a). A score for ideational fluency correlated .37 with performance of aircraft engineers whose chief work was in designing aircraft parts and the criterion was rate of increase in pay over a limited period of time (Guilford, 1956a).

The factor of adaptive flexibility has consistently shown some small relationships to performance in mathematics and in one instance to achievement in physics (Guilford, 1956a). Hills (1955) found the average correlation with achievement in mathematics to be .33 and we have found the relation to grades in physics to be .23. Among aircraft engineers a score for adaptive flexibility correlated .31 with the criterion of rate of increase in pay (Guilford, 1956a). Quantitative thinking that involves relatively novel problems seems generally to be related to adaptive flexibility.

A study of creativity of graduate engineers was made by Sprecher (1957). With criteria including ratings of inventiveness and also performance on original, technical problems, multiple correlations involving a few tests of the creativity factors were found in the range from .3 to .5.

Tests of creative factors did not predict which employees would contribute ideas in a suggestion box, but it was found that many other determiners were at work. For example, some creative individuals had incidental reasons for not offering contributions (Chorness and Nottelmann, 1957). The same tests were found to correlate significantly with some evaluations of the expressive aspects of teaching performance (Chorness and Nottelmann, 1956). Scores from the same tests were found to be related to incidence of certain kinds of creative hobbies as reported in biographical-information inventories (Gerry, De-Veau, and Chorness, 1957).

TRAINING FOR CREATIVITY

There has been considerable popular interest in training individuals for increased creativity. A large number of courses have been instituted in this country whose aim is to develop creativity of individuals, some of the courses being in universities, some in industry, and some in governmental agencies. The methods of instruction have been somewhat varied, for no one knows at this stage what are the most effective ways of bringing about greater creative performance. The brainstorming method introduced by Osborn (1953) is one of the common devices. Although it is reported to bring about increased quantity of thinking production and to have some lasting, beneficial effects upon participants, there have been almost no reports of rigorous experiments designed specifically to test these impressions.

There are indications that some methods of training, at least, lead to increased originality of performance at the expense of fluency. Using a combination of training methods, including Osborn's brainstorming procedure and Arnold's (1954) "out-of-this-world" exercise, Gerry, DeVeau, and Chorness (1957) found that there were significant gains in scores for originality but probably some losses in scores for ideational fluency. In some unpublished data on ten-year-old children, it appears that a short course on creative writing was also followed by higher performance on tests of originality and lower on tests of ideational fluency, as compared with a matched, control group. A finding that bears indirectly upon the same problem is that when examinees are instructed to give clever titles to story plots in a test they tend to lose in total productivity but to gain in the number of clever responses as well as in the average level of rated cleverness as compared with examinees who have instructions that say nothing about cleverness (Christensen, Guilford, and Wilson, 1957). The general implication from these few studies is that attention to creativity and efforts to increase it are likely to yield improvements in quality of responses at the expense of quantity. In everyday life, where there is much more time available than there is in tests of fluency, a slackened rate of flow of ideas should probably cause little concern.

SUMMARY

This paper has attempted briefly, first, to point out some of the reasons for the spontaneous interests that have sprung up in recent years in connection with the subject of creativity. It has suggested reasons for psychology's general postponement of serious investigations of the subject and has emphasized the importance of a trait approach to the subject in order to find the necessary working concepts.

There followed a brief review of aptitude traits that belong most clearly logically in the area of creativity and that have been discovered by factor analysis, many of them within the past ten years. These include factors of fluency of thinking and of flexibility of thinking, as well as originality, sensitivity to problems, redefinition, and elaboration.

A number of relationships between certain nonaptitude traits and creative performance in tests have been indicated. The two forms of flexibility of thinking seem clearly to be opposites to two forms of rigidity in thinking. Redefinition seems logically opposite to the quality known as "functional fixedness." Other traits of temperament and of motivation seem to bear small relationships to performances in tests of fluency, flexibility, and particularly tests of originality.

Most of the aptitude factors identifiable as belonging in the category of creativity are classifiable in a group of divergent-thinking abilities. These abilities, by contrast to convergent-thinking abilities, emphasize searching activities with freedom to go in different directions, if not a necessity to do so in order to achieve an excellent performance. Convergent-thinking activities proceed toward one right answer, or one that is more or less clearly demanded by the given information.

Other abilities contributing to creative performances find their places, also, in a three-dimensional, solid figure, in which the primary abilities are distinguished in terms of the kinds of material dealt with, the kinds of operations applied to the material, and the kinds of products resulting. It is theorized that a whole area of abilities, comprising what has sometimes been called "social intelligence" and sometimes "empathy," will be found parallel to other areas now distinguished along the lines of materials of thought—figural, symbolic, and semantic.

A limited number of studies of validity tend to indicate that tests of some of the creative-thinking factors, such as adaptive flexibility and originality, have both construct validity and predictive validity.

Efforts made toward improving creativity through training have given informal indications of some measure of success. Experiments tend to indicate that training yields some improvement in performance on tests of originality but some possible loss on tests of ideational fluency. Awareness of the nature of the traits of creativity should provide a much better basis than formerly for systematic methods of education in this important area.

11

Creativity and Problem-solving

ERNEST R. HILGARD

The capacity to create useful or beautiful products and to find ways of resolving perplexity is not limited to the highly gifted person, but is the birthright of every person of average talent. Because I believe these Symposia to be concerned primarily with ways of bringing the best out of people, I have chosen to consider how we might best encourage creativity and a problem-solving approach among those with whom we deal, whether they be children in our homes, students in our classes, or workers in our factories, offices, and laboratories.

Professor Theodore Schultz, who heads the Department of Economics at the University of Chicago, told me an interesting story about Nehru of India when he was Professor Schultz's guest. He wanted to see some ordinary Americans in their homes, and Mr. Schultz took him to see some small-town people of his acquaintance. Mr. Nehru asked to see their family Bibles, and was particularly interested to ask them what sorts of things they felt inclined to write down. In addition to the usual tabulation of birthdates and the like, nearly all of the people, with a little embarrassment, showed bits of poetry or narrative that they had thought worth preserving. Sometimes it described a trip they had taken, sometimes an unusually exciting or happy event. But what impressed Mr. Schultz was the sensitivity with which Nehru sought out what had personal value for these simple people, and how he had uncovered aspects of creativity that we do not expect of them.

A somewhat less romantic story of creative problem-solving by a common unlettered man centers around the development of hybrid corn. Henry Wallace and William Brown (1956) tell of the important contribution of an uneducated dirt farmer, George Krug, of Woodford County in Central Illinois. He defied the trend toward "show corn" in favor of a higher yield, arguing simply enough that his horses and cows didn't care whether the corn was in even rows on the cob. When he brought his unprepossessing corn to the County Agent to enter into the contest, the agent almost sent him away. But over 3 years it yielded the best of over 120 varieties and became one of the important ingredients in the new hybrid corn now grown all over the world. His main contribution lay in his simple refusal to be coerced by the times: he saved the seed from heavy ears with oily kernels and disregarded the appearance, which at the time was winning the prizes at the corn shows.

My purpose in telling of Nehru's visit to the homes of ordinary midwestern folks, and of George Krug's contribution to hybrid corn is merely to reiterate that with which I began. In discussing creativity I do not wish to write especially about the Shakespeares, Beethovens, Newtons or Einsteins, but rather about the creativity (whether latent or expressed) in each and every one of us.

I write as a psychologist, and I feel some obligation to tell the reader a little of what my colleagues have done in investigating this field. It is only fitting, however, that I should warn you that the field is in a rather unsatisfactory state, and psychologists have thus far raised more questions than they have answered. There have been two major types of approach to problem-solving and creativity. The first of these relates problem-solving to learning and thinking, as a type of "higher mental process" or "cognitive process," to which problem-solving certainly belongs. The second approach, supplementary rather than contradictory to the first, sees creative problem-solving as a manifestation of personality and looks for social and motivational determinants instead of (or in addition to) the purely cognitive ones. It is not surprising that these two approaches deal also with somewhat different topics. The approach via learning tends to emphasize problem-solving in which a high-order product emerges, although not necessarily a highly original one, whereas the approach via personality tends to seek out somewhat more the elements of creative imagination and novelty.

After sampling these two approaches I shall return to some speculations as to how we may best set the climate for eliciting creative
problem-solving.

The main cleavage within the theoretical approaches to the psychology of learning has been between the stimulus-response psychologists, in the tradition of Thorndike, Hull, and Skinner, who view
learning as the formation of habits or conditioned responses, and the
tradition of gestalt psychology, represented by Köhler and Wertheimer, and, in a special version, by Tolman. The latter group pays
more attention to the way in which a problem is presented, and how
the problem-solver restructures the problem in his approach to solution. The characteristic solution, according to the stimulus-response
psychologist, is by trial-and-error; the characteristic solution, according to the gestalt psychologist, is with insight.

I do not wish to take time to review old controversies, except to
point out how long some kinds of misunderstandings persist. Stimulus-
response psychologists in order to incorporarte the facts of insightful
learning within their schemes, have tended to note one-trial solution
as the chief characteristic of insightful learning. Suppose a chimpanzee
finds himself for the first time alone in a room with a box and a
banana suspended from the ceiling. If he moves the box under the
banana, climbs upon it and secures his reward, he has solved the problem in a single trial, and presumably with insight. The gestalt psychologist will say that he perceives the essential relationships, performs
the "detour" away from the food in order to make the box serve as
means to his end, and then completes the act. The stimulus-response
psychologist will say that he has used prior experience and is now
engaging in trial-and-error learning but of the extreme form in which
either (1) transfer of training accounts for the performance (Mc-
Geoch, 1952) or (2) an acquired learning set accounts for it (Harlow,
1949). They rest their case because what they seek to account for is
one-trial learning.

Actually, what is meant by insight is by no means exhausted by
one-trial learning, and, in fact, insightful learning may require many
trials. Something else is involved. What is intended by insight is a

perception of the essential requirements of a problem so that past experience can be brought to bear in a manner appropriate to the present. Sometimes a problem has to be rearranged before this is possible. This may have the appearance of trial-and-error, but in the strictly historical sense trial-and-error should mean the eliciting of habits already in one's repertoire in the order determined by their position in a habit hierarchy. Thus the fact that past experience affects insightful learning does not reduce insightful learning to trial-and-error. The real issue comes in describing *how* past experience is used appropriate to the demands of the problem. According to stimulus-response theory sufficient past experience should *guarantee* the solution; according to the insight theory, sufficient past experience will *not* guarantee the solution unless the problem is so arranged that the relevant experiences are appropriately brought to bear. Many problems are not sufficiently analyzed to force a decision as between these competing interpretations; in any case we wish to avoid glib statements either that all problem-solving is "mere" trial-and-error, or that all significant solutions require insight.

Instead of dwelling further upon the trial-and-error versus insight issue, I prefer to go on to some of the findings that are likely to have more importance for those of us not interested in the quarrels of psychologists.

Among the generalizations arising out of studies of human problem-solving in the laboratory, I wish to select for consideration one *favorable* and one *unfavorable* circumstance for problem-solving.

FAVORABLE CIRCUMSTANCE

The favorable circumstance is that the problem should be sensible and meaningful for the learner. By contrast, solutions learned by rote processes or by not-understood formulas are likely to be less well remembered and less satisfactorily applied to new situations.

In studying the role of understood relationships my collaborators and I (Hilgard, Irvine, and Whipple, 1953; Hilgard, Edgren, and Irvine, 1954) repeated, with slight modifications, some card-trick problems first used by Katona (1940), one of the gestalt group. If you prearrange six ordinary playing cards in the order Red-Black-Black-Black-Red-Red, then you can perform a simple trick which gives the type of problem set by the more difficult tricks. You place the first card on the table face up. It is Red. Then you place one card on the bottom of the pack, and place the next card on the table, alongside the first. It is Black. Then you skip another card, and place the next face up. It is Red. By repeatedly skipping one card, the cards that turn up are alternately Red and Black. The gimmick in the trick is that some cards get used more than once, as they come up from the bottom of the pack, and the trick is of course solved if you can arrange the cards in the right order to begin with. You can either remember the right order, here R-B-B-B-R-R, or you can figure some systematic way to arrange the cards which will make it unnecessary for you to remember. (For an exercise in problem-solving, you might try to figure out how to arrive at the arrangement. In the experiment, half the subjects are shown a way to do it.) Some subjects just memorize the order. They can do the trick. Other subjects learn how to construct the order. Then they, too, can do the trick. It takes longer to teach the "understanding" group, that is, those who have to learn how to construct the order.

Katona points out that results achieved by understanding are retained longer than those learned by rote. Over a shorter interval than he used (only a single day) our subjects who learned by rote did about as well at remembering the trick as those who learned by understanding, so this is a limiting case for his generalization. But when it came to transfer, we agreed entirely with him. Those who learned by understanding were much better able to do other similar tricks, such as substituting even and odd for red and black, changing the length of the series, skipping two instead of skipping one, and so on.

One interesting by-product of our first experiments came out of the large number of failures of transfer in the understanding group. (These experiments were done with high school seniors.) Although better than the rote learning group, they were far from perfect, so that new problems were set by their failures. Some of the failures were evident. For example, having solved the problems by constructing the list, the subject sometimes converted the problem to a rote one by learning the final order and trying to reproduce it the next day instead of troubling to work it out again. Or the degree of understanding was very imperfect, so that the method used was in reality a formula learned by rote and not really comprehended. Then there were the usual careless errors, made in haste. But even these errors had a somewhat systematic character which has led us to look into them further. We are convinced that there is no sharp dividing line between rote learning and understanding. This should be evident from what we know about the effect of meaningfulness within rote learning: meaningful materials are learned more easily by rote than nonsense ones, hence some role must already be played by understanding even in memorization by repetition. And understanding must itself have degrees, from the rather blind application of a formula, to the full appreciation of the relationships and principles involved.

The lesson to be learned from these studies is that the extra time and effort needed to learn by understanding pay off when it comes to dealing with new problems similar to but at the same time different from the ones used in training.

The interpretation of meaningfulness and of understanding has been furthered by recent studies of information theory. It is somewhat helpful to think of our past information as being "coded" before it is stored. Meaningful and understood relationships are coded in a manner that keeps them ready for use. Miscellaneous uncoded facts, stored in memory as isolated fragments, overtax our systems, so that we cannot use these facts well in solving problems (Miller, 1956).

UNFAVORABLE CIRCUMSTANCE

The unfavorable circumstance for problem-solving to which I wish to call attention is that of too much persistence in following in a single direction that is no longer appropriate. The ability to break such a direction or "set" is one mark of the good thinker. Some illustrations from scientific discovery are the detection of penicillin as an antibiotic and not merely a disturbing impurity, of the plant hormone 2-4-D as not only a growth hormone but a potential weed poison, the shift from the propeller to jet propulsion of airplanes.

Although past learning often makes it easier to learn something new, most of us have at one time or another found old habits interfering with new ones, as when we move from driving a car with conventional gear shift to one with automatic shift. An interesting illustration of such interference by prior knowledge in a problem-solving situation was pointed out some years ago by Duncker (1945), another gestalt psychologist. He showed experimentally that if you used something (say a pair of pliers) in its familiar use (perhaps pulling a staple out of a board) then it becomes more difficult to convert the pliers to a novel use based on the requirements of a problem, such as using it for a pendulum-bob, or as a leg to support a small stand. When the pair of pliers was just lying around, and not previously used, subjects could more easily convert them to these new uses. This "freezing" the use-meaning of the object by making use of it in its familiar way was called by Duncker "functional fixation."

This idea seemed to us to be sufficiently germinal to be worth restudying, both to confirm its generality and to learn something more of its conditions. Parallels suggest themselves in familiar problems, when we get so "set" on one way of regarding things that we fail to consider other possibilities. We lose flexibility because we have a course of action that is plausible, and no longer look around. Adamson (1952) then an assistant on the Stanford project, was able to show that Duncker's experiments are reproducible, so that we can accept the principle of functional fixedness as a genuine one: the pre-utilization of a tool or object in its normal use restricts its availability for novel uses by the subject who has just used it in the regular way.

The next step is to find some limiting conditions. One question asked (and answered) by Adamson and Taylor (1954) was the following: Does the inhibition against novel use decrease with lapse of time following the normal use of the tool or the object? In other words, is recency of normal use one of the conditions of functional fixedness? The answer came out in the affirmative: the more time that elapsed between the normal use and the novel use, the less the functional fixedness. This may help to explain why a baffling problem is sometimes solved upon our return to it after a time away from it. Perhaps during our vacation from the problem our "functional fixednesses" have declined.

These two illustrations of experimental findings—one on the positive value of meaningfulness and understanding, the other on the negative influence of functional fixedness—suggest the kinds of leads that can come from the experimental laboratory.

Many other kinds of experiments have been done on cognitive processes; for example, those on concept formation by Heidbreder,

Bensley, and Ivy (1948); Grant (1951); Hovland and Weiss (1953); Bruner, Goodnow, and Austin (1956); and others. Unfortunately I do not find many suggestions in these studies that bear on our more practical problems of developing creative imagination, valuable as the studies are for elucidating some sticky problems on the borderlines between psychology and logic.

PROBLEM-SOLVING FROM THE POINT OF VIEW OF PERSONALITY AND SOCIAL PSYCHOLOGY

The problem-solver is one and indivisible, so that there is some artificiality in viewing him first as a subject for study by investigators in the field of learning and now as a subject for study by investigators of individual differences, personality, and social psychology. As he solves his problems the individual does not say to himself: "Today I shall demonstrate trial-and-error, tomorrow insight; the day after that I'll show the influence of social conformity, and the next day I'll reveal my masculinity in how I attack my problems." He does all these things at once, and it is only the investigator who chooses to abstract one or the other facet from the totality of his problem-solving.

In our Stanford studies of problem-solving we soon found that personality variables were important, even in the solution of simple laboratory-type problems that seemed almost purely "cognitive." In fact, I am inclined to believe, in retrospect, that the personality studies opened up more useful leads than the learning studies.

The distinction is, of course, not an absolute one, because students of learning are also interested in the motivational influence of persistent anxiety, achievement orientation, and the like, while students of personality are interested also in how these dispositions are acquired.

For example, no matter what controls were used, there appeared a sex difference favoring men when the problems to be solved were of the kind requiring some restructuring of the problem before it could be solved. When a masculinity-femininity test was administered to men and women, those among the subjects who showed the more masculine orientation (whether among men or women) were the better problem-solvers (Milton, 1957). It thus appears that some subtle social process, leading to identification with the male role, makes for better problem-solving. At this point there is no reason to assign the difference to the difference between male and female chromosomes.

Another difference was that between those who are *social conforming* and those who hold their ground independently of others. The experiments were performed by Nakamura (1955). The test of social conformity was of the type made familiar by Asch (1956), in which a subject has to assert his convictions when he is a minority of one against a majority, in this case, of four others who disagree with him. The nonconformist in this situation turns out to be the better problem-solver.

Although social processes may be responsible for some of the persistent attitudes and traits that make a person a good or a poor problem-solver, there is also a more temporary influence of group composition and activity that affects problem-solving. In this day of team research we often hear voices crying for the return of privacy, arguing that thinking goes on better in one head at a time.

The question whether the group or the individual does better thinking is not easily answered, for the meaning of the question is not altogether clear. The question may mean, for example, will the group thinking be better than that of any representative member of the group working alone? Or it may mean, will its product be better than that of the best member of the group? Or, again, will the total product be better than if the group members had worked alone or in smaller groups?

Careful experimentation has tended to leave the results at about a draw, so far as laboratory problems are concerned. That is, the group does better than the individual, but has not really increased efficiency over a number of individuals working separately and pooling their findings (Taylor and McNemar, 1955).

A more recent investigation by Taylor, Berry, and Block (1957) extends the study to that popular method of group thinking known as "Brainstorming" (Osborn, 1957). The method, in wide use among businessmen and others, consists in suggesting ideas in rapid-fire succession under rules in which criticism is taboo, wild ideas are welcomed, quantity is sought, and people try to build upon and improve each other's suggestions. It was found that the group process did *not* yield proportionately more ideas, more unique ideas, or ideas of higher quality. In fact, it could be supposed that in some way the group process *inhibits* creative thinking!

This conclusion has to be tempered by several considerations. (1) The general idea behind brainstorming is to create a mood for free flow of ideas. Once this mood is created, the group process is not essential to its validity. (2) It may be that brainstorming in groups is a good method for teaching creative thinking, even though individuals, once taught, will do as good thinking alone. (3) The individual thinking will *not* be as good as the group, unless the ideas are pooled. Perhaps it is easier to pool ideas by having brainstorming go on in groups, despite some minor inefficiencies involved.

In any case, we see that it is possible to subject these processes to study, and we need not depend upon the romantic appeal of an idea or procedure as a basis for establishing its validity.

ORIGINALITY AS STUDIED BY FACTOR ANALYSIS

Most of the problem-solving that I have talked about so far is a kind of intellectual guessing-game in which there is a correct answer that the experimenter has in mind, and it is the subject's problem to find this answer, that is, the correct solution to the problem. These are tasks calling for high orders of ability and of skill, and they deserve the attention that they are getting. Perhaps we can think of them most conveniently as the kinds of problems solved in mathematics, where a relationship is to be proven, or a logical flaw detected.

There are kinds of creative thinking, however, that go beyond these "correct-answer" problems. There are solutions that, even if correct, are highly original, and are to be judged by their originality rather than by their correctness. There are problems that are invented or discovered—and detecting the problem is as important as finding the answer. There are inventions that open up entirely new fields of human endeavor and enjoyment.

Then, of course, there are the creative products of literature, art, and music that defy description according to the ordinary formulas of problem-solving.

Lest we go on to think of this higher creativity as a matter of genius or inspiration, and not subject to investigation at all, let me try to remain (for a while at least) with feet on the ground by considering some of the empirical material bearing on originality and creativity as distinct from the fixed-answer kind of problem-solving.

Guilford and his associates have been carrying out a number of studies concerned with reasoning, creativity, planning, and evaluation, all by the method of factor analysis of test scores. Guilford's (1950) study of creativity stressed the problem of measuring *originality*, in the form of ability to produce original ideas (Wilson, Guilford, *et al.*, 1954). The judgment as to what is an original idea turns out to be very difficult, especially if one wishes to reject triviality and nonsense. A remark once made by the philosopher Morris Cohen has always stuck with me: the most original ideas, he said, are *nonsense*, because all sensible ideas have some non-original connection with previously existing facts or relationships. Guilford and his co-workers settled upon three variables, for which they could construct tests:

1. *Uncommonness* of response (as in a word association test). If to "table" you say "leg," that is a common response. If you reply "carved" or "antique," such a response is less common, hence more original.

Actually, they used other forms of tests of uncommon or rare responses. For example, they asked for six or seven uses of an object, say a newspaper. Although the common use is, of course, "for reading," more remote possibilities are to line shelves, to swat flies, to place under your mattress to keep warm.

2. The ability to make requested *remote associations* was the second aspect of originality. Given two words, the subject has to find a word connecting the two. If the gap is a wide one, then his ability to associate is tested. A simple illustration is given by the words Indian—money, to be replied to by penny, nickel, or wampum, each of which relates to both Indian and money.

3. The third test was named *cleverness*. In order to test cleverness, the subject reads the plots of two brief stories. Then he tries to write clever titles for these stories. Cleverness has to be estimated by a competent judge, but scoring scales can be found.

When included in a battery of tests of creative thinking, the scores on these tests all showed a weighting on a common factor, named originality, because that is what the tests were intended to measure.

The creativity study came out with some fourteen factors, of which originality was but one. Others included *sensitivity to problems*, associational fluency, and redefinition. I shall not go into these further at this time.

One difficulty with the factor-analytic approach is that there is little external reference inherent in the method. The four hundred air cadets and student officers who took the tests undoubtedly included highly original people, yet the stringent physical requirements for becoming one of their number, and other selective features, mean that the results necessarily lack something in generality. We have no way of knowing, from the test scores themselves, whether the high-scoring subjects were effectively creative people.

Gough (1957) has also been carrying on factor-analytic studies of the personality and motivational factors that predispose to originality. His list of five factors strikes me (intuitively) as somewhat richer than those of Guilford and his associates. Here is his lists: Intellectual competence; Inquiringness as a habit of mind; Cognitive flexibility; Aesthetic sensitivity; Sense of destiny.

Although there is some overlap between the Guilford factors and the Gough ones, I wish to call attention particularly to Gough's last two: "aesthetic sensitivity" and "sense of destiny." What I said earlier about the limitations of factor analysis I must again re-emphasize. You can achieve a certain purification through factor analysis, but as a technique of discovery it is limited (a) by what the tester includes in his battery and (b) by the people he finds to test. If his tests are limited, or his subjects limited, so will his results be limited. Because the Guilford group did not test for "aesthetic sensitivity" or "sense of destiny," they did not find it; because Gough looked for these items, he found them. We do not yet know how important they are, plausible as they may be.

What these less familiar facets mean can be put in his words.

Aesthetic sensitivity is "a deep-seated preference for and appreciation of elegance of form and of thought, of harmony wrought from complexity, and of style as a medium of expression." (As an aside, does this conjure up a classroom of Guilford's airforce cadets?)

Sense of destiny. "This includes something of resoluteness and gone certainty of the worth and validity of one's own future and (naturally) of egotism, but over and above these a belief in the fore-attainment."

Gough has gone on to test his ideas against people judged to be high (or low) in research originality and creativity, and reports preliminary correlations of the order of +.40 or +.45 between their rated excellence and their scores on his Differential Reaction Schedule. This is a test consisting of 132 true-false items, taking fifteen to twenty minutes to administer.

I feel that I have now done sufficient justice to the careful research investigations of my psychological colleagues. I go on now to some conjectures about creativity that are not grounded in laboratory or test findings.

THE CREATIVE URGE: NORMAL OR NEUROTIC?

My purpose in reviewing studies of problem-solving and creativity has been to prepare a background for some recommendations for producing (or releasing) the creativity of those under our guidance or influence. But I am not yet ready for the recommendations. Another question, and that a very serious one, has to be faced.

This is the question of the relation between creativity and neuroticism. There is an old theory that superior creativity is a kind of creative madness, or at least creative instability. Many great artists and writers suffered deeply, were poor husbands and fathers, unconventional or even perverse, occasionally ending their careers in suicide. One need only mention such names as Van Gogh, Beethoven, Coleridge, Oscar Wilde, Hawthorne, or, in our day, Eugene O'Neill, Picasso, or Dali, to show that some creative people, at least, do not lead conventionally well-adjusted lives.

One has to be careful about the selection of instances. Perhaps a longer list could be made up of outstanding people who are normal and well-adjusted in all essential respects. I believe that we can all agree, however, that *some* creative people are unstable. Let us first talk about them.

The question of more than academic interest about an unstable or neurotic creative person is whether or not his neurotic conflicts are a *source* of his creativity. We may put it another way: would successful psychotherapy *decrease* such a person's creativity?

There are no firm or pat answers to these questions, although they have often been asked and their answers often attempted. I suppose that Rollo May in a preceding symposium must have wrestled with these issues, for psychoanalysts face them all the time.

Let me state my own prejudices in this matter.

1. For *some* artists and writers, the themes that haunt them and form the content of their creative efforts are in a large measure autobiographical, and in that sense may reflect their own unresolved conflicts. This was apparently the case with Eugene O'Neill, whose "conscious" autobiography appears in the play *Long Day's Journey Into Night*, whereas his "unconscious" autobiography is perhaps revealed in *Desire Under the Elms* (Weissman, 1957).

2. Such writers are not necessarily narcissistic or egoistic; that is, they do not write just for themselves, out of inner compulsion, but they generalize their experiences to meet a larger audience. In such a case, the purposes served and the satisfactions achieved are not of the kind to be destroyed by psychotherapy. (It is doubtful if many such writers would even accept the psychotherapeutic relationship.)

3. A writer or an artist who comes for psychotherapy usually does so because his conflicts, far from serving his creativity, are making it impossible for him to create. For him, successful therapy makes it possible for him to *return* to his typewriter or his canvas.

4. A writer or an artist who comes for psychotherapy and as a consequence *gives* up his artistic pursuit was probably not a very gifted person in the first place and so, in giving up his pretense to great originality, was becoming more realistic and, in a sense, less fraudulent.

This last point is a really difficult and ambiguous one, and I shall return to it presently.

Let me now, at the risk of overgeneralizing, say something about what may be the common characteristics of at least some fraction of neurotic creators. This is speculative, but let me hope that the speculations are not idle.

I wish to call attention to some immature or childlike qualities manifested among these creative people. Among these qualities I would list: (1) *dependency* upon others, with refusal to accept (or carry out) the ordinary social responsibilities of adult life; (2) *defiance* of authority or convention; (3) a sense of *omnipotence*, or what Gough has called sense of destiny; and (4) *gullibility*, or uncritical acceptance in some intellectual sphere, no matter how critical in others. Dependency, defiance, omnipotence, and gullibility are common enough in childhood so that it is not unfair, if creative people have these qualities, to describe them as in some respects immature. What kind of evidence do I have? Most of it is uncriticized evidence, but I shall call it to your attention for what it may be worth.

The improvidence and unrealism of artists about their economic existence is well known. Often they do not marry; when they do they often take little responsibility for wife and children. The occasional sexual inversion may in part be a sign of the same thing; unwillingness to accept the normal responsible fulfillment of sexual attachment to a member of the opposite sex. Even an Einstein, sitting around the house with uncut hair, in his bathrobe and slippers, is behaving in some respects like a child who needs to be taken care of.

The defiant, rebellious nature of the creative person can take many forms, including that of legitimate social reform. But it may be merely the child's desire to play at his own games, in his own way, without interference. The artist, writer, or scientist goes at his work as the child goes at his play, with the intense absorption of self-initiated activity. Social convention, like mother's call to dinner, is an unwelcome intrusion upon a private world.

The sense of omnipotence, of destiny, is part of a child's heroic make-believe, but it is also a sustaining aspect of the neurotically creative person, who must leave his mark upon the world as only a genius can. We use the expression "prima donna" to refer to the high self-esteem in which some artists hold themselves. We can equally well think of them as master magicians.

Finally, as to guillibility, I can refer to an article by Ernest Jones (1957a) in which he speaks of Goethe, Copernicus, Newton, and Darwin as illustrative cases. Thomas Mann referring to Goethe is quoted as commenting upon "The union in one human being of the greatest intellectual gifts with the most amazing naïveté."

Copernicus, famed for his refutation of the Ptolemaic theory of epicycles and the substitution of the view that the planets revolve about the sun, came upon this good conclusion for the wrong reason. Actually, he was so romantically attached to Aristotle's notion that the perfection of the Divine Creator required circular motion that he forced himself to find a theory providing for circular motion.

Sir Isaac Newton, often mentioned for his hard-boiled scientific objectivism in which he repudiated hypotheses and insisted that the facts speak for themselves, was, in fact, intensely preoccupied with theology, a field in which his writing seems particularly bizarre. He came to unbelievably fantastic conclusions about the symbolism of the Books of Daniel and of Revelations. It is known that he suffered paranoid delusions later in life; it is significant that he never fell in love or married. Merton (1957) has discussed Newton's heated controversy with Leibniz over the priority of invention of calculus, and other childish behavior of scientists.

Charles Darwin was a very different kind of person than Newton. His neuroticism showed more particularly in a succession of what today would be called psychosomatic symptoms. But surely he was not gullible or tenderminded? In fact he was. Despite the power of his own evolutionary theory, he never gave up the Lamarckian position that acquired changes can be inherited, and he developed a curious notion of "pangenesis" that only historians of science now remember.

Ernest Jones's point is that there may be a possible correlation between the credulousness of these great men and the characteristically receptive nature of genius.

If some of these great men have these childlike characteristics we may either call it neuroticism or see it as a condition for creativity. We can find Biblical texts recommending that it is only those who can perceive the world as little children who will enter the Kingdom of Heaven.

I return now to the question of whether or not psychotherapy may injure creativity. I earlier stated that I thought in most cases it did not; that when a person needed therapy because he could not create, and then gave up his aspirations after therapy, it was probably because his creative urge was weak in the first place, or his talents limited.

It is possible, however, that a psychotherapist's insistence upon maturity may, in fact, weaken creativity, no matter what else it does. A man who takes more responsibility for his wife and children, and works harder at his job, may have less time for his hobbies: and he may conceivably be more creative at his hobbies than on his job. Responsibility, social adjustment, being a good citizen, accepting a conforming role—these have their costs, too. It is not too surprising that relatively few English professors are first-rate creative writers. A man can hardly meet his classes regularly, take his committee responsibilities, and grade his papers conscientiously and still have the irresponsible attitude toward those about him that we often find associated with genius. There are ethical issues here, as well as psychological ones, but we must not fool ourselves that good social adjustment is the best condition for all human production.

Sometimes psychotherapy releases people, makes them freer and more creative. Sometimes, however, it deadens affect by making the person more guarded in what he does, more sensitive about his impression upon others. Under such circumstances he may be less creative than he was. There is no one outcome of psychological treatment any more than there is only one outcome of surgical or drug treatments.

This has been a rather long digression on the neuroticism and childishness of creative people, but I believe it important to recognize that some such exist, and we should be tolerant of them.

Are they the only species of creative man? I think not. I see no corner on creativity by people who are disturbed and suffering and irresponsible to those about them. There must be those geniuses who fit Carlyle's dictum that "genius is first of all a transcendent capacity for taking trouble" or Edison's: "genius is 2 per cent inspiration and 98 per cent perspiration."

IMPLICATIONS FOR COLLEGE TEACHING

Now I am ready to return to the place where I started and to say something about training for creativity in ordinary people. The scattered things I have called attention to—studies of learning and problem-solving, factor-analytic studies of originality, and some speculations about normality and neuroticism in creative people—give a background for what I am about to say. I am going to direct my remarks to college teaching, although they apply *mutatis mutandis* to other levels of instruction as well.

Let me first express the fear that the wrong methods of instruction may destroy the inquiring attitude, may quench the spark of creativity. It would be a terrible thing if college injured students through its efforts to help them. A little disquieting evidence with respect to what happens in the last year of high school comes from the study recently released by the Fund for the Advancement of Education (1957) of the college success of the boys and girls with three years of high school compared with an equated control group who spent all four years in high school. In nearly every comparison involved in the study those with less high school did better than those with more high school. This does not mean that every student did well, but the averages suggested that something may well be wrong with the last year of high school or the first year of college. Whether or not college was more exciting for those with but three years of high school, we should ask ourselves why we cannot make it exciting and bring out the best in all the students. Many of the students who spent four years in high school complained that they got very little out of their last year.

It may be a comfort for college teachers to have a scapegoat in the high school, but there is some evidence that similar things may be happening in college. The "sophomore slump" is a well-known phenomenon, where the enthusiastic freshman has already become jaded by the end of his first year. Some teachers report less satisfactory class discussions with seniors than with freshmen.

On the positive side, we find a number of promising indications that creativity can be encouraged in college, and not only for the very bright students. I wish to stress again that I am not here urging honors programs and the like for the exceptional student. I believe in them, but I believe also in providing opportunities for self-expression by all the students.

At Princeton, for example, the senior essay is required of all students, regardless of their standing in the class. According to Professor Oates, who has given the program much attention, this often turns out to be most valuable for the mediocre student, who for the first time really learns to expect something of himself that can be judged on its own terms by a standard of excellence that does not compare him with fellow students writing on common topics.

At Colby College, an experiment reported by President Bixler (1957) shows what can be done with a small group of fifteen selected *not* on the basis of their records but for their interest.

The conditions for creativity will have to be carefully nourished if we want more creativity to be demonstrated. All of our evidence shows that we must keep search alive, and we must allow sensitivity to new ideas, perhaps tolerating a little foolishness. We must not develop critical abilities to the point that anything unproven is stupid or that anything weak is altogether wrong. We must not insist upon conformity, or we will end with traditionalists rather than with innovators.

So that my own position can be given a little greater concreteness, I am going to suggest a series of questions that can be asked of an educational program to find out whether or not it is encouraging creativity in the sense in which I meant it. I say "educational program" advisedly, because I do not refer necessarily to a single course (although a course can be judged in this way) but to the total impact of the educational community.

1. Does the student *initiate* inquiry on his own, or only inquire along lines set by others?

2. Is there opportunity to *exhibit* and *take responsibility for*, successive evidences of creativity, even though the created items are not "distinguished"? That is, does the student learn to take satisfaction in *small evidences* of creativity?

3. Are there opportunities for the student's original work to be judged according to *individual progress* rather than according to group norms?

4. Is there time in the program for a substantial investment of time in *idiosyncratic specialization*? By this I mean unusual interests which do not necessarily lie within the standard academic disciplines, e.g., the history of boating on the Missouri River, the role of herbs in human affairs, home-made musical instruments, the changing patterns of the comic strips, etc.

5. Is there evidence that the progressive changes during the academic year are toward *greater diversity of talent* rather than toward greater conformity?

A program that would score well on these five items would be a very bright spot indeed on the collegiate horizon.

12

Creativity in Education

GEORGE D. STODDARD

CREATIVITY came close to being a lost cause in American education. Progressive education, a phenomenon rarely observed in pure form, helped to revive its spirit. Education, frequently viewed as an aggregation of facts or the preparatory stages of a prosaic life, carried on the scholastic tradition. The urge to inquire, to invent, to perform was stifled in millions of school children, now grown up, who did not get above rote learning, or at least did not stay above it. Their final culture pattern is all about us.

CREATIVITY AND CONFORMITY

Conformity rules, not because people crave it but because they fear deviation. Which way, for example, does a window look—*out* or *in?* Persons outside do not have to look in; there are other vistas available. Persons inside the home do want to look out occasionally if only to ease the tension in their eyeballs. The so-called "picture window" rules otherwise; it is made to be seen from the outside—to create the illusion that you are looking into the charming recesses of home life. It is a false image. It covers up like a decoy what really happens inside the house and obstructs the view of the world outside. Its significance lies in a common lack of nerve.

Inside the school, many teachers and textbooks (refrigerated versions of teachers stamped and sealed) pay homage to the same god of conformity. It used to be thought that this made little difference in mathematics, physical science, and grammar, but we were wrong even there. Three hundred years of standard instruction in these disciplines have produced populations whose chief reliance is on the conditioned response, the repetitive act, the voice of authority.

In the words of Oscar Handlin (1957, pp. 110–113):

> With few exceptions (the textbook) is dogmatic and dull, an obstacle rather than an aid to learning . . . Excellent illustrations and maps, thoughtful design and layout, and good paper and binding are characteristic of today's publishing. But there has been no alteration in the basic assumption of the text that learning consists of remembering and that the function of the book is to supply the material to be remembered . . . Only a few textbooks have ventured to break through the pattern of dogmatism and dullness which is characteristic of the species. Generally, publishers, authors, and teachers follow one another in a frustrating circle that strengthens the pattern. The publisher is constrained by the market to turn out books for existing courses; the author writes what will be published; and the teacher shapes his course by the available texts. The result is endless imitation.

Now we know that memory has a part to play in learning; speaking any language, including our own, involves a vast number of correlated impressions on call. The trouble is that in textbooks far removed from original sources, we are fed fragments that conform neither to the logical demands of an intellectual discipline nor to the psychological needs of the learner. Devoid of form, many a textbook renders its authors wholly unexciting. Our search for creativity therefore demands a new role for the textbook—a lesser one in the totality of the school day, but a deeper one. Its main purpose should be introductory. It should stir the student to ask, and find answers for, key questions. It should send him to original readings, experiments and experiences not otherwise occurring to him; it should transport him across the barrier of words to sights, sounds, feelings, and emotions. Such a work viewed as map, ticket, or guidebook is defensible; not itself creative, a good textbook can show the way to creativeness.

The alternative is to regard creativity as beyond the reach of most children still in school. Everything is against them in a world of slogans and mass responses. It is hard nowadays to sell anything to anybody on the strength of deviation from others; it is still harder to monopolize economic, military, or political power in a people given to self-analysis and free choice.

To be creative, in short, is to be unpredictable; it is to be decidedly suspect in the world of affairs. The creative aspect of life is rightly viewed as action. Never simply contemplative, the creative act at its highest brings about notable differences in things, thoughts, works of art, and social structures. What is to be changed fights back, perhaps with success. Even in science, the truly novel or radical person has a hard time of it. For this, we need not go back to the ancient Greeks, or even to Copernicus, Galileo, or Darwin. In our day an Einstein or an Oppenheimer is viewed with different emotions by different elements in our society.

Of course, some children will not give in to restrictive measures designed to make them into little conformers. They go about their internal business—the business of thinking and creating—hampered at times by the environment but managing to select from it concepts that are stimulating. Although almost everybody else falls behind in the race, they keep ahead. Such persistence characterizes genius but it is found elsewhere. It thrives on good teaching.

Creativity, a precious attribute of thought and deed, can be circumscribed through academic prejudice. Who would deny Sir Richard Livingstone's (1944) claim that frequently in teaching we confuse means and ends? How far we should follow him as he spells out this deficiency is another matter. For example, in *The Future in Education*, he says:

It would take too long to apply this distinction of means and ends to all the subjects in education. Most of them are concerned with what I have called subordinate purposes or ends. Mathematics, for instance. The pupil learns it in order to become an engineer or an accountant or to add up marks or his house books or for some similar purpose; and also perhaps because it trains the mind. But mathematics is not concerned with the ultimate end of life; no one is the wiser about that for the hours he spends with Godfrey and Price's *Arithmetic* or Durell's *Geometry*. So with most subjects in Education. Languages are not concerned with the supreme ends of life, especially if they are studied for the purposes of conversation or commerce; nor are science, or geography, or economics, or sewing, or cookery. I do not question the importance of these subjects; all are elements in the nourishment of the human being, but they are destitute, or almost destitute, of this essential vitamin. . . I suggest then that the best way of bringing order into this chaos of the curriculum is for the teacher to have clearly in his mind this distinction of means and ends, and the need for higher ends, to feel that he is training his pupils to live a life that is a symphony and not a series of disconnected noises—even if they are beautiful noises—to see that while they acquire the means which they need for the practical purposes of life, they should also form an idea of the end at which they should aim.

The mathematicians I know have a different feeling about their subject. There is relatively little mathematics in the work of the engineer and much less in the work of the accountant. And let us not revive the fallacy of mental discipline; neither mathematics nor any other subject "trains the mind." But pure mathematics is so glorious that nothing in the visions of men recorded elsewhere really surpasses it. In the ingredient of imagination, the work of a Newton, a Kepler, or an Einstein deserves to rank with the creations of a Dante, a Milton, or a Shakespeare. Is it not futile to attempt to play off history and literature against science? We should not compare the low levels of one discipline with the highest ranges of another. What counts is the depth of the abstract principles. This is not to say that one field of work can be equated with another. Some fields are predominantly physical or mechanical in their content and must therefore be given a separate treatment. "Vocational" is itself a slippery concept. The minister-member of a college board proclaiming the inherent virtue of Hebrew, Greek, and Latin as humanizing nonvocational subjects is suspect. For him these languages are vocational and professional; he needs them in order to understand scriptural texts and commentaries. This can be said of language teachers proclaiming the virtues of language study, or of teachers approving pedagogy. A truly nonvocational approach will deepen insight, adjustment and enjoyment regardless of one's vocation. A mastery of one's native tongue is a good example, as is familiarity with history, philosophy, and science, or with the innumerable manifestations of the fine arts in the cultures of the world. There is a psychology not reserved for the psychologist; there is art beyond the artist's domain.

Such insights are good for all persons. If we do not understand and enjoy art as revealed in certain basic principles we will waste time on what is bad. For many decades we have done just that: witness the architecture and decoration of the late 1800's in America as reflected in the nation's school buildings. The specialists were in part to blame, for they could have done better by the people even if the people were innocent. Just as the lay person has a right to expect a bridge to endure even though he does not understand the underlying mechanics, so the people have a right to ask their artists to avoid what is ugly or shoddy. Granted that criteria in science and technology are more firm than they will ever be in the graphic, plastic, and structural arts, I stick to the charge that thousands of American schoolhouses and courthouses were bad by any known principles of design, safety, or function. The artist, like the expert in any other field, ought to be ahead of the public. If he gives in to irresponsible and untrained pressure groups, he will lose his self-respect at the time and eventually he will lose the confidence of the groups, less ignorant now, that he deceived in the first place. It is no part of the democratic procedure to replace good decisions in art by a counting of noses among the uninformed.

The real safeguard for the public is to become better educated in those general fields upon which intellectual, emotional, and artistic progress will depend. It is not a case of the public giving *carte blanche* to the specialist but rather of asking the specialist to be special, that is, wise and imaginative beyond a common awareness of standards.

To get creativity in society viewed as a whole, we must make it mean more to each person. We must start early in the life of the child.

We observe in children the use of imaginative forms from "patty-cake" on. There is rhythm. There is often a strong splashing sense of color. The child tends to put first things first not in the categories of art but in terms of the way it seems to him. The head, eyes, ears, and mouth predominate in his so-called figure drawings, while limbs often appear as simple appendages. He is reaching into a world of confusing stimuli, but very soon he extracts from it what is closest to him. His vocabulary grows the same way—from the inside out, as it were. His first act of creativity is to get in relation symbolically to something or somebody outside himself. This will appear as language and soon as play, for in play the child begins the never-ending struggle to understand both his world and the world as conceived by others. Play is preparation and it is a bridge. It demands that the child himself accept a role. To be creative at these incipient stages, acts must conform to a child's need. His lines, blots, or circles mean, as Alice said of words, what he wants them to mean—for a time. With growth, the idea of convention comes in and it need not be forced. Creativity finally produces a merger, combining what the child feels and wants to express with what others respond to. When he finds his imaginary world carrying weight outside and making impressions even on grown-ups, the child will accept the discipline of a medium without feeling maligned. The action components impose their disciplines first. To skate beautifully, you must first skate, and so it is for acting, dancing, or musical performance. Creativity involves a reforming of first impressions and achievements, not because somebody demands it, but because the maturing personality senses that children's games are not forever satisfying. The educational problem is to relate new imaginative elements to new concepts of the world.

Creative impulses may be fostered if we ask the child to cross from one medium to another—to describe a landscape or an event, to illustrate a story, to set words to music. Generally the pupil is asked to describe his own images. Since these are private, failure may lie in either the image-forming or language phase of creativeness.

One way to test the situation is to present the same images to a group. Paul Witty's (1956) study of the use of films in identifying talented pupils is a case in point. He used a film entitled *The Hunter and the Forest—a Story Without Words*. Of two thousand compositions written by grade pupils following a showing of this film, Witty judged that 10 per cent showed superior promise in writing. One fifth-grade example will indicate the power of this wordless film to evoke an imaginative response in words:

Once upon a time there was a beautiful forest. In it were the graceful deer, the comical grouse, and the beauty of flowers and trees. Near this forest lived a hunter, oblivious to these things. He was out for sport. He walked through the beautiful forest, crushing the tender blossoms, and breaking boughs of lovely trees. He saw a grouse, done up in feather finery, and killed it. He then put one of its tail feathers in his hat. Then he went home, satisfied with the day's kill. Then a rain came. The flowers, sprinkled with shining diamonds, did their exotic rain ballet. The trees swayed too, with the gentle beat of the rain. The next day, the hunter again went into the forest. He set up a net for some unwary animal. Then something caught his eye. It was a deer family, grazing peacefully by the water. His hand touched the trigger. Just then something wonderful happened. As a flower opens, slowly, slowly, so the hunter's heart and eyes opened, slowly, slowly. The hunter, the destroyer of nature awoke. Why, this wasn't something to destroy. It was something beautiful, sacred, it was the unspoiled perfect beauty of God and nature. The hunter took down his net, lowered his gun and started home. Instead of a stalk, his steps were light and springy. The birds chirped. The squirrels chattered. Why hadn't he seen this before? He threw down the grouse feather, the symbol of his slaughter, and put in its place a delicate flower. He walked along, whistling.

It was thus that the hunter found what so many long to find, a new world, a heaven on earth, a paradise. It's everywhere. It's beauty, purity, exotic grace. It is beauty of Venus, the Kingdom of Pan, the haunts of Diana. Here, there is no past, no future, just now. Beautiful, happy, now!

Beyond any motion picture lies the world of firsthand reality, but to be real it must be touched, tasted, smelled, seen, and heard in manifold ways, over and over again. A single mountain view changes with the time of day, the weather, the season, and, more subtly, with the mood of the observer. What we see and respond to may be affected by pressure from economic, political, or religious sources, thereby losing a measure of its individuality and of its truth. Creativity in any medium suffers from the *imposition* of content, form, or message. If, beholden to politicians, we demand that certain things be not only looked for but found and expressed, artistic integrity is lost. The end-product is poster art, presently rampant in Russia. The creative life at any age may or may not accept norms of behavior, but to flourish at all it must be given a free choice. Many conformists fear contemporary education for its insistence upon a freedom of the mind they have learned to do without.

Creativity is a phenomenon that appears along a continuum of personal and social growth. We may postulate that everybody has some spark that education can blow upon and make brighter. Certainly that is an educational imperative, no less for special talent than for general ability. We aim to give the child something to think about, something to be and to do. By definition the child will never perform beyond his capacity and most likely he will fall far short. If he succeeds according to any criterion, then he could have done so, but even if he fails he might have succeeded, and may yet. Although the American school takes the long view and the long chance, in the creative aspects of its program it is demonstrably defective. The lock-step of curriculum, textbook, and a teaching habit of all eyes front is hard to break. What many critics derisively speak of as progressive education is simply an attempt—often a good attempt—to break through this crust of conformity and passivity. Memorized forms, as useful as bricks are to a building, create nothing. Steel, concrete, and glass may be made into the meanest of structures, failing in all respects, and the reference is not to changing styles. So for the pupils, row on row. What nursery school teacher has not observed with joy the curiosity of children before they get fitted into the neat slots of a rigid grade system? What chance does the pupil have to go all out in any direction that suits his fancy, even when he is willing to pay the price of hard work and good performance in culture-patterned content?

We need to counteract the drab effects of generations of mass conformity in the arts. Americans, by and large, are at the mercy of the cheap trick in sound, sight, or word. Still, there is progress and university centers deserve credit for raising the standards. The dance and the theater, for example, are fed by fresh talent and audience acceptance across the land. On the campus creative art, music, and writing are no longer alien, and the campus will eventually reproduce itself in the American community. Slowly we are becoming a nation of college alumni, as we are already one of high school graduates. But the critical start is made in the elementary school. Let us look there.

A Dual Progress Plan for Elementary Education

It is not clear that we can introduce more creativity without reforms in teaching methods and grade organization.

The typical classroom teacher is swamped with chores. She is supposed to act as a tutor, even with 30 pupils in the classroom, but she does not really know their minds. Technical aids are regarded as luxuries. We have spent billions of dollars on kitchen equipment in order to free the homemaker, but to free the teacher is regarded as sinful.

At the precise moment of learning, what takes place inside the mind of the learner? Learning is a private experience, even in a group. Our methods of teaching do not permit a full application of this basic principle. Thus learning calls for self-study and group practice and motivation hinges upon dramatic experience. Self-study in cubicles with the aid of films, records, and tape recordings may iron out common errors and increase the confidence of the learner. These mechanical aids to learning are impersonal. They do not embarrass the learner. Although they are unable to show affection, neither do they have a capacity for insult.

It is easy to put a finger upon defects in elementary education. It is not easy to set up a new plan. However, some of us at New York University are attempting to do so. Basically the plan calls for team-teaching by special teachers not only in music and the arts but also in science and mathematics.

The pupils in grades one through six will remain with their respective home-room teachers for the half-day devoted to reading, writing, speech, and the social studies. The rest of the day they will be under special teachers in mathematics, science, music, arts and crafts, recreation, and health, these teachers to work as a team responsible for instruction up through the grades. Thus a special teacher will offer work on a longitudinal basis, regrouping the pupils according to the needs of each child rather than on an age-grade distribution. He will also help pupils to form social clubs, based on content interests. Home-room and special teachers will meet together regularly to discuss common problems.

This *dual progress plan* emphasizes the ambivalent nature of the child in a given culture pattern. This is the way child, youth, and adult are really tested in our society. The graded steps—regular school grades, made more elastic by the plan—represent the accepted, averaged core. These steps rest essentially on a grasp of the language arts and the social studies. A concept of general maturation is retained in the new plan. Certain aspects of science and the fine arts penetrate these "core" layers or grades, but in descriptive terms—knowledge *about* science and technology, music, art, and literature. Thus, mathematical terms and physical equations, like singing, composing, sculpturing, acting, and dancing, are really special in our culture; by themselves, they should neither retard nor advance the scholastic progress of the child. In order to give these disciplines free play, we should exempt them from the concept of age-linked grades.

This plan, in essence, would give up the unsuccessful, century-old struggle to find grade teachers who really like mathematics, science, art, and music and are sufficiently competent to guide pupils in every one of these studies. It presents a means of progress for pupils of special talent, without doing violence to the concept of general maturation. It should encourage the home-room teachers to become truly expert in the language and descriptive arts, capable of teaching through the spectrum that runs from remedial reading and speech correction to imaginative writing. Teachers who "hate" mathematics will not be expected to teach it.

The plan involves a fundamental shift in our attitude toward child development and behavior. It applies to the child what is more conspicuous for the adult, namely, that general education is based on language, social studies, and the descriptive aspects of natural science, technology, and the contemporary scene. Sentence structure, history, literature, and current affairs—these are of the cultural currency; they carry a strong potential for either embarrassment or personal satisfaction, depending upon the scantiness or the abundance of the supply.

Technical proficiency in art, music, crafts, mathematics, science, or recreation is a wonderful asset to anyone who possesses it, but in our society there is no insistence. Nobody hands us a violin, a chisel, a mathematical formula, saying *play, sculpture, solve*. As a rule, we do not know rocks, plants, animals, or stars in a scientific way. Except as uncomfortable amateurs, we are not expected to sing, dance, recite poetry, or take a dramatic role. But a few double negatives or historical misquotations mark us as ignoramuses. Sensing this, children respond in a perfunctory way to what should be immensely appealing and satisfying.

In any event, all children should make the best progress they are capable of in the home room, which is the nearest to the parental situation from which they have come at age 5 or 6 and to which they return for half of each waking day for 185 days on the calendar. In the longitudinal programs they will have new opportunities to stretch their minds. They will be guided by teachers who themselves have reached into the upper levels of knowledge and performance.

Creativity in the plan I have described is envisaged as a resolution of four forces: the child, the teacher, the school, and the culture pattern. Children are not equally creative in all disciplines, and they vary enormously in intelligence. Nevertheless, regardless of talent, they must be encouraged to make progress in the arts of communication and social living. A large number will need tutorial attention, usually in English and speech.

The teacher—home-room or special—should understand and like

children and, further, be skilled in the art of teaching. This skill is denied a person who lacks firsthand contact with the higher levels of a given academic discipline. For English, the social studies, and current events, the problem is met by the accessibility of descriptive and imaginative writing. The third-grade teacher, like everyone else, is bathed in this culture. But in mathematics and abstract science there is no comparable support from the culture, the grade teacher rarely reading anything in higher mathematics, physics, or chemistry.

The changes contemplated affect all school grades, but they are specially relevant from grade three through the junior high school. Eventually the design of classrooms will catch up. When a pupil needs to be alone—perhaps in a cubicle with mechanical devices that offer no occasion for classroom mockery—then he is indeed alone. When he needs social interchange, it is available. Under the dual progress plan pupils will be placed in grades only to the extent that the culture pattern demands age-related progress. In their work under teams of specialists they will be free to slide up or down without pressure, for these are the tasks in which adults themselves accept elastic achievement norms. The same Americans who freely apply such words as "moron" or "dumbbell" to children who cannot or will not master English, avoid bad French by not speaking French—a double standard.

So, we discern the culture pattern for our day and nation, as it shapes Livingstone's question: *What are the ends sought?*

In partial answer, let me insert a statement by one of our most richly endowed philosophers, Robert Ulich (1956). A Harvard professor, born abroad and steeped in the European tradition, he says:

One often blames the American school for its shortcomings in learning. Indeed, much needs to be done. We are no longer in the frontier situation but absorbed in the highly competitive world of today. Hence, we must raise our young minds up to the level where they would be in the most advanced countries of the world. But in doing so let us not forget that countries with the most highly trained intelligentsia broke down miserably, partly because they had neglected what we have cultivated: sound human relations among the various classes of society, a healthy— sometimes even too great—suspicion of "book-learning," an undogmatic openness to new experiences. There has been a healthy instinct in the Anglo-Saxon nations that the brain alone does not make a man.

Of course, merely neglecting the brain does not make a man either, nor does it guarantee a healthy nation. Rather we should take more seriously the admonition of the great Swiss Johann Heinrich Pestalozzi that true human education cultivates not only the head, but also the heart and the hand.

A Turner, a Morrill, a Lincoln could scarcely have done better than this imported man has done to express the truth at the core of the land-grant college movement. And now a warning note from Professor Ulich:

We have many testimonies of those who can claim to have possessed the quality of creativeness in superior fashion. Most of them were specialists of a kind, otherwise they would have been mere dilettantes. But they were more than specialists. Their stubbornness in the pursuit of the aim in mind was accompanied by a wealth of associations. They were not one-dimensional but multidimensional. They were not only logical, they were also intuitive. The "creative hunch" that led them into new areas of perception did not spring from a mere accumulation of knowledge and technique. Many forgotten men were their superiors in that respect. It came from an often unconscious source they themselves could describe only in symbols.

It is exactly this source of creative intuition which should interest us—that quality which so clearly distinguishes the great man of business from the mere moneymaker, the statesman from the politician, the truly rational man from the mere dialectician, the scholar from the recorder, and the artist from the reproducer. Strange though it sounds, if our colleges and universities forget about this intuitive center of the human mind, their instruction, however accurate and diligent, may bury creativeness.

We have all come here not to bury creativeness but to praise it. The Symposium is well-timed. In creativity we have the essence of what is worth saving; in education we have the means.

CREATIVITY IN THE GRAPHIC ARTS

Since we expect to find creativity to a high degree in the graphic arts, let us examine this medium more closely.

Many an abstract painting, seeking to probe the unconscious depths of personality, may fail to communicate. After all, the particular experience, graphically stated, must also have general significance; in a sense it must be part of everyone's unconscious. Further, since every form of expression is a language, to the uninformed the thought stays hidden beneath the symbols. Art has to go further to be in the great circle of human events. If art is altogether private, few will bother to pay attention.

Perhaps only a unified people can develop that further probing which great art exemplifies, whether the new vision be alluring or devastating. As of now, no forked devils or stations in Hell are as frightening as the image of hordes of New Yorkers, Chicagoans, or Detroiters being burned, dissolved, and vaporized. There is enough horror in the specter of tomorrow's Hiroshimas to feed our conscious and unconscious fears for all time.

In any event, creativity in the graphic and plastic arts is a treasure at all maturity levels, from the swabbing efforts of the child to the touch of genius. Light, shadow, color, reflection, and movement play many a trick. Distortion is common enough, even to the camera eye. The final mental impression is what counts. The function of the cortex is to transmute images so as to establish certain conventions in the interpretation of lines and forms in space. Thus images are automatically reversed in the vertical plane, distance is perceived through converging lines, a third dimension is easily added, and colors are related to what is adjacent. But these are only psychological events. It is the work of a master to make of these little illusions the organic great one that permits plastic or pigment to glow with the essence of a reality that transcends ordinary vision—to be realer than the real object as perceived.

Hence we should not overemphasize the technique of vision. We cannot think with the eyes, and we may think without them. Vision brings in the data, the raw materials, and the cues that guide our steps. The eye is an invaluable sense organ, a true part of the brain through its optic nerve, but the frontal lobes preside over the problems created and they are not to be denied. The artist is a man seeing and thinking—both at once; his cunning is in his brain. It is not enough for him to experience beauty or love or hate; he must get it down on something at least two-dimensional. The artist is uncommon because speech is common. If man had kept to visual patterns and had not developed speech except in a gifted few, speech might have become the main vehicle of artistic endeavor. If everybody talked by drawing, and only a few by speaking, we would regard every manifestation of speech as a work of art—good, bad, or unintelligible. In fact, primitive Norsemen did regard writing as a form of magic and therefore reprehensible. Talking has made babblers of us all, so that only the low idiots lack the gift to some degree. For us the difference between speech and graphic art is that in art few try. The painting, unless it carries the impact of a blinker sign, is regarded as tough reading with no reader's guide.

Still, through a mild uniformity of culture, art is attention-getting. We tend to see the same things, provided we have the same experiences and aspirations. The only forms we know well are those found in nature, but their emotional content varies. Consider rain. It may be a gentle soporific, a bringer of buds, a hope of plenty, a seeming answer to public prayer; it may also be a spoiler of picnics, ball games, or commencement exercises, a sinker of ships.

The artist seeks the meaning that is lost in the casual. If he achieves it for himself, he still cannot achieve it for us, but only offer us a better basis for finding the meaning than we might otherwise discover. He works hard at the task. He extracts, selects, arranges, does what we have little time or talent to do. Admittedly, if he fails to communicate, the failure may be in us. It is wrong to hold, however, that the failure is *always* in us—the observers—for to do so would make painting as empty as a crystal ball. The archaic picture on the cave wall meant something that needed no reference to words to make it a passion to its creator fresh from the hunt. He saw; he felt. He transmitted, sometimes with wonderfully accurate drawing, the essence of the experience. Such works, devoid of borrowing from a culture pattern, are close to the heart of creativity.

Today, war and the fear of war are overriding, and nobody sees a way out. Casualties through disease, crime, and accident are almost of the same order as losses in battle. We carry a terrible burden of shock, anxiety, and remorse in the cumulative effect of the killing and maiming of loved ones.

These events and others like them, real or imagined, lead to another great trouble—the splitting of personality through sheer inability to cope with life. It appears in all degrees, some not immediately harmful. The neurotic develops emotional peculiarities which he confines to certain areas. He learns to live with these defects and compulsions; his friends and associates permit him to do so. They are rarely a part of his charm but through overcompensation they may be useful in his work. The person devoid of such drives is not necessarily the most normal. He is too much like an old man without wrinkles—the smooth face of complete adjustment may mask an indifference to real problems. The Greek poets and dramatists were the first to see this, and the psychologists, under the impetus of Freud, have made a science of this penetration into basic drives.

I feel that artistic expression in all the media is needed more than ever before as a means of channeling good and bad emotions. It is not enough to follow the saintly Spinoza into a world of sweetness and light. The heavy involvements of violence are always with us. They cannot be counterbalanced by kind thoughts. They can be overcome only by positive actions based on love and companionship.

What is new in creativity is a realization that our conscious life is superimposed upon an intricate structure of the unconscious. A person differs from every other person not only in genetic and physical structure but also in mental content. Identical twins soon cease to be alike in the habits of thinking. Differing sense data differently interpreted build up a unique mental apparatus for each person. Hidden meanings, marvelously complex, characterize our dreams but are not confined to them. Speaking, writing, performing, composing, drawing, sculpturing—let us say behaving symbolically—draw from these deep wells of personality. They dredge up strange forms and actions, strange not because they are unnatural but for two other reasons: first, they are not needed in a life of 2 plus 2 equals 4, and, second, they undergo censorship even before exposure to the inner self.

Thus paintings may show regression to the more carefree days of childhood; they may depict wish fulfillment through dream elements; they may go beyond illusion to delusion. Paintings may, in a word, be to the painter what the reclining couch is to the psychiatric patient. If through such graphic or plastic freedom a new personal unity is achieved, we need not hold this against art. On the contrary, let us encourage such forms of therapy; they are powerful, even if the subject matter happens to lie in personal despair.

Art is one way of telling a truth—or an untruth. It is not science. It is not technology. It is not factual in a statistical sense. If it becomes simply illustrative, it still tells the truth, but in a limited ephemeral way. Classic art generally tells beautiful, ennobling, inspiring truths—hence the poet's equation: *Beauty is truth, truth beauty.* In the hands of lesser men such art runs the risk of becoming sweet, sensuous, or imitative. The creative power of the early Italian masters, for example, could not be transmitted to the unseeing, unknowing, or uncaring.

Let me restate this for the artist. If the artist says that life has no meaning and man no claim on existence, present or future, he may paint accordingly—dots, dashes, zigzags, or contrivances—and this act of such a painter painting is a fact, a truth. What he tells us is another matter. He may carry the idea of destruction to what he regards as a logical conclusion. He may leave man out. But he cannot leave himself out. Painting, to such a man, may sink to an automatic activity, a perseveration, carried on while the person is occupied elsewhere or perhaps nowhere.

Now this is different from an urge to define the new environment. In music a Stravinsky introduces sounds and rhythms that push against us like pistons. They are put together as cunningly as any machine and the final effect may be overwhelming. The graphic artist has the same privilege and opportunity. Visual creativity goes beyond faces and landscapes into the dark recesses of the mind. Psychology is replacing nature study. Still, it will not be enough to depict horror or confusion—to show life as it once was or might be. What we seek is a sense of growth and inner power. Should we celebrate at once the triumph of machines and the defeat of the men who made them? Machines were supposed to rescue us from drudgery—to expand our creative energies. Can we discover what has gone wrong?

Creativity is an active force. It may thrive for a time under tyranny but tyranny itself is weakened by free creative acts. Plato held that art should be the basis of education. Modern psychologists—James, Dewey, Piaget, and the gestalt workers—give art a high place. The habit of thought without art was not intended to override thought through art. In the words of Moholy-Nagy: "Every man has energies which he can develop into creative work. I do not believe so much in art as in mankind. Every man reveals himself. Much of it is art."

The truth beyond science cannot be found by a preoccupation with science. It will not be in conflict with science, for it takes up where science leaves off. It flourishes in the realm of choices, values and excitements that transcend the factual or predictable. Beauty offers one path to this excitement. There is no need to explain its crucial place in the world of art. Redon said: "Painting is not mere representation of three-dimensional forms, but human beauty adorned with the prestige of thought." The love of beauty is an inspiring phenomenon in the world. Let us hope that no assignment in morality, mental hygiene, or public service will stamp it out. In the long run, whatever man accomplishes along enduring lines will be a by-product of his devotion to the beautiful. There lies one sure entry into human thought; to go around it, except by way of new discovery, is to diminish man.

In stable societies there is an accepted currency for beauty, as there is for exaltation. Saints will wear their halos for a long time, at home with the humble and the elite, and fat Buddhas are not easily slenderized. Still, religion as a stimulus for our highest thought and best design—for what curators will assiduously collect as the art of our day —may prove barren or at best imitative. Inexorably man himself moves into the center of what is known or can be found out. There is no longer anything creative about creating new gods, or shoring up old ones for that matter. Except for humanism time is running out. The essence remains; it is *love*.

An episode in organic evolution, man has just become aware of himself. Small wonder that the nonobjective artist hits pay dirt as he digs into the unconscious. The full communication of human tragedy will require a mastery of psychology and all the arts, especially the performing arts. As in pain or shock, the organism raises barriers against revelations that get too close to the inner self. The split mind, protecting itself, reveals much to the analyst or the artist but it rarely is again creative. The enormous talent of a Nijinsky or an Ezra Pound peters out. It appears that, granting sequential and cyclical states, creativity and pathology are incompatible as concurrent conditions.

It is a function of education—a creative function—to open the mind to self-revelation, thus unifying the personality. In so doing, education clears the channels of communication. As we ponder the self-revelations of others in any creative aspect of art, science, or behavior, we may tap the springs of some small creativity within ourselves.

CREATIVITY AND HUMAN RELATIONS

Although inevitably we turn to creativeness in the fine arts, we should recognize it elsewhere, and especially in the emergence of personality. Here we run into a sex difference that some persons regard as deplorable and therefore nonexistent. To me, the difference is not only understandable in the long cultural history of the race; it is still a force in natural selection. A woman creates the child far beyond events in egg or sperm, and, having done so, she has a different outlook on life. For one thing, she sees through pseudo abstractions. Accused often of loquaciousness, she cares little for words, formulas, or themes as such; for most women words take on meaning only as they define persons and external events. This trait has proved to be a strong antidote to the mental excesses of men. In our immediate monstrous future of big rockets and little men, the superior ability of women to get back to fundamentals—back to persons—may prove to be the glory of the human race.

As I said nearly ten years ago (Stoddard, 1950)—

Instead of fretting about the disinterest of women in the mechanical, we should be thankful for this saving part of our culture. Home and community life, the fine arts and humanities, freedom—these are the cultural goods transferable across all boundaries. Work in science, technology, commerce, agriculture, and politics provides the strong supporting structures, but it should not fly the flag at the mast. The *know-what* should rise above the *know-how*. A new division of labor will not only encourage more crossing of occupational and cultural lines between the sexes; it will also form a new concept of teamwork. By concentrating on original creations, women can save themselves centuries of scholastic cultivation which has gone to seed.

In my opinion, educational programs from elementary school to college will lack distinction if they continue to ignore differences allied to sex. The sexes have much in common in our culture pattern, and these elements determine the nature of undifferentiated curriculums. Language is the chief example, with social and political studies closely following. Beyond that, personal association, the performing arts, and religion may become a passion for women, as for many men, but among the latter especially is found the power to create abstract forms and patterns. So, if we want to waste talent on a huge scale, let us follow the Russians; let us try to produce physicists and engineers by inducting girls en masse. The Russians will indeed get some additional scientists from among the women, but they will alienate many more, perhaps to the point of neurotic despair, for creativity along technical lines is reserved to a small population of persons—chiefly males. It is to them and their works—to basic research like that of Lee and Yang—that the United States should turn in order to develop scientific creativity on a big scale.

In education, at times with a fierce concentration on motivating the child, we have neglected the social matrix. We have not only failed to set up the conditions. We have discouraged whole communities from paying attention to the creative energies of any child—to the need for form and beauty and originality. The straight utilitarian finds a miserly virtue in the ugliness of factories, homes, and schools. Let us nail this down: builders who are paid for ugly structures are paid for the ugliness as well as for the utility.

As aesthetic values rise, and they are rising notably in America, the level of expectation for each person rises. Music in Austria, opera in Italy, graphic arts in Japan, and the dance in Southeast Asia are so interwoven with the culture as to be inseparable. What creativity is asked of every American boy or girl? There is no clear answer. I would place high on the list an awareness of contemporary architecture and a feeling for the performing arts. Also, we move painfully toward the realization of human rights fully alive in the individual. To set the stage not for great art alone, but for the steady support of creative manifestations in any child, youth, or adult, our schools should get beyond the dull, the safe, the orthodox. Any excitement lost to our schools will be lost to our communities ten times over.

We should not forget that the wonderful efficiency of the oyster succeeds only in producing more oysters. So it goes for thousands of species that have been able to maintain themselves for eons in a stable environment. We are different. Our environment changes from place to place and we modify it ourselves, often dangerously. We build huge cities close to the ocean and far from the sources of food. We manage these cities through an intricate system of public utilities. The system is vulnerable in a time of emergency and the sea carries new dangers. We face the prospect of hundreds of enemy submarines outside the harbor prepared to deliver atomic bombs on target from a submerged position.

We are told by one and all to face reality. The question is, *whose* reality? Dense, hungry populations, needing more hands for crude labor, are prolific, but life is held cheap. In that ancient cycle characteristic of the Orient, human misery is compounded. The creative imagination that regards tools as substitutes for human drudgery is held back, snuffed out in the first walking, working days of the child. The adult peasant cannot invent a machine to lessen his toil, but the tractor will teach him.

We need a new rapport between the creative potential of individual intelligence and the social pattern. Man, viewed as an animal, changes little in ten thousand years, but the elasticity of his nervous system engenders new structures of thought and society. Through education he must nourish this one source of growth and achievement. Everything else about human tissue appears to be headed for simple duplication or deterioration. We do not grow stronger; our sense organs are as weak as ever. It is only when we develop external aids— the tool, the lens, the machine, the drug—and work together in unity that anything is added to our biological efficiency.

Now all these increments are the by-products of creativity. Seen close at hand as in the emergence of art, science, government, or human rights they give us a sense of pride and accomplishment. We have come far from the caves of our ancestors. Unhappily, we still carry the burden of tribal identification. The new reality to be faced is the saturating one of mobilizing creativity across all national and racial barriers into one responsible force: Man united! The nations, also united, will have their place, as do states, cities, and villages, but they will have lost the sovereign power to kill. To hold that this ideal is beyond the power of social creativity is to seal us off from further progress; it is to invite catastrophe.

To maintain that, with business, government, technology, and religion in full control of the social structure, there is no longer a need for the freely creating mind is to condemn us to unending dreariness. This is the constant threat of authoritarianism; to resist it is to fight for freedom in every realm.

Extreme danger makes internationalists of us all, and drives us to seek again the principles of world brotherhood. It is easier to change the reality than the form; to change the latter might call for recantation. Everybody is for peace as a matter of conscience and religious doctrine. The true conversion comes when the consequences of a war, win or lose, are deeply felt to be suicidal. As this view simmers down to our schools, the great push for missiles and bombs, necessary now, will first be matched and then replaced by a demand for the structure of world government. Any other answer to the saturating question of our time will eliminate the last flicker of creativity in the human race. Our cerebral cortex tells us this, but habit patterns seem to say, "perish the thought."

Is there time?

To win the battle of creativity, we must win the battle of the human race. At the end of 500,000 years of human and social evolution, an Einstein produced the formula for ultimate natural power. Taken by itself, it is one of the greatest single creative acts in the history of thought. We may now mobilize vast new energy sources, or with equal facility and perhaps greater likelihood, bring all living forms to a nasty death. One giant Hitlerlike misstep at this moment of world history will suffice to ruin us—to deflect the well-documented forces of natural selection to the forms of life found in the ocean depths. In a billion years these forms might work toward the surface, the fish walking again, creating a new cycle.

Is this gloomy picture the "new look" in creativity viewed as a life force? Yes, it is, unless we can find, and find fast, a solution to our political problems. In a recent past, science and art have proved to be creative, but we cling to dead dogmas and dead forms of government. The first act of most new nations is to arm to the teeth. Against what? Against other nations, old or new, and their combinations. Although the United Nations is a new and valuable political structure, it represents only a halting step toward world peace. Henceforth, to have elegance in science, beauty in art, or love among men, we must have creativity in politics. For once, we cannot shoot our way out. The situation is desperate unless we use creatively what time is left. Sums such as $30 billion (earmarked for roads) and $20 billion (proposed for bomb shelters) if spent purposely on a program of world peace, fast-moving through the United Nations to a world government, would at least be a start. No less creative a scheme in world affairs will offer any hope to the men, now children, whose dreams carry them into outer space.

Education, above all, gives us the leisure when young to think about these issues and to work a lifetime toward their solution. Perhaps, in future, adult education in many forms will give new and extended meaning to the constant search. Every unit of work for work's sake should be matched, and overmatched, by measures of thought and art and brotherhood.

13

The Social Setting of Creativity

HAROLD D. LASSWELL

CREATIVITY is the disposition to make and to recognize valuable innovations.

CASES OF CREATIVITY

Suppose we begin by looking at some cases. A favorable intellectual exercise in this country and abroad is characterizing the institutions of the United States according to their contribution to human culture. Let us note some judgments often made in this exercise (Almond, 1950).

Consider *law and government*. We are congratulated for having created a unique, although transferable, institution in the Supreme Court, with its authority to disallow acts inconsistent with its version of the Constitution. Also singled out for comment is the Federal system itself, one feature of which is the limitation of central authority on behalf of individuals as well as States. The presidential form has been emulated in several versions, which provide for a direct link between the chief executive officer of the government and the electorate.

In recent years the comment is often heard that the originality of American society has found expression in a distinctive version of capitalism featuring a subtle interplay of public and private channels, an expanding stream of investment, human and materials engineering on a vast scale, high levels of consumption, high though variable levels of productive employment, declining hours of gainful labor, spreading automation (and certain other traits).

The creativity of American life has been exemplified in negative and positive form in institutions that impinge directly upon respect relationships. The dissolution of the traditionally subordinated status of women and children has gone hand in hand with the growth of a fraternal tone of life and an accent upon individual merit.

The ingenuity of Americans in taking advantage of new materials and energy sources has been remarked from an early day. The topic has received impressive treatment in the thoroughly documented work of Giedion (1949) in matters of architecture, and in the study of early American science (Struik, 1948). The cultivation of skill has been encouraged by a public and private system of specialized structures devoted to education throughout the span of life.

In journalism, in the use of film, and, in fact, in all media of mass communication the United States has been original. At higher levels of enlightenment it is not always overlooked that the United States has sired, or at least cradled, a major system of philosophy, namely, pragmatism.

American civilization has been originative in systems of ethical guidance and transempirical revelation. We have given to the world the *Book of Mormon* and *Science and Health*, to say nothing of inspirations that bloom in the peculiar circumstances of Southern California. Our imposing network of charitable and civic enterprises is often interpreted as signalizing a general sense of social responsibility.

Observers of the national scene, struck by America's concern with physical comfort and health, have been impressed by the war against dirt, pain, distress of mind, and the boredom of waiting. The inventory includes a bathroom without dirt, a dentist's office free of pain, a drugstore that relaxes, and a bank of instant service.

So far as intimacy and congeniality are concerned, many institutions and routines for the expression of friendliness thrive among us, if foreign commentators are to be believed.

I have been making a token check list of our civilization in terms of the institutions and practices relatively specialized to the shaping and sharing of such value outcomes as power, wealth, respect, skill, enlightenment, rectitude, well-being, and affection (Lasswell and Kaplan, 1950). A similar check could be made for every known society with a distinctive culture; for every social class within every society; for every interest found within every class or cutting across class lines; for every level of crisis (high, middle, or low) in the life of every group.

In our individualistic tradition it is natural to look for the creative individual: the Benthams in politics, the Adam Smiths in economics, the Aknatons in ethics and religion, the da Vincis in prodigality of skilled expression, the Galileos in the march of human enlightenment, the Great Emancipators in the history of respect for human dignity and the overcoming of caste, the Pasteurs in the overcoming of disease, the Rousseaus in the creation of styles in intimacy of expression.

THE CONFLUENCE OF INNOVATION AND RECOGNITION

The foregoing allusions have served their purpose if they recall the formidable scope of the problem with which this symposium deals. Even the examples of creativeness are in dispute. They have been controversial over decades, and no doubt will continue to be. At first glance the task of saying anything sensible about creativity may appear to be comparable with the problem of developing the biology of the Lake Monster or the Himalayan Snowman, or the physics of Unidentified Flying Objects. On second thought the subject loses some of its ambiguity and takes its place alongside typical objects of study in the sciences of society. We have to do with event-patterns in which changing, though ascertainable, patterns of subjective events are crucial.

As we said at the beginning, two complex processes must jell before we can identify a completed instance of creativeness: an innovation must be essential; and it must elicit a certain degree of recognition as valuable. Subsequently the recognition may be withdrawn, reinstated, and withdrawn again through many cycles. A creative pattern is completed, however, each time an affirmative consensus (of a specified degree) is attained.

It was a grandiose act of creativeness when the intellectual riches of Greece and Rome were accepted in Italy and elsewhere in Europe during the revival of learning. In our day busy archeologists are making it possible for us to recognize the formidable contributions of Sumerian civilization in the Near East and of pre-Columbian civilizations in this hemisphere Our acts of recognition are not only later than previous patterns of acceptance; they are affected by a radically different constellation of factors.

For classificatory purposes we can set our critical frequencies in such a manner that social contexts of many degrees of inclusiveness can be made eligible for examination. In the vast context of time and space that embraces prehistory and history, the domestication of animals or the making of fire or the cave drawings will presumably find a place in the list of major creative emergents. The context may be systematically reduced in time and space until eventually we arrive at the characterization of the person recognized to be most creative in the laboratory of an industrial chemical plant, in an art show, or at a committee meeting.

The hidden complexities of the double process of innovation and recognition are among the factors that have helped to keep the idea of creativity alive. *Norms of expectation* are involved in perceiving novelty or the lack of it in a given pattern. *Evaluative norms* are obviously involved in judging that an innovation is also "valuable."

How are we to classify a phenomenon that, when assessed by the same person in terms of several values, seems creative in one dimension, but not in others? The fluctuating reputation of Machiavelli is a striking case (Benoist, 1936; Meinecke, 1957). For the most part he was hailed, with varying intensity of vituperation, as an enemy of morals and religion. The difficult task for the scholar is to make up his mind whether the audience of a period agreed that Machiavelli's generalizations, although "immoral," were sufficiently novel and probable to be accepted as contributing to enlightenment about man in politics. Psychotics often say or do novel things; here, too, the task is to recognize valuable emergents despite the immediate setting.

In many cases judgment can be focused by appraising a pattern according to its intrinsic features; that is, according to the arrangement of component elements. This is a question of style; and when style is invoked in the appraisal of an innovation, we speak of "the skill value."

The Recognition Process

We explore the recognition process first. The chances that an *individual* will recognize innovations are improved if he expects to maximize his value position by innovative rather than repetitive patterns. It is improved if he takes an active, not merely a passive, posture toward the discovery of innovators. (This is a demand upon the Self by the Self; it is supported by the expectation of benefiting from innovations.) The prospects of recognizing a new pattern are increased if the individual has certain capabilities (base values) at his disposal in the social setting under study.

Referring to the group context as a whole, we can venture the proposition that the chance of recognitions during a given period is improved if there is a high frequency of the expectation of value advantages following from innovation rather than repetition; if there is a high frequency of the demand on the self (by the self) to search actively for worthy innovators; if potential recognizers have capabilities (base values) at their disposal for establishing contact with innovators.

More narrowly, the chances that a potential recognizer will focus his attention upon an innovator (or an innovation) during a given period is fostered by similarity of position in the social context, and by similarity of personality structure. Do they belong to the same cultures, social classes, interests, and levels of participation in crisis? Each of these major positions defines a detailed life pattern in which are included a diversity of roles specialized to situations in the various value-institutions, together with a timetable of performance.

By referring to Figure 1 some of the implications of these statements can be specified: A represents the innovation and the innovator. The first circle of broken lines that surrounds A stands for the persons who require no intermediary to have an opportunity to focus their attention upon the innovator, the innovation (if it can be given external form), or a description of the innovator. The second circle of broken lines surrounding A represents all persons who owe their opportunity to focus upon the innovation (or a description) to the mediation of one person other than the innovator (that is, to someone in the first circle). The history of an innovation in the social process is a sequence of specific events of the kind here referred to. If we were to draw a circle for every new intermediary the circles would in many cases run into many millions.

It will be observed that the process referred to here involves both communication and collaboration.

Let the first broken-line circle B around A stand for ten friends to

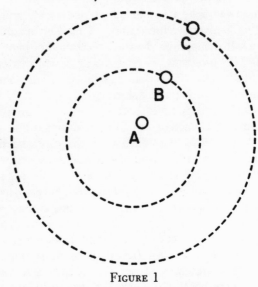

FIGURE 1

whom an innovator has shown his novelty. Let small circle B represent one of the friends who recognizes an innovation and expects to make money by exploiting it. In our terminology B expects to be better off in terms of the wealth value by promoting the novelty than by doing nothing about it. Allow small circle C to stand for an investor who is spoken to by B and made aware of A. Thus B acts as part of the environment of C and undertakes to mobilize C's predispositions in such a way that C will expect to be better off by investing in A than by seizing other opportunities.

It is not to be assumed that the friends in the first circle respond only in terms of wealth. Let B stand for one who sees in the novelty (a jet engine mock-up) a means of enhancing the political power of the Western Alliance. C may be a highly placed official in the armed services of the United States. It may be that B's dominant evaluations are in terms of respect, and that he is looking for some means of restoring the damaged prestige of the Navy. Or B may be concerned with nothing more complicated than showing his friendship to A (the affection value). Possibly B is a highly neurotic person who suffers pangs of anxiety whenever anyone asks him for help. He may respond by seeking to reduce his anxiety, thus contributing to his own well-being, by turning to C. Or B may be a very responsible individual who takes any appeal for help as a legitimate claim upon his time for serious consideration. (We call this the rectitude value.) It can be that B is a trained engineer who is sufficiently skilled to assess the innovation technically. He may turn to C largely on behalf of encouraging excellence in technology. Possibly B is more concerned with enlightenment than with other values, and desires to assist A as a means of advancing fundamental knowledge of the natural world.

We have indicated that all formal and informal interactions are multiples of the circle-pattern sketched here. The chains of communication-collaboration comprise all the value-institution patterns of the social context (all the significant outcomes, pre-outcomes and effects), and all the major divisions that conveniently distinguish the cultures, classes, interests, crisis levels (and distribution of personality structures).

Looking anywhere within a social context it is, in principle, possible to predict the route that will be taken by the recognizers of any innovation, and to follow the routes from center to center and among various zones within the society. Thus, if an innovation is made in the laboratory of a large engineering and manufacturing concern that has an élite position in the estimate of the U.S. Department of Defense, we can predict the possible route of the recognition response if we keep our trend information up to date. The first circle outside the laboratory might be within the plant and would include officials who occupy various formal positions in the organization chart, and who had received advance briefing on contingencies. The circles would extend outside the plant, perhaps following discernible lines of formal and informal liaison with the Department of Defense. The extending circle would follow describable routes—formal and informal—within the Department and also within the Federal government's executive structure. The Congress could become involved through both types of channels, the sequence running perhaps from the staff and membership of committees specialized to the armed services directly to other personnel on the Hill. At some stage the first intermediaries connected with mass and specialized channels of communication might become involved, and disseminate news stories and other content throughout the nation and perhaps the world. Test demonstrations, trial orders, and all the vast routine of putting an innovation to work provide occasion for new recognizers to commit themselves.

A fruitful way to examine any social context is to locate the *facilitators* and *inhibtors* of recognition. Built-in practices operate both ways, some aiding the process, some providing defenses against innovation.

It would be a rewarding and gigantic task to appraise our entire civilization from this point of view. What are the facilitators of which innovations? What are the inhibitors of which? We need to examine every cluster of value-institution practices with these questions in mind. Beliefs, faiths and loyalties are relevant; so, too, are the operational arrangements of every organized body (and of every unorganized, though patterned, activity). Every structure contains specialized situations, and these situations contain *roles*, some of whose consequences put them among the facilitators or the inhibitors of recognition. A reminder:

Law and government. The open forum receives protection as a means of encouraging the recognition of new ideas. There are also arrangements in fact and in form for degrees of censorship, police inquisition, and harassment. During various periods, where does the balance lie as it affects facilitation or inhibition?

Economics. The huge saving and investment operations of modern capitalism have given scope and recognition to a host of specialized innovations. To what extent has business failed to recognize creative cultural expansion?

Social classes. The color caste system in the United States is breaking up, removing the barriers to the recognition of many patterns previously overlooked, rejected, or denied. Will the subculture, once the barriers are effectively down, have enough self-respect to recognize the creative significance of more of its own expressions?

Skill. Are taboos still operating so effectively that Oriental civilization, for instance, is still unrecognized in basic education, so that many forms of expressive style are overlooked?

Well-being. Is enough recognition of creativity in the health field given to those who give individuals and groups an awareness of worth?

Enlightenment. Do the educational institutions equip enough students to recognize the significance of the principal questions and traditions in man's destiny, and their relation to the space age?

Rectitude. Is integrity, coupled with ingenuity, in mediation, arbitration, and adjudication vividly enough perceived and endorsed?

Affection. Has our culture given too much recognition to the cleverness and charm of "good mixers," "smoothies," and manipulators?

We turn to the other confluent stream, innovation. The first question concerns innovation in general; then we look at the problem of explaining detailed innovations.

THE INNOVATION PROCESS

INNOVATION IN GENERAL

Some innovations appear to owe more to the mutual impact of collective influences than to factors within the inner life of individuals. The American Constitution, for instance, seems much more of a collective product than Freud's psychoanalysis. To account for psychoanalysis we must undoubtedly concentrate upon the stream of subjective events in the mind of Freud. But it would be a mistake to disregard the social setting in which these events took place and with which they were in perpetual interaction, even as they interacted among themselves. To explain Freud's creativity one does not overlook the exposure to Jewish culture during formative years (modified by the presence of a by now famous Catholic nurse); or the fact that Freud's family setting was middle class, with characteristic demands to rise in the world; or the influence of the special interests of a neurologist and physician provided with opportunity to study hypnotic supplements to chemical, physical, and other currently standard modes of therapy; or the significance of a conflictful personality dominated by the mechanisms of defense of which his work enables us to take cognizance; or the cultural richness and tension of late nineteenth- and early twentieth-century Vienna (to name a few factors in the social setting) (Jones, 1953–1957). When we try to explain Freud's creativity we are dealing with endless chains of interactive events in which the emphasis in some instances is upon an impact originating in the environment; at other times the emphasis moves to an inner preoccupation with lonely observation and reading, to sequences of critical reflection and rumination, to partial regressions that mediate permissive contact with unconscious yearnings for dependency[1] (or, for example, desire for the annihilation of a rival or for illicit peeping into the psychosexual evolution of another human being).

Each factor can be scrutinized by the scientific observer in a context sufficiently rich to disclose the fact that, far from being a unique occurrence, these phenomena are bound in varying degree to specifiable configurations within the event-manifold that constitutes history. The pattern of private observation and reading, for instance, was not limited to physicians in Vienna; and the giving of intervals of the day and night to partially regressed communion with the "secret places of the heart" was limited neither to physicians, nor the middle class, nor Jews—nor Viennese, for that matter. Yet detailed observation would undoubtedly establish the fact that all people do not spend the same amount of time conforming to these conduct patterns, and that distinctive profiles of "autism," for instance, exist among all the groups mentioned.

The multiple impact that a factor may exert upon a complex process such as creativity is well shown in the case of the established expectation that Vienna was a great creative center of culture, notably in medicine. The personnel of the university, and especially of the faculty of medicine, was under the pressure of the environment (including one another) to add to scientific and medical knowledge. From the earliest days of student competition the accepted goal was defined broadly in such challenging terms. Little wonder that the self-system incorporated these perspectives, making them of the self about the self. In Freud's case, at least, the self-system was predisposed by interaction with the pre-university social setting to remodel itself along these lines.

Hypotheses about innovation are closely allied to the factors already considered as determining recognition. The chances that an individual will innovate are improved when he expects to maximize values through innovation, and when demands upon the self are made by the self to make an innovative contribution. The probability of such an outcome is increased if the individual's capabilities (base values) support projects of innovation.

Examining a social context, we assert that the chances of innova-

---

[1] Kris's (1952) psychoanalytic theory of art can be generalized to account for significant factors in all creativity.

tion are improved if innovation is expected with high frequency to maximize values and if demands by the self upon the self are widely distributed. The probability of innovation is enhanced if the base values available individually and collectively are applied to foster innovative results.

We will review some categories of factors that combine within the context of an individual personality or within his environment, or within the whole context of a group, to foster innovation. (It need scarcely be reiterated that all propositions found here are hypothetical, pointing toward inquiry.)

It may be useful to glance at the broken-circle sketch in Figure 1, reversing the flow from the innovator to his environment, making it from the environment to the innovator.

A precipitating factor appears to be contrasting systems of expectation. These may be invented by an individual; but more typically contrasts are communicated from the environment. It may also be that the take-off point is a new observation that gets into the stream of experience and communication.

Historians are well aware of the widely ramifying consequences of the voyages of discovery and especially of the opening of the New World. Contextual maps were vastly enlarged not only in the spatial dimension but in every other. A well-known occasion of innovation is when peoples of diverse culture intermingle, as when the Roman Empire expanded its domain. Biologists speak of "hybrid vigor"; and presumably some innovations that occur must be attributed to whatever increase of basic capability results thereform.[2] More directly obvious is the effect of intermingling upon maps of knowledge. These maps are bound to contain differences of design; contradictions or omissions are challenging gaps in the coherency and inclusiveness of a configuration.

We recognize as particularly great those innovations which sketch a map that many others labor to fill in. We are cognizant that position in regard to such great innovations is a factor that affects the creativity of groups and individuals. Mathematical physicists who came after Einstein were exposed to a preliminary version of the natural order that transformed the direction of science. I recall a

[2] The role of men marginal to two or more cultures is set forth in detail in Barnett (1953).

seminar at the University of Berlin that included Einstein and Von Neumann, then in his twenties. Einstein would sometimes put an equation on the board and presently get tangled up. Von Neumann would go to the board and with great virtuosity put things in order. I recall the remark of a participant, "Of course Einstein is partly pre-Einsteinian; young Von Neumann has the good luck to be Einsteinian from the beginning."

There have been great shifts in the direction of creativity as a consequence of change in individual or group delimitations of the self. Often the efflorescence is released by a rather sudden conversion to a larger self. We are aware of the linguistic, literary, political, and legal results of nationalistic movements; and we have observed the liberating impact upon an individual who, formerly restricted to a parochial loyalty, is suddenly ablaze with the consciousness of his identity as an "Italian" or a "German" (Deutsch, 1953). Similarly we have had occasion to take note of the creative activity after conversion to a movement or an organization whose aspirations are universal, whether secular or sacred. The transformations, of course, are not invariably from the lesser to the larger. The changeover in the self-system can be from the universality of communism to the more parochial nation; or from the nation to a neighborhood or family. (Shifts of identity are usually preceded by an inner conflict in which the older symbols of identification are stigmatized as a source of deprivation.)

When we examine the comparative history of innovation we observe that a shift in value ranking usually releases a flood of novelties. In a business society such as ours we see this process on a gigantic scale during war crises and wars, when social assets are deliberately employed to encourage ingenuity in the improvement of weapons, tactics, and strategies of destruction (Nef, 1950). A changeover in emphasis from wealth to power serves to focus attention upon new ways and means of obtaining social rewards. After wars there has typically been a prompt return to the former ordering of values.

The transformations that we have mentioned in expectation, value demand, and identification can often be tied to shifting environmental magnitudes of a given order. More precisely, innovation appears to be favored by the challenge of proportionate, not disproportionate, value changes in the environment. Once more, we do not insist upon an unvarying sequence; on the contrary, the crucial transformation in perspective may occur with no discernible precipitating occurrence in the environment. The present generalization is that great extremes of value indulgence or deprivation provide an environment unfavorable to the release of creativity, either because adversity overwhelms the persons concerned, or because the result of superindulgence is to remove incentives to make a significant innovation. We speak of the optimum range as "proportionate"; extremes of indulgence or deprivation are "disproportionate."

Systematic study of the impact of proportionate change calls for an examination of all categories of participants in the social process. Toynbee (1934–1954), among others, has partly characterized the history of cultures in such terms. Within each culture the position of every value class and institution (upper, middle, lower) can be so analyzed. So, too, can interest groups and personality systems. The hypothesis of proportionate change specifically relates to what we have called a middle-level of crisis.

The previous proposition has enough intuitive and scientific support to encourage attempts to refine it. But it is not to be assumed that an environmental impact of a given magnitude will necessarily exert the same degree of effect upon creativity. This depends upon current predispositions; and we must allow for the variable influence of disproportionate predispositions upon the outcome. If you and I were convinced that we would die tomorrow (an "extreme" deprivation) our creativity today would undoubtedly be affected. In the famous case of the French mathematician Evariste Galois, who allowed himself to be goaded into a duel with a political enemy in the turbulent year 1832, we have a spectacular instance of a threat that released the floodgates of creativity. All night before the duel, Galois, who was twenty years of age, wrote his last will and testament. As Bell (1937) put it, "What he wrote in those desperate last hours before the dawn will keep generations of mathematicians busy for hundreds of years." It may be doubted that as yet we have the tools that enable us to describe which predispositions, proportionate or disproportionate, will respond creatively to environmental challenges of great magnitude.

When we focus intensively upon the innovative process in any social setting we become aware of the phenomena of *resonators* and *dampers*.

In particular we are impressed by the peculiarly resonant relationship that successful innovators, at least, set up with individuals in their social environment. Similarly, although the means to which people resort in defeating themselves are devious and subtle, we suspect that potentially significant innovators are often stunted through lack of a friend to play the resonating role, and through dependence upon an environment only too willing to exert a dampening influence. Sometimes the identity of the resonators changes rather rapidly through the years; they may overlap; occasionally they create a small interstimulating cell of more than two.

Often the partner is an affectionate, admiring, and infinitely patient audience, playing the role of a wide-eyed younger sibling, and offering no discernible addition to the incessant flood of ideas that pour forth by free and semicontrolled association. Such a voluntarily captive audience was afforded to Adolf Hitler at one period by an age mate from the same village (Kubizek, 1955). The partner frequently performs a nursing role for the innovative person, looking after his physical needs like an all-providing mother. This is the part that wives or mistresses have so often played in the lives of creative figures. In our civilization the creative person in many lines is often an economic dependent, as Van Gogh was upon his brother, from whom he received affection and respect as well. We note, too, the conflicts, inner and outer, that the innovator may experience when his thoughts violate some ethical or religious norm. In this case a chosen intimate may provide reassurances of rectitude and absolution from guilt. If the public authorities are involved and legal issues are raised, the chosen one may be the person able and willing to stand off the threat for some time, if not indefinitely. (Galileo's life [de Santillana, 1955] is of interest in this connection.)

The greatest of all boons to an innovator is a person of kindred skill and range of enlightenment who approaches the status of a full intellectual collaborator. The variations that occur in this category of relationships cover an enormous range. Often the collaborator is a teacher who welcomes superior potentiality even when the student is "conceited, with an insufferable affectation of originality," as one teacher said of Galois (Bell, 1937). Freud's partial dependence upon the attention, encouragement, and ideas of Professor Fliess at a critical period in the growth of psychoanalysis is now documented. Karl Marx's intellectual relationship to Friedrich Engels is sometimes underestimated; Marx's economic dependence upon this remarkably generous provider is well known. In the case of the Curies we have a full-fledged collaboration; so, too, in the remarkably intense, relatively brief, and phenomenally productive-destructive association between Paul Verlaine and Arthur Rimbaud.

A recurring feature of the innovator's relationship to his social setting is the growth of a circle of "apostles," of students and collaborators. The newly emerging perspective or device may be in a primitive state at first, so that if it were exposed to general evaluation in conventional terms it would come off badly and drive the innovator into sterile disputation or despair. The withdrawal into an esoteric circle makes it possible to consolidate the new departure and to improve the chances of survival.

An *ecology of innovation* would enable us to predict the routes along which novelties would originate in a social context, together with the principal centers and zones of innovation. Changes of perspective in this context are by-products of moving people to new places, changing the function of people in old places, and multiplying the flow of messages among people in all places.

A detailed inquiry into any society or any value-institutional specialization would require an examination of the *facilitating* or *inhibiting* impact of every specific practice. It is out of the question here to do more than remind one of the continuing survey, or self-appraisal, that is needed to provide proper guidance for policy and ample challenge for science. (See again the social process map.)

PATTERNS OF INNOVATION

A science of innovation will go beyond the knowledge of who, occupying what position in the social context, will innovate; it will raise the question of what the innovation will be.

As a step in this direction it is necessary to classify the fundamental patterns of innovation. We have indicated before that an innovation can be seen as an act of completion which reorganizes a chaotic, inconsistent, or sketchy configuration.

The most original innovations make explicit a previously unassembled contour. Most innovations fulfill an already assembled contour. We may classify psychoanalysis or quantum theory among the former. In regard to psychoanalysis it is possible to show that Freud was thoroughly acquainted with the seemingly inconsistent contemporary conceptions of neurophysiology and clinical psychology (including hypnosis), and that the clinical feebleness of these tools drew attention to the omissions in the map of reality at hand. We know, too, that in all probability Freud had been exposed to some literary anticipations of the technique of free association, and that, since he had presumably read Plato, he was not unexposed to the idea of a sexually tinted unconscious apparent in dreams. The procedures and formulations of psychoanalysis make articulate connections among features of the map of knowledge in ways not achieved before. This was an act of completion in which a hitherto unassembled contour was made explicit.

Within an articulated contour, innovations move in three directions: they *particularize*, *universalize*, or *equalize*. A contour is particularized, for example, when the Darwinian view of natural selection is explored and largely confirmed in more detail; or when Communist doctrine is elaborated into a legal system expressly designed to carry it out. An original contour may be universalized to the extent that it is extended to include categories of phenomena beyond the context to which it originally applied. The biological theory of "speciation," for instance, may purportedly be generalized to include the rise and fall of cultures or nonspecies groups. Finally, innovations equalize the original contour with other patterns. Champions of a scientific theory, for example, may try to show that it covers certain phenomena as competently as rival systems. An economist may demonstrate that John Maynard Keynes's theory of the structural causes of unemployment is as capable of accounting for inflation as the classical theory. When the innovation is a material object the point may be to demonstrate by use that a pen, in addition to keeping its shape when frozen in the refrigerator or broiled in the oven or run over by a truck, will also write as well as any other pen.

What clues do we have to the constellation of factors that make for one or another of these major outcomes? Particularization, perhaps, is the easiest to grasp. We expect that innovative talent in a social context will fill in the details of contours which are explicitly recognized, and which pass unchallenged; and in which value indulgences are given to those who work faithfully within the established frame.[3]

Consider universalization first in reference to evaluative systems. Many religious and political movements have gone through a *universalizing* phase in which the inevitability of world dominion has been affirmed, celebrated and justified. This calls for more ingenuity than the relatively simple application of a theological or legal system to a particular problem of order internal to its domain. Universalization flourishes when the prospects of acceptance of an innovation are believed to be good. There is, however, another extreme; if individuals and groups are utterly impotent in the social context they withdraw into the elaboration of all-embracing myths.

Innovation takes the path of equalization when rival patterns are prominent and when the prospects of obtaining general acceptance for one's pattern are regarded as low. The universal pretensions of religious or political systems typically fade away when they confront one another for a long time and appear to make little progress toward superseding the other. Accommodation takes the form of treating the universal claim in ritual fashion, and in developing the equivalency of the systems. This is usually accomplished by ingenious thinkers who strengthen the weak spots of the original ideology.

When do great novelties come into being? Evaluative innovations, that is, striking new religious, ethical, critical, or political doctrines, are favored by highly polemical settings in which established norms are under attack. Such a situation is typically found where the level of crisis is high, and contributes to it.

It appears, on the other hand, that scientific theories of a novel kind are comparatively independent of dialectics and respond to the presence of glaring inconsistencies in the image of Nature. The disjunction between "waves" and "particles" challenged the most alert minds in physics (Planck, 1949), and the seeming inconsistency between therapy by chemicals and therapy by communication (hypnosis) kept the "mind-body" problem alive in the psychological and psychiatric field.

When we look closely at the innovating process we see that existing

[3] Particularizing a contour often displays cyclical patterns, as in Kroeber's (1957) famous case of fashions in women's clothes. The limits are set by conceptions of rectitude governing the extremes of bodily exposure, and by considerations of convenience and safety in locomotion.

patterns are partially incorporated and partially rejected. A new development necessarily rejects some present features.

Can we improve our anticipation and understanding of innovation by analyzing all the significant contours to be found in a given social context as a whole, or in selected situations within it?[4] By considering in advance a range of environmental changes, can we predict innovations? Besides collecting the contour patterns, it will be necessary to note omissions and inconsistencies and the expectations of value maximization associated with degree of probable diffusion and restriction. If we are successful it should be possible to locate the centers, routes, and zones where innovations of a given kind will occur.

I shall use a macroscopic case to indicate possible lines of inquiry. The reference is to rival political doctrines in world politics. Suppose that an analysis had been made of the probable lines of development on a world scale shortly after the Moscow seizure of power in 1917 during the October Revolution. One contingency open to examination would have been that the new regime would establish itself in the former domain of the Russian Empire. Presumably such an assumption would have gone along with the expectation that the political forces which blocked the worldwide diffusion of the new order would nevertheless undergo some changes. What would these changes be?

Suppose we begin by describing the main features of the symbol system of the new political myth. In grossly simplified form it might have been characterized as universal in scope of authority demanded, democratic in preferred pattern of political life, socialist (communist) in economic program, proletarian in main symbol of identification. Each key symbol would figure in doctrinal statements with varying degrees of elaboration.

Let us now consider the probable working of defense by partial incorporation and partial rejection (Lasswell, 1950). Disregarding for the moment the as yet unimportant "race" symbol (c. 1917) we might have thought of the following: "International" will be rejected (along with "proletarian"), and there may well be conflict over the claim to "democracy." The "proletarian dictatorship" is likely to put

---

[4] If we locate the contours we may even predict that the corresponding innovation will be made by several individuals at the same time. Gilfillan (1935) has discussed the phenomenon of concurrent invention.

the effective practice of democracy in the shadow, making it plausible to reject the "democratic" symbol and to assert that a "despotism" or a "tyranny" is in power.

"National" is the most available counterpoise to "international" (a reaffirmation of a predisposition); and "national" (and "democratic people's") may be teamed with "socialism," "communism," or "capitalism" against "international" and "despotic" "socialism," "communism," or "capitalism."

We return to "racism" once more because this turned out to be the most creative political doctrine after World War I. The language of the French Revolutionary wave (1789–) had been "political" in color; that of the Russian Revolution rejected "politics" for "economics." "Racism" was also a functional differentiation from what had gone before. By what methods might we have anticipated the role of this doctrine in the world arena?

THE TOTAL PROCESS OF CREATIVITY

The foregoing outline of creativity has proposed that the process be viewed as a confluent stream of innovation and recognition. We have spoken of the many determiners—let us label them (K)—that work toward creativity and the determiners (K—), or anti-K, that tend to inhibit either innovation or recognition. Our examination of perspectives, roles, and structures within a social context has emphasized the multiplicity of factors involved. The analysis has shown why creativity is to be expected at the *nuclear* centers of culture rather than the *peripheral* centers (Childe, 1954; Harrison, 1954). As in Vienna, cultural centers provide a rich stock of uncompleted contours, whether assembled or not, and a high incidence of awareness and positive evaluation of the creative act itself. We have indicated how the chances of individual creativity are increased by various events in the individual's context of subjectivity; how the likelihood that such events will occur is improved if such events are widely distributed throughout the community; how creative *linkages* are most probable among members of a social context of similar civilization, class, interest, personality, and level of crisis exposure.

Can we, indeed, conduct a selective and continuing survey of the distribution of predispositions to establish such linkages in both the recognition and innovation wings of the total process of creativity in a given social context? This, at least, is the challenge.

14

Creativity in Cross-cultural Perspective

MARGARET MEAD

In drawing upon anthropological materials from many different primitive cultures, we are seeking not for models but for relationships between the forms provided by a culture and the creativity of the individuals within the culture, upon which statements of regularities may be based. It is possible of course to establish some sort of hierarchical arrangement within which Culture A may be said to have more creative products—art, music, architecture, drama, science—than does Culture B. But in doing so, our criteria would be those of product, not process, and in a symposium primarily devoted to the question of mental health it is the process of individual creativity—inso far as it is relevant to mental health—that must concern us.

I shall use the term mental health to include both absence of crippling, preventable[1] mental illness and presence of active fulfillment of individual potentialities, with full recognition that neither of these conditions is at present more than an undefinable aspiration. I shall use the term creativity as a statement of process in the indi-

[1] One might of course assay a culture in terms of what role it gives to the congenitally disabled, but this would take us too far afield for this discussion. It should be remembered, however, that the degree of dignity given the handicapped and disabled—the blind, those with epilepsy, with cerebral palsy—may be used as one measure of the state of a culture. But here one must take into account the level of technology and knowledge, and it is unrewarding to try to compare the way a savage tribe handles one blind person with education of the blind to read Braille, for the difference in the achieved position of the handicapped is so heavily dependent upon the state of invention.

vidual; to the extent that a person makes, invents, thinks of something that is new to him, he may be said to have performed a creative act. From this point of view the child who rediscovers in the twentieth century that the sum of the square of the hypotenuse of a right angle triangle equals the sum of the squares of the two other sides, is performing as creative an act as did Archimedes, although the implications of the discovery for cultural tradition is zero, since this proposition is already a part of geometry (Huxley, 1924). Similarly, the child who happens upon some solution of a problem of perspective without having any sense of having learned this from the advertisements in the subway or the calendar in the kitchen may experience the full excitement of creativity and may indeed be giving a demonstration of great ability.

In making such a judgment, however, we are not considering the relative greatness of Archimedes and of the enquiring child, a question that would have to include some measurement of the difference between the imaginative leaps it was necessary to take when geometry was a matter for the speculation of the few and those necessary after it had become embodied in the construction of every article of material culture that a child encountered. If we were to engage in this sort of enquiry we should be discussing the problem of talent and ultimately of genius, which would again take us a little far from the question of mental health.[2]

So, looking at a number of cultures, we may ask: How is the problem of individual creativity handled? Which individuals, under what circumstances, have an opportunity to experience creativity? I use the word experience advisedly, because there are contexts in which the individual may be creative, but because this creativity is unrecognized, unnamed, and unrewarded, the full experience, which may be crucial from the standpoint of mental health, is missing.

When the new knowledge of psychoanalysis first led us to consider problems of creativity within a setting provided by the study of mental illness and mental aberration, the first questions we asked were prompted by very general use of the ideas of compensation and

---

[2] It should be recognized, however, that a society's ability to utilize the special talents of those born within it may, in the end, affect the mental health of every individual in the society, to the extent that unused talents may be destructive of the individual himself, of his associates and of the larger society. "Lilies that fester smell far worse than weeds." —Shakespeare, Sonnet XCIV.

sublimation. Thus, when I studied the Samoans in 1925, I described in considerable detail how their culture included provision for compensatory reversal of role—the tiniest child, usually the least in the group, beginning the dance, and a place being made in the dance even for the crippled and the mad (Mead, 1928a). The dance was seen as an area of culture within which the relative positions of child and adult, high status and low status, even sane and mad, could be reversed—an area of self-expression and creativity. This is an attitude which is still very much a part of Western thinking; we talk of how regimented children and adults are, most of the time, and we then seek to find areas in which they are free—the word is important—to create. Significantly enough, we equate these areas of freedom to areas of unimportance, in one way or another; thus, they are hobbies or amateur activities; or, in the case of those whom we recognize as artists or scientists, we may still talk about freedom from ordinary demands of everyday life as a necessary condition of being creative. Areas of creativity are counterpointed, as it were, to areas of real life where creativity is inappropriate, and only maintaining and sustaining activities are called for.

In looking at the Samoans—not only at their dance but also at the elaborations of rhetoric used by their orators and the designs painted on barkcloth by the women—I was also struck with the relationships between degree of originality and social reward. Again against the background of our own ideas, which separate so widely the product of a great imagination from all other activity, I could see that the dancer whom the Samoans applauded as having a genuine individual style had made only the most minute change in a style which was shared by all, and that the orator's turn of phrase or the barkcloth maker's variation in design was really perpetuating stability of style rather than making for innovation and change. It seemed clear, even then, that if each individual were permitted to feel that the slightest change was in fact creative, something could happen to the impulse to make major changes. Those areas to which creativity seemed most appropriate would actually be, when considered as expressions of style or as art forms, static and relatively unchanging (Mead, 1928b).

This observation threw light on the tendency of critics of Western culture to sentimentalize those cultures in which traditional arts were found to flourish as being cultures in which creativity was greater.

The critics mistook their delight in a culture in which the form of the house, the grace of the dance, the simple, pleasing, repetitive designs on barkcloth, and the slightly varied speeches of the orators together made a pattern, for meaningfulness of the details to the people themselves.

Rather it is possible to say that a culture like that of Samoa neither developed sharp individual needs to create something new nor provided the conditions within which some individuals would be driven to break a pattern which was too firm and too demanding. The style was there to hold each performer in place, to assure success if one had only mastered it properly, to provide for each slightest innovation, and to reward these so lavishly that the desire for future change might be said to have been stilled. Such a culture probably assures the greatest degree of mental health in its members, rearing them without deep and unsatisfied urges to make the world over, giving them from childhood a chance to make it new for a few minutes on the dance floor or by weaving a slightly different kind of necklace of flowers and shells. Samoan children and adults have a continuing small delight in living, and they can watch without boredom, night after night, performances that seem to the foreign eye pleasant but extraordinarily repetitive and tedious.

Another repercussion of Freudian thinking and of the general educational outlook of the 1920's was the emphasis upon creativity as something natural to childhood, which if only given freedom would blossom into works of great beauty. Small children were given crayons and paints, and when they produced what they felt to be acts of creation, these were hailed as works of art. We were then confronted with the spectacle of the gifted five-year-old weeping bitter tears over her failure to draw a human face: "What is the use of being called 'the best artist in nursery school' if I can't draw what I want to draw!" (Mead, 1931b).

This approach to small children almost completely discounted the importance of style—that style which gave each Samoan child, no matter how small and shy, a framework within which to move beautifully before the eyes of the beholder. It was during this period that I studied the Manus children of the Admiralties, children of a people who bought and sold the art work of their neighbors but who were not artists themselves (Mead, 1930). I collected some 32,000 children's drawings, in which the only traces of beauty were those of rhythm—the one aesthetic element in their parents' lives. But the Manus children drew with greater eagerness than the Samoan children. The life they led was free and untrammeled, but so empty of content, so filled with running and swimming, diving and wrestling, or making the identical string figure again and again, that they welcomed a chance to take a pencil or crayon and draw the same man over and over and over instead. Their individual versions of a rapidly established group style—which was as definite as it was empty of aesthetic appeal—became fixed and stereotyped, and twenty-five years later, when I asked grown men who had not drawn since I left Manus, in 1928, to draw for me, their work styles were still recognizable as that of Nauna or Loponiu or Pomat. It was clear that freedom alone was not enough to provide for more than an initial creative effort, which then became as repetitious as the string figures.

The importance of some kind of style for even the slightest creativity was reinforced by a study of the Arapesh culture of New Guinea (Mead, 1935, 1938). The Arapesh were a people who felt themselves unable to accomplish as much as their neighbors. They made unornamented net bags; their neighbors made patterned ones. They knew how to haft a spear-point to an uncarved shaft; their neighbors carved beautiful shafts. Their language itself, although complex in structure, with thirteeen genders, provided two mutually incompatible ways for absorbing foreign words, classified either by sound or as foreign words (Mead, 1950). Children were taught the language, bit by bit, "What is that?" "That is a mosquito" (aul), one aul; many (using an indeterminate plural to make the point) agu. Likewise, the names of the herbs used for each ceremony were taught singly, without any generalization or any opportunity to see a pattern. Ideas were so unformalized that the imagination was left very free, and if a child or adult wished to remark that the moon had come up that night to pay back the light of the pressure lamp we had just lit, no one objected. One could if one wished assign a different reason for the moon's rising every night; people would give a momentary amused attention, and then the little fancy died forever. With an occasional burst of ambition, an Arapesh man might decide to try to make something—a carved wooden plate, an ornamental bark belt—that was normally imported from far away. Without any respect for the skill and discipline that had gone into the imported object, he would attempt to reproduce it. People would comment casually: "Wutue is trying to make a belt." The belt would be a sorry failure, and no more belts would be made. The low self-esteem of the people, as a people incapable of doing what their brighter and more gifted neighbors did, was a poorer general setting for mental health than was the Samoan delighted slight inventiveness within a pattern of which they were proud. So the study of the Arapesh material added to my sense of the importance of form, within which the impulse to make something new could be channeled and given meaning.

In the 1930's visitors began bringing back accounts of the island of Bali, where every man was a musician, every woman an artist in making offerings, where people enjoyed rehearsals as much as performances—a paradise pleasing to every sense. Students of the various arts, Covarrubias (1942), de Zoete and Spies (1938), McPhee (1936), Belo (1935), wrote vivid descriptions of the continuous involvement of the Balinese in the practice of their arts. When the process by which the Balinese child became thus involved was studied in detail (Bateson and Mead, 1942; Bateson 1943) it was found that the child was subjected to continuous frustration in human relationships, particularly in relation to his mother; each sequence of relatedness was broken just before a climax was reached, and the child's feeling was turned back upon itself. But the child, teased and stimulated to a response which would then be broken off, driven to tears and desperation, was also presented with a rich and varied world of art, in which it began to participate before it could walk, learning to dance while an infant in arms, playing a xylophone before it could stand on its own, watching from a witchlike mother's arms the witch in the play being attacked but never really dying. As in Samoa, the emphasis in Bali is on slight innovation within a well-developed pattern; but the style is enormously more elaborate, drawing as it does on the rich traditions of India, Southeast Asia, and China (Belo, 1949). There is a place for straight improvisation within each form, represented by the clowns in the theatre, the carvings of kitchen gods made of wood that will soon rot, the way in which a play is given or an orchestral piece is performed. All these permitted the exercise of individual creativeness; they were appraised by an audience whose highest flattery was to stay and watch, an audience who never applauded but could easily burst into jeering laughter. The Balinese delight in the old form and in the new twist to the old form was as persistent as the Samoans', but it was no mild delight in the repetition of something lightly loved, rather, it was a preoccupation with problems of aesthetic performance. Whereas the Samoan dance was true folk performance, in Bali all dancers were professional, trained and criticized, never simply accepted because of their membership in some group or of their good intentions (Bateson, 1944; Mead, 1941, 1942).

If the Balinese are considered psychiatrically, they manifest a high degree of the kind of behavior which we associate with schizophrenia. They are withdrawn, fall into benign stupors when frightened or under strain, avoid close relationships with other people. People whose performances on tests are indistinguishable from those of individuals in our mental hosiptals are functioning members of their communities who are married, have children, and engage in some artistic activity. The forms provided by the culture are elaborate enough to encompass the feeling that is given so little outlet in human relationships. These forms are stylized in such a way that every person can perform well some part of a complex activity, can play the simplest instrument, weave the simplest container, dance in the chorus, carve the conventional costumes on the statues on temple gates. The delight in slight innovation and the stylistic provision for it—as in the role of the clowns in the theater who are expected always to make new jokes—gives a setting for creativity. Each individual can find a place for his talent, however slight, where it will seem to be part of a living new whole (McPhee, 1944; Mead, 1955; Belo, 1955).

When the Balinese are contrasted with the Samoans, in simple mental-health terms, the Samoans would probably be placed higher. They have been stimulated to desire no new beauty, to search for no new knowledge which their culture does not immediately and fully provide. In a sense the Balinese also have a culture which provides what they have, in childhood, learned to seek—art forms within which they can become deeply distant from the trying contacts of everyday life (McPhee, 1955). But the detachment that underlies the complex joking of the clown, the twisted fantasies of the little kitchen gods which mix man and animal in horrible ways and torment and distort the human form, has been learned at a greater price. And the Balinese often knew what the Samoans hardly ever experienced, an

overwhelming boredom. Their response both as creators and as spec-
tators seems to have included too many defenses against their own
disallowed personal feeling, to have been used for purposes other than
those of pure delight, for which the art forms, like tranquilizers or
stimulants, became insufficient and therefore required change. The
restless desire for change in Bali, although it kept the music fresh, the
traditional drama ever new, and gave the gifted individual a chance
to exercise his creativity, is based upon a kind of child rearing that
would perhaps be disastrous for the individual if the art forms were
not there.

The theory of Balinese creativity, as we developed it in Bali in the
late 1930's and early 1940's, was still oriented toward a psychoanalytic
model of human development, on the one hand, and an interest in
the style and artistic achievement in the culture, on the other. The
work of the 1950's, especially the work of Margaret Lowenfeld (1958)
and Edith Cobb (1959) has provided us with some new questions to
which to submit our cross-cultural materials.

This new work emphasizes the need of the growing child to respond creatively to his relationship to himself and to the universe in
which he lives, and this need is seen as comparable to the needs for
air, food, water, and sleep essential for the organism's functioning.
Edith Cobb has emphasized what she has called "the cosmic sense"
and the extent to which each human individual has to attain, in an
ecological relationship to the universe around him, something which
may be treated as speciation—comparable to what a whole species of
birds or beasts establishes phylogenetically. Margaret Lowenfeld has
stressed the distortion that arises when the child's inner image of the
world, based on its own body, especially its proprioceptive system,
fails to be brought into a four-dimensional relationship with the
world around it. The question that is asked in cultural terms is no
longer one of simple relationship between instinctive expressions of
interpersonal needs, as in the resolution of the Oedipus situation, in
which culture is seen as a form within which essentially antisocial
tendencies are tamed—with more or less success. Instead, we can ask
about balance, in each and every individual reared in particular ways,
between the proprioceptive and distance-perceptive systems, and
about the forms which the culture provides for maintaining such a
balance (Mead, 1952). Seen from this point of view, Arapesh culture

permits a little more urgent desire for form to develop in the child than the outlets which the culture provides; there is a residue of insignificant, unrewarding creativity, and in the gifted individual, a tension that has no creative outlet. When I presented the Rorschach protocol of my most gifted and imaginative informant to Rorschach specialists here, they were undecided as to whether or not to account him dangerously maladjusted (Mead, 1949). Actually, he was so completely a member of a culture low in any form of expressiveness that recently, Hunt (n.d.), writing about the lack of "real love" among savages, could select as an example my informant's account of an affair with his brother's wife. In finishing his Rorschach, Unabelin said:

Well! There are many things here. Some like ghosts, some like dreams, some like *marsalais*.[3] Some like rotten pig, some like cassowaries that have rotted, some like the things a man sees when he is mad: evil things appear then. Some like the things a man sees when he is in the hands of sorcerers, some like the corpses of men which have rotted away, some like clouds, red clouds, blue clouds, and the sky when rain is coming up, and some like façades[4] of the ceremonial houses of the Plains people.

This was all the formal substance his culture provided for the expression of an eager curiosity, a deep and intense appreciation of the poignancy and drama of life.

As the Arapesh furnish an illustration of a culture lacking in forms to meet individual needs to perceive and make sense of the surrounding world, Unabelin provided a further illustration of the individual gifted by temperament far beyond the forms his culture supplied. There were no cultural forms through which he could express this discrepancy; for such men as he, a higher degree of suspiciousness about the sorcery of their neighbors, a greater degree of sensitivity to insult or neglect were the only channels for that greater intensity.

Samoa contrasts with Arapesh in that the growing child is provided with forms easy to master, pleasing and complete, requiring no extreme emotional experience to give them meaning. The child is encouraged to ask no questions, to strive for no new meaning; it is discouraged from being in any way outstanding or precocious; and, at the same time, beautiful, flowing, formal words are ready for its lips

[3] Supernaturals who sometimes took the form of serpents.
[4] Elaborate, painted, repetitive semi-anthropomorphic designs.

and graceful dance steps for its feet. No frightening or repelling experiences throw the child back upon itself to sharpen and distort the impressions received from its own body, no hands reach out to stretch its capabilities beyond the lowest limit. The amount of creativity which such a child needs is there, every day, every evening, for the asking. But the Samoans make no contribution to the world beyond that of being—an art form in themselves, untranslatable, noncumulative.

We may see the Manus as a people who developed in their children a need for activity of mind greater than the culture fulfilled; the child's attention was directed outward, with a demand for the child to master the world around him, swim, climb, name, count, fish, and for a corresponding inattention to introspection and fantasy. This learned habit of activity without imagination again lacked balance. It produced a people very ready to change, caught in no self-rewarding circle like that of the Samoans, but eager to fill up a vacuum in their lives. Their creativity was in their willingness to take a new path, try a new method (Mead, 1931a).

This then is one way of classifying cultures; those whose members' creativity lies in faithful reproduction with only sight innovations in a traditional form, like the Samoans'; those whose members' creativity lacks form and flounders in helpless ineffectuality in the present, like that of the Arapesh; and those, who lack form but have developed a restless seeking, a reaching-out for the new, like the Manus so that they become not the inheritors of tradition but the willing originators of forms of which they are virtually ignorant.

Anthropological investigations have gone on long enough so that re-studies are possible of the ways in which these different forms of culturally induced creativity are now expressed in the modern world (Mead, 1959). The Samoans are suffering today from overpopulation; well-adjusted, contented, they have bred far beyond the resources of their small islands. As they responded to the new cultural ideas brought to them from the West, these were assimilated into the pleasant, mild round of their way of life. Chastity was a requirement for church members, so one became a church member after marriage; prayers, even of deep repentance, were public exercises in graceful oratory. The intensity of each innovation was reduced to fit the existing cultural style; there was no movement out, no plan for some

Samoans to become part of the wider world. Today, forced out, they are discontented and unadjusted, lost without their pleasant round of slight expressiveness, and, especially in the New Zealand Trust Territory, Samoans who remain have turned toward an aggressive nativism, "Samoa for the Samoans." The system which seemed so well devised to reduce conflict and provide a charming, if culturally nonproductive, way of life proved successful for absorbing foreign ideas, but not for adaptation to a wider social system.

The Manus, on the other hand, who, thirty years ago appeared to be so aggressive, so overactive, so empty of imagination, with their children's well-stimulated desire for intelligent activity petering out in rough-and-tumble games or in the 200th drawing of the same scene, have been able to turn their restless dissatisfaction into a whole new system (Mead, 1955; Schwartz, 1958). The form of their new way of life, with its paraphernalia of modern democracy, was provided by the imagination of a leader, Paliau, of the little island of Baluan, who was not a Manus. Thus, twenty-five years ago Baluan stood out as a society more interested in the arts and graces of life than that of the grim, energetic, practical Manus. Paliau planned this new way in which Manus life was to be modeled on the life of the white man, and the Manus, village by village, eagerly participated. Where before in one village one or two houses a year had been built, fifty were built in a few weeks. There was a great burst of creative energy in this ability to inaugurate a new social system, which was felt to be both based on a foreign model—that of the white man and especially of the American—and also "something that really belongs to us, ourselves, we, the South Coast Manus."

The Balinese, no longer a colony but part of the Republic of Indonesia, face a different problem. Their system, like that of the Samoans, was a closed one, a delicate adjustment between spectator and performer, between the supply of originality and the demand for originality. Under the old system, most artists most of the time did traditional work, but there was room to express new ideas, either by slight changes in the more serious forms, as in sculptures of gods, or by riotous originality in the less serious forms, such as the kitchen gods and the masks and antics of the clowns. No man was goaded to originality, and the Balinese believed that too great success was bad for any artist; a man did better when he cultivated his rice fields by day, and at night or on special feast days played in the orchestra, danced in the theater, or carved the temple gate.

A tourist demand for Balinese artistic products began in the 1930's; dances were shortened and adapted to the tourist audience from the big ships; the same carvings of girls with high headdresses and boys with twisted headcloths were made over and over again. The level of execution was lowered for these repetitious works. At the same time the European premium upon originality began to affect the Balinese through a sophisticated high-level club formed under the patronage of European artists, which accepted original works of art—carvings and paintings—to be sent abroad or to be sold for high prices.

After World War II, the Balinese were confronted by a new kind of tourist, not the former European and American patron of alien arts but the recently educated Indonesian or Chinese clerk on a holiday, interested less in style or form than in sensation. And the carver and the painter—particularly the carver—were presented with an insatiable world market for "original" Balinese products. No longer sufficient were mass-produced "heads of dancing girls," which could be turned out repeatedly with the same dreamy, slight involvement characteristic of the old traditional carving. Artists must now be original, and so today each artist copies himself and half-a-dozen less "original" artists copy him, in order to supply the curio shops of the world. The slight originality which once satisfied the exuberant creativity which expressed itself mainly in the reproduction of traditional forms, in playing old music in a new way, has been overstrained and cheapened. The dilemma of the Balinese today presents dramatically the paradox of identifying creativity with originality—with product rather than with process (Mead, 1958).

We are here brought back to process, although it has been necessary in discussing the light that cross-cultural studies can throw on the problems of creativity to introduce product after all. If we are to evaluate any system of balance between the way in which individuals are reared—including the forms their culture offers them for creativity—and mental health, we shall find that the kind of balance that may look mentally healthy in one situation may in twenty-five years be altered and the balance be lost, and a state that looked less mentally healthy may be in fact healthier. This suggests that we need to know a great deal more about the kinds of balance and imbalance which can be maintained, in differently endowed children, between traditional forms for the imagination, opportunities for rediscovery and originality, and degrees of essential dissatisfaction (Mead, 1952).

We need to know more about the consequences of reliance upon psychologically adequate cultural forms—whether ballet or baseball, embroidery or do-it-yourself tile-laying, tennis or bowling, or reliance on the slight, ephemeral satisfaction of painting a bad picture, writing a bad poem, or composing a poor piece of music. We need to know not only how these forms make children more at home with themselves and the world and can give contrapuntal meaning to over-mechanized modern life but also what kind of adults such children become. Barzun (1956) has suggested that a nation so busy playing music that it has no time to listen and produce composers may provide an ideal audience when the composer arises. Being called the "best artist in nursery school" may be a road to becoming a painter. Giving each child a set of ready-made images and clichés through which to view the world may effectively reduce a need for new creativity among all but the most gifted. In the light of these questions and these hypotheses cross-cultural material is suggestive, but it does not provide answers.

Above all, we need research to show the difference between the sense of discovery or of creativity and the quality of the discovery or the creativity. We take for granted, without grounds for this belief, that the effect on a child of discovering something that is mathematically true will be different in kind from the pseudo discovery of something that is not true. But is this so? And we take even less seriously the question of whether creating something that is aesthetically good is somehow more satisfying than creating something that is aesthetically bad. Granted that the determination of what is aesthetically good is fraught with tremendous complications—cultural, historical, and temperamental; it is still valid to ask whether such a writer as Poe got more or less satisfaction from writing a passage in which his obsession with a personal childhood trauma can be shown to be dominant than he did when he wrote verse less specifically compromised by his past (Bonaparte, 1949). It may be that there is no such correspondence, that the individual derives as much creative satisfaction from a discovery without truth value and a production without merit as from activities which, viewed against man's history, can be seen to be true and/or beautiful. In the context of evolution this seems an unlikely possibility, but it should be explored.

We may find that there is an intrinsic gain for the individual in re-creating forms and ideas that are already known. At the same time, there is an intrinsic gain for society as a whole in maintaining traditions of art and science in which only genuinely new contributions count. In the second case we shall need to develop new educational methods, in which children's guided rediscovery of known mathematical and scientific relationships is a reliable prelude to new discoveries. We shall also need to invent some method by which children who are themselves relatively ungifted in any artistic medium may be able to create forms which will satisfy their cosmic sense.

It is here that Margaret Lowenfeld's World Technique seems important. This is a form of therapeutic play in which the child—or adult—is presented with a tray of sand and water and with a large supply of small-scale models of "everything in the world," people, cattle, cars and planes, policemen, letter-boxes, bridges, trucks, wild animals, guns, and so on, and also with standard fantasy creatures such as witches, Red Indians, and dragons. Each child, working with these materials—in which the sand and water provide a fluid medium and the rest, fixed and solid, represent the intractability of both material world and culturally patterned fantasies—can present to himself and to the therapist or educator an original creation which relates him as a perceiving organism to the universe and to his own culture. By placing such activities in a definitely therapeutic or educational context, we avoid the degradation of art and science which permits a child to claim for slender, meager work the role of "best artist in nursery school," or to feel falsely proud and contemptuous of the past as he redoes the thinking of Archimedes. At the same time we may provide a medium through which each child may experience the kind of creativity most necessary to full development or, in the sense of this symposium, to mental health.

15

Creativity in Perspective

HAROLD H. ANDERSON

In examining the fourteen chapters on creativity, one notes a tremendous scope of coverage from seeing a rose to solving problems of world government. Historically, these authors take us from Genesis to Gamow and from the theoretical first explosion that sent stars spinning into space to a hypothetical projection of social evolution into infinity. Diversity was planned in the interdisciplinary character of the Symposia. Diversity was also hoped for in the relatively openended invitation to each of the contributors. Each author was thus free to make his own outline, select his own examples and documentation, and place his emphases where he would. It was therefore not expected that each author would cover the same topics or make the same points.

In spite of this freedom and the consequent diversity of treatment, the reader nevertheless gradually becomes aware of certain basic ideas, an essential unity, consistency, even unanimity running through this variety of perspectives on creativity.

A perceptible autobiographical note is found in each of the chapters. Perhaps this is necessarily so. There is little research to cite and hence few persons to quote. Each author was, moreover, asked to give us what *he* thinks. It is my judgment that as scientists they have written not only with originality and personal conviction but also with charm and occasionally with poetic candor.

In writing this concluding chapter I find myself in the several roles of participant, observer, questioner, and reviewer.

What are the characteristics of a creative person? Is creativity a process or a product, and what difference does it make how one regards it? What is the role of intuition, insight, inspiration, and just plain hard work in creativity? How do these authors regard the relation of the unconscious to the conscious in creativity? What is the relation of neurosis and mental health to creativity? What is the relation of intelligence and talent to creativity? Is creativity properly reserved for the genius, the person of "high level talent" in the arts or sciences? What is the range of activities included under creativity? What is the nature, function, and meaning of evaluation? How do these authors deal with the scientists' perennial problem of "scientific" criteria for creativity? What in the environment do these authors regard as related to creativity? What concern need we have with the developmental process from birth to death?

Whatever these authors can contribute toward answers must be regarded mainly as hypotheses or definitions. Many of the answers reflect assumptions out of which definitions are derived. There are no "right" definitions or "wrong" definitions. Our problem here is to understand the meaning which each author has tried to communicate and to search for clarity, consistency, and inconsistency.

CHARACTERISTICS OF THE CREATIVE PERSON

For Sinnott creativity is life itself. For Dow it is a way of life. For Anderson it is optimum growth in social interaction. For Maslow it is a maximum of self-actualizing. We could extend the range and fill in details with examples from the other authors. If creativity is a broad way of life, then the characteristics of the creative person would be those characteristics which describe a person in the full, vigorous adventure of living. Affection for an idea, absorption, concentration, intensity of encounter, peak experience, delight, ecstasy—such words are used by the authors of this volume in describing the creative experience.

These authors have departed from a long tradition in psychology and philosophy. They have questioned the separated meanings of cognition and learning on the one hand and the priority which these have been given over emotion, personality, and motivation on the other. Hilgard spoke of the totality of problem-solving. He said that the problem-solver is one and indivisible and that it is only the experimenter who chooses to abstract one or the other facet of the totality for study. He found personality variables were important, even in the solution of simple laboratory type problems that seemed almost purely "cognitive." In retrospect he reported that the personality studies opened up more useful leads than the learning studies.

Guilford began his research in creativity with studies of "higher thought processes" as related to originality and creativity. He now thinks "it is reasonable to suggest that the same operations and products apply in the area of social intelligence or empathy." Dow reported that in designing a house "the things that made this house good did not start with reason. Ideas seemed to come out of the blue and then were recognized as reasonable." May discussed at length the necessity of emotional involvement in creativity. Ecstasy, a "level of intensity of consciousness which occurs in the creative act . . . brings intellectual, volitional, and emotional functions into play altogether. . . . We cannot really see the object unless we have some emotional involvement with it." Stoddard, pointing out that most of school instruction is oriented about so-called cognitive learning, deplored the lack of opportunity for affect or personal involvement in the child's school experiences.

Other characteristics mentioned in these chapters are: desire to grow, capacity to be puzzled, awareness, spontaneity, spontaneous flexibility, adaptive flexibility, originality, divergent thinking, learning, openness to new experience, no boundaries, permeability of boundaries, yielding, readiness to yield, abandoning, letting go, being born every day, discarding the irrelevant, ability to toy with elements, change of activity, persistence, hard work, composition, decomposition, recomposition, differentiation, integration, being at peace with the world, harmony, honesty, humility, enthusiasm, integrity, inner maturity, self-actualizing, skepticism, boldness, faith, courage, willingnes to be alone, *I* see, *I* feel, *I* think, gust for temporary chaos, security in uncertainty, tolerance of ambiguity. These words or their synonyms and many others are representative of most of the chapters. They have practically no internal inconsistencies, and are offered by their authors as essentials of the creative process.

CREATIVE INTERACTING WITH PERSONS

The characteritics of the "creative person" listed above are not enough, by themselves, to represent the creative process as discussed in this collection of papers. In fact, some authors (for example, May and Anderson) question whether it is meaningful to continue talking about characteristics of "a creative person." Is there such a thing as a creative person? Or, are there creative processes, creative relatings in which persons are involved? Instead of: What are the characteristics of a creative person? would a more proper question be: What is the nature of the creative interacting between the person and his meaningful environment?

Is the English language adequate to describe what is out there for us to see? Three authors have mentioned specifically the difficulty of subject-object structure of our thinking which the English language imposes upon us. That is, if something is created, we are required to have something or someone that creates. Is the search for internal characteristics of the creative person, for personality traits, character traits, attitudes, a search for something that is not really there? Do we need to invent new concepts to communicate to each other what we think we see? Are we trying to describe something like a bridge which, by definition, must have two ends, but which, from our foggy perspective, seems to some of us to have only one end, with such traffic as there is going out, and to others to have two ends with two-way traffic going both ways? These authors have used many expressions to describe what the process of interacting seems to be.

May wrote, ". . . world is interrelated to the existing person at every moment. A continual dialectical process goes on between world and self, and self and world; one implies the other, and neither can be defined by omitting the other. This is why you can never localize creativity as a subjective phenomenon; you can never study it in terms simply of what goes on within the person. The pole of world is an inseparable part of the creativity of the given individual. As mentioned above, we cannot speak of a 'creative person'; we can only speak of a creative act. For what is occurring is always a process, a doing; specifically a process interrelating the person and his world."

Anderson discussed at length the two-way process of interrelating and used the term socially integrative behavior, a kind of circular behavior which he called the creative growth circle. He used such phrases as the confronting and free interplay of differences, the use of power with others, working with others, two-way communication, interweaving of differences, interrelating of spontaneities. "Learning in the interacting of persons is an activity-between. The infant cannot be separated from his environment, nor can he be considered separate from it. The infant is within the environment and the environment is within the infant."

Dow has diagramed the interrelatedness of individual rightness and social rightness which together constitute a way of life. He explained the dynamics of this relating in his discussion of action-reaction, ". . . the resultant of these two forces becomes greater than the original force. In other words, the original idea when confronted with the reaction, absorbs some of the reaction idea with its own and thereby makes the final idea a combination of ideas, which in truth is a new idea." An illustration of this action-reaction was the spontaneous production of a motion picture in which everyone participated.

Murray's dyadic examples illustrate creativeness where human relating is superordinate. In dyadic creativity, "we shall be dealing with two interdependent regions of imagination operating as a single system. Also, both members of the dyad will be endeavoring to translate their imaginations into actual, overt reciprocations and collaborations. It will be like two people singing a duet and making up the music as they go along."

Eyring gave examples of fruitful interaction among scientists in the chemistry laboratories. In a broader social context Lasswell referred to the occasion of innovation when peoples of diverse cultures intermingle. He reminded us that biologists speak of "hybrid vigor."

Fromm expressed the interrelating of self and others in different words. He called attention to the unity or oneness but expressed it with an emphasis on the outgoing response: "To respond in a realistic sense means that I respond with my real human power, that of suffering, of joy, of understanding, to the reality of the 'object' which experiences something . . . the object ceases to be an object. I become one with it. I cease to be the observer. I cease to be the judge. This kind of response occurs in a situation of complete relatedness, in which seer and seen, observer and observed, become one, although at the same time they remain two. . . . One transcends the boundaries of his own person, and at the very moment when he feels 'I am' he also feels 'I am you,' I am one with the whole world."

In contrast with the writers cited above, the creative potentialities of the interacting process have been given no emphasis by Rogers, Maslow, or Guilford. Rogers used such phrases as desire to communicate, to relate to the world, constructiveness for others, other-enhancing, and personal and social constructiveness. The phrases seem to have more of a connotation of communication, energy, stimuli flowing outward, as for Fromm, than of a vigorous, dyadic, two-way communication implied by the other writers.

For Maslow such flow of human relating as was presented was also outward. Self-actualizing creativity for Maslow represented something that happens within the person. It is an inner experience, an expressive or Being quality that is " 'emitted,' like radioactivity." It is synonymous with health, or the fullest humanness. This state of well-being is achieved for the average person by healing a split within the person which is likened to a civil war, i.e., to a setting of one part of the person against another part. The creative interaction is internal.

One might ask whether the "split" or the "civil war" does not present a strange paradox for the concept of self-actualizing creativity. Maslow discussed the healing of the split within the person almost to the exclusion of mention of persons in the environment. Would it be acceptable to Maslow to perceive the conflict as a foreign war rather than a civil war? It is not clear who started this encapsulated civil war nor when it was started. Maslow's subjects were adults. It is difficult to form an image of the nature of such a civil war even in an adult. Would it help to clarify the figure of speech by asking what would be the difference between a civil war at age 50 and one at age 5 years or 5 months? We could scarcely expect such a thing to be the same or even similar at these different ages.

My hypothesis would be that the conflict was environmental in origin and was probably started, or its basis laid, when the individual was very young. From this point of view the "war" is more likely a "foreign invasion" with overwhelming odds against the child. In the child guidance clinics one sees examples of such environmental onslaughts against children. These clinical observations are supported by research on parent-child relations and research on child rearing practices. Even if the conflict were originated in adulthood, it would seem more likely an outside invasion than a civil war. Fromm had a figure of speech quite different from Maslow's when he likened the conflict over creativity to "I think," versus "It thinks in me." As Fromm has stated it, the conflict again would seem like a foreign invasion.

It may be a naïve question, but I would even ask whether there can be such a thing as a split or a civil war within a person? If part of me is assumed to be set against another part of me, I assume that one part is me, and the other part represents a well-advanced and insidious infiltration by someone else, a symbolic pretender, who is definitely *not me*. This, with conventional uses of symbolism, I can well imagine. Moreover, once I can identify the foreign invaders or infiltrators I have a better chance of rediscovering the *me* which is myself. To do this much would be healthy and would appear to be a step toward self-actualizing. In all probability, according to several of our authors, there is a tremendous cultural infiltration of the individuality of small children, so that by the time they come to adulthood they no longer recognize the self which they have been prevented from actualizing.

If this is the nature of the problem, then one cannot discuss self-actualizing without giving attention to the significant persons in the environment as well as to the individual himself. When, however, one has successfully differentiated oneself from the invaders (let us say the aggregate of the *Its* that have been in me)—or, in Maslow's terms, healed the split or transcended the civil war—and only then—is one ready for the level of creativity in the dyadic or socially integrative relating. Regardless of one's choice of figure of speech, the questions which cannot be neglected are: Who started it? How? When? Where? Even, Why? In his conclusion Maslow spoke of a "suppressed potential" and he asked: Why was it lost? How much is left? How much can be recovered? The orientation of these questions was still internal, and Maslow made no reference to the possibility that the lost potential could be associated with an environmentally restricting interaction or environmental obstruction or pressure.

PROCESS OR PRODUCT

Is creativity a process or a product, and what difference does it make how one regards it? It is traditional to associate creativity with a product, a painting, sculpture, invention, sonnet, drama, something that can be seen, studied, experienced, enjoyed. The product, however, took time to produce; it did not happen all at once. In the conception and the making of the product there may have been several attempts, stages, phases, transitions, failures, revisions. It is known that manuscripts have been revised; paintings have been painted over and rearranged. There are even unfinished symphonies. In this sense creativity must be thought of as a process; a process of planning, experiencing, acting, and interacting by the person who is creating the product.

In the past creativity as product has been given greater attention or emphasis than creativity as process. The process is often obscure, unknown, unperceived, unverbalized, even by the person himself, and therefore uncommunicated to others. In fact, neither history nor science has developed a method or means for recording or evaluating process, except by the comparison of cross-sections in time. The struggle involved in learning or in conceiving and producing an object of creativity is inferred and not directly measured. Even the motion picture is an illusion of process and motion. The product and process are both important. Without the process there would not be the product. Without the product or evidence of action or achievement there might not be more than fantasy. That creativity is to be regarded as both process and product, including intangible productions such as discussions and decisions of committee meetings, is consistent with the views expressed or implied by each of the authors in this book. The question is unimportant unless joined with the crucial problem of evaluation of the product. On the subject of evaluation, which will be discussed below, we find wide disagreement among our authors.

INTUITION, INSPIRATION, INSIGHT, AND HARD WORK

Sinnott expressed the keynote of authors who verbalized their thinking on these points: ". . . inspiration, it is well recognized, rarely comes unless an individual has immersed himself in a subject. He must have a rich background of knowledge and experience in it." May, speaking of unconscious insights, or the answers to problems that come in reverie, said that they do not come hit or miss. "They come only in the areas to which the person is intensively committed in his conscious living. . . . they come in those areas in which the person has worked laboriously and with dedication in his conscious experience." Similar points of view were expressed by Eyring, Stoddard, and Dow. Guilford, referring to Anne Roe's studies of leading artists and of leading scientists in several fields, said that she found "only one trait that stood out in common among individuals. This was a willingness to work hard and to work long hours."

RELATION OF THE UNCONSCIOUS TO CREATIVITY

The variability of treatment of the unconscious among these chapters ranges from complete absence to extended discussions by Sinnott and Stoddard. Such emphasis as is given is focused on positive, organizational, truthful functions of the unconscious in providing innovations. According to these reports, however, the content of the unconscious can be healthy or unhealthy. To the extent that it is expressed in art or symbolism it reflects the quality of the health or illness in the person himself. What is left out is *why* we think of the unconscious as healthy or unhealthy, or *why* we find it related to creativity.

Freud, who formulated the concept of the unconscious, worked with unhappy and unproductive persons. He found in the unconscious sexual and pathological content. Freud saw disease. He dealt with disease. Some of his basic concepts were negative. Anything positive that was related to these negative instincts was regarded by Freud as a substitute for the negative.

Giving Freud full acclaim for originating the concept of the unconscious and discovering the dynamisms does not mean that we should expect the examination of the concept to stop with Freud. I think that we need to revise his hypotheses and assumptions in order to make the assumptions consistent with positive concepts about creativity and with the world as we see it today. Instead of assuming that death, hostility, hate, aggression, and destruction are instinctive, it is more consistent to assume that the basic, primary things in the universe are directional: love, life, growth, harmony, evolution, and progressing integration with the cosmos. From the first cell that developed a spark of life and was able to reproduce itself there is presumably a healthy, enduring continuity. The most valid assumptions that concern living things are evolution, differentiation, integration, creativity, a flowing originality. If we can make these assumptions, then we must go back and re-examine the meaning and function of the unconscious. When we do that we see some of the same things that Freud saw. We see horrible nightmares, but we also see things of beauty, intuitive and inspired things of beauty, symbols of unity, harmony, truth and grace in the arts, the letters, and the sciences.

Since the unconscious cannot be seen, it cannot be described by one person for another. Since the unconscious must be inferred, the idea of the unconscious must be constructed by each person for himself. Even so, some communication of these inferences is possible. The unconscious is thus many things to many persons. It is an attic, a dark cellar, a chamber of horrors, or even a space under the bed where in childhood one stores things precious to oneself, hides things, or has things swept away from him which someone—*someone else*— thinks should not be in sight. What is the function or purpose of the nightmares? Are they necessary—to whom—and for what?

At the same time the unconscious seems to be a place where one's real self, his simple, efficient, evolving self, can crawl away momentarily from a world of crass, hostile, preoccupied, fearsome adults, and in a symbolic way enjoy beauty, live simply and efficiently, and be truthful to himself and to others, and unafraid. Consciousness by itself does not seem to be able to produce things of beauty, truth, and harmony, or at least not to do it so well as when it can draw on the so-called depths of the unconscious, the truth within the self.

A person is a more or less whole organism, biologically and psychologically, as Sinnott and others have maintained. Creativity, as these authors have emphasized, represents a reorganization, a composition, decomposition, recomposition, which includes as an essential the rejection of the irrelevant—the irrelevant as *one himself sees the irrelevant*. In the conscious life of any person there are some stimulating, harmonious, socially integrative experiences. But there is also much that is irrelevant that needs to be discarded. There is much cultural coercion, domination, and conformity in the conscious life of everyone. One seeks to avoid this. The artist goes to a secluded studio, the scientist to a quiet laboratory where it is easier to concentrate, easier to become emotionally involved with an idea, to think simply and symbolically and reject the traditional, reject the stereotyped and other conservative patterns of thinking and acting, to say nothing of rejecting what is erroneous and contradictory to one's own experience. Even the child needs some corner of the house where he can occasionally be alone and be himself and have his possessions respected.

Is the unconscious the region—the attic, or perhaps the cellar—where one can crawl away from the threatening and unrelenting noise and babble and be himself? Most of these authors, as well as Freud, were concerned with efforts to bring out truth from the person himself. But when they do that, what they actually get is communication of truth in some guarded, symbolic way. The cultural world has not yet discovered the meaning of respect for the individual person. The conscious and cultural world of the individual is intolerant of truth and beauty as the person himself sees it. The quality of the symbolism is thus degraded by the extent of the necessity to cloak and disguise it in the double-talk which a judging, evaluating culture requires. The true self in the culture must behave defensively, like a foreigner in a land of preoccupied, unsympathetic, and hostile adults. In one's conscious behavior he displays to the culture only so much of himself as it is safe to display. The remainder of his conscious behavior is sham, falseness, camouflage, veneer, dissimulation, which he learns very early and painfully but very well, as a child in the "socializing" process.

With this idea of consciousness it is easy to understand the many reports of artists, poets, scientists who have worked hard, exhaustingly, and unsuccessfully at a conscious level on some problem. Only in some moment of relaxation or detachment from the business of the day, at breakfast, stepping on a bus, setting out alone on a brisk walk in a snowstorm, in an early morning hour when the culture has receded—at some moment when the self is alone, momentarily safe from the onslaught of the culture—that the solution, the idea, comes to him so neatly, so deftly, that it seems to come without effort. Among primitive peoples the experience is so strange that they have ascribed it to direct communication with a deity, an animal, a person outside themselves. Who can yet tell? But it could also be that the idea, the solution, the inspiration, was there for some time. It could be that it is at such inspired moments that the person himself can cast off the trappings of sham, camouflage, the strains of cultural misrepresentation and defense with which he is obliged to live and which color his conscious thinking, his planning, his communicating, his acting and behaving.

Is this the meaning of rejecting the irrelevant, that one finds rare moments when one can reject all that has not yet become meaningfully *me*? Is this insightful experience the expression of the *true me* that can respond to the universe without socialized sham and cultural *impedimenta*? If the problem of discovering and utilizing the unconscious is mainly one of helping each individual to jettison part of his cultural baggage, that would not simplify our problem, though it would definitely change it. The question would still remain: What baggage to discard? Eyring said that creative chemists are those who can themselves discard the cultural irrelevancies of traditional science. "Individual success in research was accompanied by a shedding of any undue veneration for the embalmed science of the past." Stoddard, Lasswell, and others have pointed out clearly that we still cling to obsolete forms of human organization and human relations that are irrelevant to human needs.

One more comment seems in order. Viewing the unconscious in this way raises the question how much one understands of the person—the child, the artist, the poet, the scientist, the chemist, the creative engineer—if one does not also understand the reality of the human interacting? How can one regard even a sunset or a rose, how can one enjoy a painting, how can one respond to the *impersonal* part of nature that is pleasant and beautiful when one has been told many times that only work is good, play is sinful, art is sissy, and beauty foolishness? If only part of this is true then the *restricting* impact of the culture is involved in every aesthetic sensitivity of the child and of the adult. The socially integrating relating, which I have regarded as a *facilitator* of creativity in personality development, is now seen to become a condition of high facilitation of creative expression in every form of art, letters, or science, and at every level of competence or skill. The socially integrating relating reduces the defensive distortions in one's perceptions and makes it possible for one to be himself and to live and to communicate truthfully. In the process of socially integrating relating the unconscious can safely come nearest to the conscious. At such moments—moments so rare even for the genius that we call them inspired moments—at such propitious moments of unity, harmony, and security in his interacting with the universe does one sense his originality, become creative.

Is this the meaning of creative genius, that only a few persons are able to live in such truth to themselves and to others? High intelligence and talent alone are not sufficient to bring out creative truth. Is this the meaning of the encounter, that one can shed the falseness, the error, the trappings of his culture and be open to the totality of his own experience and even for brief moments live consciously with his unconscious?

RELATION OF MENTAL HEALTH AND OF NEUROSIS TO CREATIVITY

There is essential agreement among those authors who comment on these topics, and no disagreement among them, that mental health and high utilization of one's creative potentials are closely associated. Except in the chapter by Mead, the term mental health is scarcely mentioned in the book. The whole volume, however, is an attempt to define the positive qualities and characteristics of a healthy life process, a way of life, the activity and relating of a fully functioning person, the self-actualizing individual, the person of courage and integrity who is also at peace with his neighbors. The consensus of these authors is that creativity is an expression of a mentally or psychologically healthy person, that creativity is associated with wholeness, unity, honesty, integrity, personal involvement, enthusiasm, high motivation, and action.

There is also agreement that neurosis either accompanies or causes a degraded quality of one's creativity. For neurotic persons and persons with other forms of mental disease, such assumptions as the following are offered: that these persons are creative in spite of their disease; that they are producing below the achievements they would show without the disease; that they are on the downgrade, or that they are pseudo creative, that is, they may have brilliant original ideas which, because of the neurosis, they do not consummate.

RELATION OF INTELLIGENCE AND TALENT TO CREATIVITY

What is the relation of intelligence and talent to creativity? Is creativity properly reserved for the genius, the person with "high level talent" in the arts or the sciences? The answers provided by these authors depend on their assumptions and definitions. Lasswell, for example, defined creativity as "the disposition to make and to recognize valuable innovations." If the product must be valuable, and recognized by others as both novel and valuable, the definition almost requires performance by one of high intelligence and talent. Most of the authors, however, regarded creativity as within the province of everyone, including all ages. This assumption is found in Sinnott, Dow, Fromm, May, Rogers, Maslow, Murray, Anderson, Hilgard, Stoddard, and Mead. Eyring expects both intelligence and high-level talent for creativity in the chemistry laboratory. But for Eyring and Lasswell, as for most of the others, intelligence is not enough, and brilliance can be accompanied by creative sterility. Guilford's research was designed for the study of the higher thought processes in adults in relation to creativity.

RANGE OF ACTIVITIES INCLUDED UNDER CREATIVITY

If creativity is a potentiality of everyone and at all ages, as eleven of our contributors have assumed, then it follows that the range of activities to be included under creativity would be very wide indeed. Rogers, for example, by definition, "makes no distinction regarding the degree of creativity. . . . The action of the child inventing a new game with his playmates; Einstein formulating a theory of relativity; the housewife devising a new sauce for the meat; a young author writing his first novel; all of these are, in terms of our definition, creative, and there is no attempt to set them in order of more or less creative."

The question will then occur to some whether the concept of creativity thus becomes so general as to have lost its meaning. The first step toward an answer to this question is to ask, "Meaning for whom?" The answers are different if we consider meaning for father, for mother, the boss, a vice president, an employer, or other authority figure, or even for *any other* person, than if we consider meaning for the *individual person himself.* The concept of creativity as developed in this book is indeed broad and general, but it has not thereby lost its meaning. To develop an answer to the question, "Meaning for whom?" we must consider the critical and controversial problem of evaluation, which we shall discuss below.

INFLUENCE OF THE ENVIRONMENT ON CREATIVITY

We have already mentioned in part the role of the environment in creativity when we raised questions above as to the nature of the interacting between the individual and his environment and also as to the meaning of the unconscious.

None of the authors has attempted to address himself to the question of the relation of heredity versus environment to creativity. Sinnott discussed genetic variation and also creativity as response to environment. He said the changes of the mind are not dependent on genetic change. "Rather are they the result of the enormously varied responses of a given genetic constitution to environmental differences. . . . much of the variety of all organic life is due to environmental variety." Eyring said, "Undoubtedly the prospective scientist should arrange to be born with the right genes. Anyone who has examined the variations to be found among individuals with ostensibly equivalent training cannot escape this conclusion. Even the gifted individual, however, requires a stimulating environment. . . ." Eyring's view is directly supported by most authors and is not contradicted by any.

Lasswell's entire paper was on the social setting of creativity. For Lasswell the environment serves as facilitator and as restrictor both in the innovation process itself and in the process of discovery and recognition of the innovation. Lasswell's discussion of the social processes underlying Freud's development of psychoanalysis is an exposition of the dynamic interrelating between a genius and his cultural environment. "To account for psychoanalysis we must undoubtedly concentrate upon the stream of subjective events in the mind of Freud. But it would be a mistake to disregard the social setting in which these events took place and with which they were in perpetual interaction, even as they interacted among themselves. . . . When we try to explain Freud's creativity we are dealing with endless chains of interactive events. . . ."

Mead discussed creativity in cross-cultural perspective. She analyzed and documented "the relationships between the forms provided by a culture and the creativity of the individuals within the culture."

Rogers said, "This tendency [to actualize himself, to become his potentialities] . . . exists in every individual and awaits only the proper conditions to be released and expressed."

Dow maintained that "this quality [of creative personality in each person] should be taken for granted. The real problem is to discover what outside influences or forces prevent creativeness, or prevent anyone from becoming a complete personality. . . . we are guided in our productiveness in either of two ways—by the narrow, deadening boundaries of conformity, or by the intellectual or spiritual guidance of truth or . . . the process of love or growth."

It is neither necessary nor fruitful to extend the review of the details submitted by these authors as to what is a propitious and what an unpropitious environment. For each of the remaining authors (excepting perhaps Guilford) the environment serves as a facilitator or as a restrictor of individual creativity. Eyring enumerated environmental facilitators of creativity in chemistry laboratories. Hilgard discussed programs designed to facilitate creativity at the college level. Stoddard described a dual-progress program of education in actual operation, the purpose of which is to facilitate creativity in elementary school children.

It will be mentioned below that the propitious environment for creativity is the "Open System" and that the unpropitious environment is one that tends to close the life space of the individual.

Responding to Persons and to Things

In this volume there has not been sufficient distinction between the psychological import of the environment of persons and that of the environment of things. There are only occasional allusions to the differences.

There is only one way in which a person can treat a thing: that is, in a manipulative or dominative way. One can change the form or position of a thing; he can care for it or push it around. Man can be inspired by a thing. But regardless of how the person feels about the thing or what the person does to the thing, the thing will not respond to the person. The thing has no intentionality toward a person as a unique individual.

A person, however, does have intentionality toward another person. There are two ways in which a person can respond to a person: one can work *with* another or work *against* him. In human relations, on a person-to-person basis as on a nation-to-nation basis, there probably is no such circumstance as responding with neutrality. Socially integrative behavior (the creative growth circle) can occur only between persons; this is the positive meaning of treating a person as a person. To work against a person, to dominate, attack, threaten, ridicule a person (the uncreative vicious circle) is to show lack of respect for the dignity of the person as an individual and to treat him as a thing. To treat a person as a thing is to obstruct the creative growth processes in the person. The distinction is important because the culture is still in process of learning the meaning of treating persons as persons, and of abandoning the ancient historical and primitive practices of treating persons as things.

Stoddard pointed out that "mechanical aids to learning are impersonal. They do not embarrass the learner. Though they are unable to show affection, neither do they have a capacity for insult." It is precisely this quality of interacting, either positively or negatively, the capacity for love and affection and the capacity for insult and attack, which distinguishes the environment of persons from the environment of things. The distinction between persons and things is the thesis of a little book by Buber (1937), has been discussed by Mooney (1956), and has been elaborated more recently by Tagiuri and Petrullo (1958).

THE OPEN SYSTEM VERSUS THE CLOSED SYSTEM

Rogers mentioned as one of the inner conditions for constructive creativity "Openness to experience extensionality," as the opposite of psychological defensiveness. Rogers' phrase was quoted by Maslow, who used the term with the same meaning as openness of awareness. Similar ideas have been expressed in other words by May, Fromm, and others. Anderson used the term "Open System" as a quality of the responding process between persons in the environment and the individual himself. The open system is an environment of beckoning horizons in which the person finds security and mutual stimulation in his relations with others. He does not actually need to be in the presence of others. He can be painting, inventing, or viewing a landscape by himself. But the open system means that to the extent of its openness the persons in one's meaningful environment are permitting or even encouraging him to be himself and to make adventures into the unknown. It follows that the openness to experience can happen only within an open system. For to the extent that one's life space is closed to a person by another it makes the person defensive and self-protective, which for Rogers is the opposite of openness or extensionality.

Openness for Rogers and Maslow is in reality two-way relating, although the words and the context and the emphasis on the self may give the impression of one-way relating. If the environment is propitious for one it should also be propitious for the others in the inter-relating. This is the meaning of an open system. Anything less than this represents a partially closed life space, a life space restricted in some way by a person or a symbol of a person or persons in the environment.

The open system is thus the ideal, propitious environment for creativity, and anything in the environment that tends to close the system makes the environment unpropitious for creativity. This assumption must be qualified to admit the interweaving of desires and activities and the free interplay of differences out of which is developed the permeability of boundaries which is also a positive characteristic of the propitious environment. Propitious means propitious for the process of interacting. It means freedom of each person to respond truthfully with his whole person as he sees and understands the truth.

CREATIVITY IN CHILDREN AND ADULTS—A DEVELOPMENTAL PROCESS

Most of the authors in this book have written about adults and have drawn their illustrations from research on adults or from adult behavior. At the same time, most of them have mentioned children and have called attention to the similarities between the behavior of creative adults and the behavior of children. It is almost as though creative adults are those who somehow did not lose their childlike qualities.

Fromm asked, "What are the conditions of the creative attitude, of seeing and responding, of being aware and being sensitive to what one is aware of? First of all, it requires a capacity to be puzzled. Children still have the capacity to be puzzled. Their whole effort is one of attempting to orient themselves in a new world, to grasp the ever new things which they learn to experience. They are puzzled, surprised, capable of wondering, and that is what makes their reaction a creative one." It is difficult to imagine that the infant or the very young child can do very much of anything else. On the way to adulthood, however, something happens. Fromm continued, "But once they are through the process of education, most people lose the capacity of wondering, of being surprised. They feel they ought to know everything, and hence that it is a sign of ignorance to be surprised at, or puzzled by anything. . . . it would be much closer to the truth to state that most people are not aware of, and do not respond to anything."

How did Maslow compare self-actualizing creativeness in adults with the behavior of children? It "was in many respects like the creativeness of *all* happy and secure children. It was spontaneous, effortless, innocent, easy, a kind of freedom from stereotypes and clichés. Again it seemed to be made up largely of 'innocent' freedom of perception and 'innocent,' uninhibited spontaneity and expressiveness. Almost any child can perceive more freely, without a *priori* expectations about what ought to be there or what must be there or what has always been there. And almost any child can compose a song or a poem or a dance or a painting or a play or a game on the spur of the moment, without planning or previous intent. It was in this childlike sense that my subjects were creative."

Maslow, too, had some ideas as to what happens between childhood and adulthood: ". . . this all sounds as if we are dealing with a fundamental characteristic, inherent in human nature, a potentiality given to all or most human beings at birth, which most often is lost or buried or inhibited as the person gets enculturated." Maslow explained at length wherein his creative adults were different from average adults, who, for Maslow, are fearful persons, frightened by the unknown, the mysterious, the puzzling.

Rogers dealt mostly with adults. He gave as an example of creativity, however, "the child inventing a new game with his playmates," said that the teacher and parent as well as the therapist could foster creativity by accepting the individual as of unconditional worth. As adults, Rogers said, we are "a generally passive and culture-bound people" with "a strong tendency toward conformity, toward stereotypy."

Stoddard has given a detailed, consistent, and sustained treatment of how creativity as a way of life has been lost to most American adults. "The urge to inquire, to invent, to perform, was stifled in millions of school children, now grown up, who did not get above rote learning, or at least did not stay above it. Their final culture pattern is all about us. Conformity rules, not because people crave it, but because they fear deviation. . . . To get creativity in society viewed as a whole, we must make it mean more to each person. We must start early in the life of the child." It is not appropriate to review here the vast range of documentation which Stoddard presented for his point of view and the dual-progress plan which he has proposed for elementary education.

Can we learn a lesson from a page out of the life of an artist? Two of our authors have mentioned Picasso. Here is a brief statement on Picasso's respect for the integrity of the child and the process of interacting. I quote from the narrative of Duncan (1958) on Picasso, children, things, power with, open systems, and what happens.

There was but one Great Law in that house: DO NOT MOVE ANYTHING! Everything had its place and even its own dust pattern. To move anything out of its place, or pattern, might easily destroy a composition, unseen by anyone else, which Picasso had been watching, thinking about, and turning into other forms in his mind. It had to be remembered, constantly, that the house and garden constituted almost the entire physical world seen by Picasso, and that he was terribly dependent upon them in many ways.

Delightfully, this law did not apply to children or to animals. In Picasso's world children were born to run free. If a child moved things, even canvases themselves, he would say only "Good . . . Good!" or "How droll!" and nothing more, apparently having already accepted the compositional changes as the functioning of a law greater than any of his own. During all of the months that I was a guest at the villa, while Kathy and her friend Martine and, later, other children played endlessly—and Lump and Yan and the goat frolicked all around the place—I never heard the word "Don't" nor saw a child or pet punished . . . and nothing was ever broken.

A conspicuous gap in this book is the lack of any significant discussion of the role of child rearing practices in facilitating or restricting creativity in the child. There is no delineation of what in the culture is relevant to the way of life of the average person at his peak of creativity: his early childhood. Does the family teach the child to have the *It* think in him before he quite discovers the *I* in himself? Does he thereby become "conditioned" to the *It*, and fearful of and lacking in confidence in the *I*? These are questions of the first magnitude for a research approach to creativity.

That life is creative and that children are born with qualities and capacities for creativity were major premises of most of our authors and were not denied by any. That adults are not creative, that they are passive, fearful conformists, was admitted and bemoaned. Perhaps the most consistent protest in the book is against *conformity*. Our authors used such expressions as: break through this crust of conformity and passivity; how is the fabric of custom and habit so rent that something emerges; the narrow, deadening boundaries of conformity—the tool of fear or ignorance; generally passive and culture-bound people; deeply buried under layer after layer of encrusted psychological defenses; enculturation; socialization; brainwashing; closed system—these are the phrases and the figures of speech which represent the protests of these writers.

The view of our authors that American adulthood is dull and has lost the spark is expressed for another culture by Antoine de Saint-Exupéry (1939), a French writer-pilot who commented on a conversation overheard on a bus that took him to the airport. For the discovery of this quotation and of other ideas on the open spirit of adventure I am indebted to Wilfred Noyce (1958):

I heard them talking to one another in murmurs and whispers. They talked about illness, money, shabby domestic cares. Their talk painted the walls of the dismal prison in which these men had locked themselves up. And suddenly I had a vision of the face of destiny.

Old bureaucrat, my comrade, it is not you who are to blame. No one ever helped you to escape. You, like a termite, built your peace by blocking up with cement every chink and cranny through which the light might pierce. You rolled yourself up into a ball in your genteel security, in routine, in the stifling convention of provincial life, raising a modest rampart against the winds and the tides and the stars. You have chosen not to be perturbed by great problems, having trouble enough to forget your own fate as man. You are not the dweller upon an errant planet and do not ask yourself questions to which there are no answers. You are a petty bourgeois of Toulouse. Nobody grasped you by the shoulder while there was still time. Now the clay of which you were shaped has dried and hardened, and naught in you will ever awaken the sleeping musician, the poet, the astronomer that possibly inhabited you in the beginning.

What does it mean to show respect for the individual child? What does it mean to treat children as human beings and not as things?

How is it possible for children to grow to adulthood with courage to be themselves? Do we need a new level of affection which will reserve a place for the dignity and individuality of the child? What has culture achieved by the stifling in childhood of the vast creative potentials of the human race?

EVALUATION OF CREATIVITY

In considering the evaluation of creativity we should in fairness to our authors recall that they were not given specific topics to discuss. Evaluation of creativity has been treated or given emphasis by each author as it fitted his discourse. Some authors have taken more than one position without elaborating on the nature of the differences.

Lasswell spoke of the time element in evaluating. Others deplored the cultural time lag in evaluating the products of creativity. In both theoretical and applied science there is a solid tradition of an external evaluation of a created product; yet neither in art nor in science do we find valid criteria for this evaluation. The history of science reveals the scientist's blind spots in viewing and evaluating the "goodness" of the productions of his colleagues.

Several of our authors have pointed out that the more novel the idea, the more likely it is to be judged as evil or worthless. Dyson (1958), writing on innovations in physics, said, "When the great innovation appears, it will almost certainly be in a muddled, incomplete, and confusing form. To the discoverer himself it will be only half-understood; to everybody else it will be a mystery. For any speculation which does not at first glance look crazy, there is no hope."

The invalidity of contemporary judgments is found on the frontiers of all human disciplines. Fabulous sums are paid today for paintings by artists of an earlier day who died in poverty and scorn. Ghosts of persons burned at the stake by previous generations are sainted today with cold regard for the unfortunate individuals who are now being excommunicated. The cultural lag in evaluation of what is new and what is also good or acceptable is found as well among physicists, chemists, and psychologists. The big gap in dealing "objectively" with creativity is the lack of criteria for assessing the products or productions of creativity.

The evaluation of the product has many other obscurities. We know little about the development of social acclaim. Presumably a painting by Gauguin had some meaning to Gauguin, some worth, some value, even when his colleagues were laughing at him and the market would not offer him a meal for his product. Artists, economists, philosophers, and psychologists cannot explain what happens in the transition from individual value by the artist himself (the satisfaction of self-expression) to a status of social recognition and approval. The evaluation by contemporaries has so often been reversed by a succeeding generation as to place upon contemporaries a great burden to justify any evaluation whatsoever. Even if we could invent a correction for the time lag in our evaluation of the creativity of others the problem of evaluation would still be with us. There would be a kind of academic futility in discussing evaluation if we had to confine ourselves to the Gauguins, the Benjamin Franklins, and to Nobel prize winners. Where is the cutting line for discriminating the "top level" of creativity from any other level of importance? Is it less creative to make a mud pie at the age of two than to bake a cake at the age of twenty? The process of creativity is operating both at the age of two and at the age of twenty. If we knew more about the process of creativity and if we could recognize it as process at two and at twenty, would the problem of criteria be simplified by identifying the process instead of trying to evaluate the product? If we could think of creativity as process, would that make it possible for us to dispense with the question of value and of social approval? Are we really interested in Benjamin Franklins or in lightning rods, in persons or in things? If we are interested in persons, do we find that we have lightning rods, too?

Three defined sources of evaluation were discussed in these chapters, each with one or more quite explicit advocates or interpreters: (1) external evaluation, required by Lasswell; (2) internal locus of evaluation (with the exclusion of external evaluation) required by Rogers; and (3) mutual, dyadic, or participating evaluation, proposed by Murray. We shall summarize these three points of view as presented by the authors and then re-examine their relations to creativity.

1. *External evaluation.* Lasswell gave his definition of creativity in his opening sentence: "Creativity is the disposition to make and to recognize valuable innovations." He further elaborated this defini-

tion: "Two complex processes must jell before we can identify a completed instance of creativeness. An innovation is essential; and it must elicit a certain degree of recognition as valuable." By this definition Lasswell ruled out such things as the daily activities of the ordinary person, the creative games of the child, the sequences of experience in the developmental process, and all other undiscovered instances of originality. His range of innovations, however, is still broad. Lasswell regarded the process of *recognition* of novelty and of value as crucial. He discussed recognition even before he treated the innovation process itself. He regarded the social mechanism for recognition as a facilitator of further innovation and developed an elaborate scheme for explaining the communication and collaboration of intermediaries through whose efforts innovators and innovations become known.

The motives of Lasswell's intermediaries are varied. An example is a friend "who recognizes an innovation and expects to make money by exploiting it." The friend communicates with an investor who in turn expects to be better off by investing in this innovation than by seizing other opportunities. Other motives for recognizing and collaborating with an innovator are: enhancing one's political power, increasing one's status of respect or prestige, expressing affection for the innovator, reducing personal anxiety, expressing rectitude values, encouraging excellence in technology, and advancing knowledge that is enlightening and fundamental. Lasswell did not elaborate on a method or technology for making a valid judgment of an innovation, for example, for recognizing those inventions which would also be good investments. Neither did he elaborate on the possible differences in psychological meaning for an inventor who receives support for his invention on the one hand as an expression of affection for the inventor and on the other hand as an ambition of an investor who expects thereby to make a profit for his company.

Lasswell's definition is similar to definitions used by industrial psychologists who are concerned with the "identification, selection, and training of creative high level talent in organizational, administrative, and scientific functions of industry." Stein (1956), for example, for his purposes of empirical research in industry, has defined creativity as follows: "Creativity is that process that results in 'a novel work that is accepted as tenable or useful or satisfying by a significant group at some point in time.' . . . By virtue of this definition we limit ourselves to studying individuals who are regarded as creative by significant others in their environment. Some . . . may regard this definition as 'too social' but I submit that almost any criterion in this area has its roots in the judgment of others."

The problem of external evaluation has been a topic of interest at two conferences on the identification of creative scientific talent, reported by Taylor (1956, 1958). The reports of these conferences and other publications reveal that the determination of a criterion for identifying and evaluating the creative person, or even for judging his product, is a bewildering, confusing and baffling problem.

Although validation has not been a feature of Guilford's current plan of basic research, he was not unmindful of the traditional "scientific" expectation of validation of test scores. He did cite reports by other investigators who correlated performance on some of his tests with such external criteria as ratings of degree of originality, grades in small classes of mathematics courses, average grades in science and mathematics courses, grades in physics courses, evaluation of the expressive aspects of teaching performance, and incidence of certain kinds of creative hobbies as reported in biographical information inventories. Merely to mention these correlations illustrates the desperate degrees to which scientists are forced by the cultural traditions of their craft to grope for criteria of validity.

Hilgard confined his review of problem-solving almost exclusively to "fixed answer" problems. This is a kind of learning, common to arithmetic, chemistry, physics, and mathematics courses. It is also the kind of learning most widely studied in animal laboratories and in experiments in psychological learning and problem-solving situations. The answers, determined in advance, are found in the back of the book or in the experimenter's head. The predetermined answer is the external criterion of evaluation of this kind of learning. Such a criterion, however, makes the problem a kind of closed system, with originality of the subject restricted to methods of approach to the "solution" and not permitted in form or content of the solution. In problem-solving of this sort, the subject does not create anything that is new to the experimenter, and the "learner" in a certain sense conforms to the thought processes of the teacher. Hilgard was aware of this limitation and spoke of "material bearing on originality and creativity as distinct from the fixed answer kind of problem-solving." He said, ". . . there are the creative products of literature, art, and music that defy description according to the ordinary formulas of problem-solving."

For Eyring, creativity in chemistry was the discovery of a new proof not known to the teacher. Eyring required an external criterion for creativity in that the new proof must be for a process or event that is repeatable. Creativity for Eyring was mainly the process of putting more and more answers in the back of the scientific book.

Murray defined creativity as either process or "the *resultant* of this process, a new composition, regardless of its value, destiny, or consequences." This definition does not admit of an external criterion. Murray is mentioned here, however, because he qualified his definition for certain "contexts of the present discourse" to include the criterion of " 'valuable' [which] will mean *either* intrinsically or extrinsically valuable *as such* to one or more persons, . . ." This addition does not seem to represent Murray's own position, which appears instead to emphasize the intrinsic or internal evaluation by the person himself, or the mutual evaluation through meaningful interaction. Concerning the external criterion of "valuable" Murray raised a host of difficult scientific questions, including finally the impossible necessity of judging the evaluators, and after that the evaluation of the judges who judged the evaluators, and so on.

2. *Internal locus of evaluation*. Eight of our authors have taken the position directly or by implication that the locus of evaluation of creativity should be internal. This position is diametrically opposed to that held by those who require or attempt to use an external criterion. It is furthermore maintained by some of these writers that the use of an *outside judgment* of novelty and value is detrimental to the very process of creativity itself. Rogers was explicit on this view.

"Perhaps the most fundamental condition of creativity is that the source or locus of evaluative judgment is internal. The value of his product is, for the creative person, established not by the praise or criticism of others, but by himself. Have I created something satisfying to me? Does it express a part of me—my feeling or my thought, my pain or my ecstasy? These are the only questions which really matter to the creative person, or to any person when he is being creative.

"This does not mean that he is oblivious to, or unwilling to be aware of, the judgments of others. It is simply that the basis of evaluation lies within himself, in his own organismic reaction to and appraisal of his product. If to the person it has the 'feel' of being 'me in action,' of being an actualization of potentialities in himself which heretofore have not existed and are now emerging into existence, then it is satisfying and creative, and no outside evaluation can change that fundamental fact."

Rogers' statement of conditions which foster creativity included further, "Providing a climate in which external evaluation is absent. When we cease to form judgments of the other individual from our own locus of evaluation, we are fostering creativity. For the individual to find himself in an atmosphere in which he is not being evaluated, not being measured by some external standard, is enormously freeing. Evaluation is always a threat, always creates a need for defensiveness, always means that some portion of experience must be denied to awareness."

The definition of creativity offered by Fromm as the ability to *see*, *to be aware*, and *to respond* requires an internal locus of evaluation. In the situation of complete relatedness, "the object ceases to be an object. I become one with it. I cease to be the observer. I cease to be the judge. . . ." The internal locus of evaluation is consistent with the positions of May, Maslow, Stoddard, and Anderson. Eyring's statement concerning "the rejection of superficial explanations of one's own as well as of others" requires an internal evaluation enroute to the discovery of proof. Murray required honesty and integrity for creative dyadic interacting. Dow's test of values, including honesty, humility, and enthusiasm, was used on the products of others as well as on one's own. But his intuitive thinking, which he regarded as the most valuable kind of thinking, represents one's own honest thought "unruled by conformity," and thus has an internal locus of evaluation.

3. *Mutual, dyadic, participating evaluation.* A third possible way of regarding evaluation is to see it as emerging through a process of participation, of two-way communication, mutuality, interweaving of desires, goals, purposes, through spontaneous, meaningful change in interacting with others. Murray, in his content analysis of what happens in this process, found a high level of evaluation to be one of

the emergents of his dyadic example: ". . . one last determinant should be listed, namely, an above-normal capacity to evaluate with fine discrimination—in terms of some enlightened standard (Va)— the worth and relevance of what has been brought forth, coupled with the disposition to reject (Na) what is unacceptable in those scales and to incorporate (Ca) whatever is fitting and propitious."

This mutual, participating experience seems not unlike that in Dow's creative action-reaction, in Anderson's socially integrative behavior, Fromm's I-become-you, Rogers' interaction with one's environment which "tends to be constructive both for himself and others," May's dialectical process between the individual and his world, and Eyring's interaction among scientists in the laboratory and during informal private discussions. It is possible to include here Lasswell's examples of the invention of the Federal system and the Supreme Court, which were unquestionably devised through participating processes of intercommunication. The evaluation of such governmental structures as valuable was probably mutual or dyadic.

PSYCHOLOGICAL MEANING OF EVALUATION OF CREATIVITY

We have presented a range of perspectives on evaluation of creativity. Let us now examine these three kinds of evaluation in terms of their psychological meaning for creativity.

1. *External evaluation.* The hypothesis which I propose here is that external evaluation is distinguished from internal and dyadic evaluations only as it is related to power over the innovator. This power over may be real, potential, or symbolic. It may be intentional or unintentional. The net result of power over another is the ultimate achievement of conformity by the individual to external standards. It denies to the creating person the opportunity and the right to be himself. It is thus a prime source of anxiety in the person and an instigator of resistant defenses. It detracts by that much from the "originality" of the behavior.

Examples of power over combined with external evaluation are seen in the use of rewards and punishments, praise and reproof which constitute the chief techniques of child rearing practices and of education of the young. Children are taught not to think for themselves but to seek and be content with rewards and approval as social substitutes for the satisfactions of intrinsic and meaningful originality.

They are also taught to avoid punishment and reproof. This is part of the vast practice by which the culture degrades the quality of creative behavior. This is the source of the encrustation, the enculturation of uniqueness, the building, as our authors say, of layer after layer of defenses, of sham and pretense and falseness that often can be opened up again only by prolonged psychotherapy. Children brought up on a diet of rewards and punishment become the adults our authors have described.

External evaluation when associated with power over another becomes an instrument of all the negative polarities discussed in these chapters. It means the creating of defenses, the instigation of conflict, working against another, showing disrespect for the person as an individual human being, treating a person as a thing, socialization, the vicious circle, the unpropitious environment, the closed system, brainwashing, and conformity. External evaluation when associated with power over another becomes the chief restrictor of individual creativity. Power over another does not exist without external evaluation.

External evaluation *without* power over another is something entirely different: it becomes the confronting of differences and the free interplay of differences. It becomes the free intermingling, interweaving of internal evaluations; it becomes the dyadic, mutual, evolving process of evaluating. There is a much-quoted example attributed to Voltaire of external evaluation without the intentionality of power over the other: "I heartily disagree with what you say but I will defend with my life your right to say it." In such a relating each can be truthful to himself and to the other, without jeopardy or the necessity for defenses. But without power over the other the external evaluation becomes the nonthreatening interplay of internal evaluations. The example from Voltaire falls short of the mutually stimulating and invigorating process of interacting; but in that example neither one attempts to close the life space of the other.

2. *Internal evaluation.* My hypothesis is that, given an internal locus of evaluation, one's creativity depends upon one's perception of the strength or absence of intentionality in others to use power over him. The range of intentionality or of degree of power over one may be vast. It may extend from relative absence of it, as in the socially integrative relating, through increasing degrees of subtle and

symbolic expressions of social control and socializing, to severe examples such as have been found in concentration camps.

Where there is no intentionality to use power over him, creativity would be at a maximum. Rogers took care of this problem by requiring the absence of external evaluation. People in one's environment would thus respect the dignity of the individual as a person and treat the person as a person and not as a thing. The objection is not to external evaluation, as such, but to the use of power over the creating person.

3. *Mutual, dyadic, or participating evaluation.* The hypothesis for the mutual, participating, or dyadic relating is that, because it is relatively devoid of power over each other, it offers the maximum interplay of true perceptions, maximum of communication, of understanding, of spontaneity, and of harmony. This is what is meant by vigorous, mutually stimulating, creative relating; this is socially integrative behavior. This relating is associated with all the positive polarities discussed in these chapters: the use of power with others, mutual stimulation, originality, seeing, doing, thinking, feeling for oneself, encountering, open system, propitious environment, growth circle, resonators, and facilitators in the environment.

Why is it difficult to define a position on this problem of evaluation of creativity? Validity is a basic tenet of science. An external criterion would theoretically be most desirable. Internal consistency of several less desirable measures would be acceptable. But there seems to be no suitable external criterion to be found.

Is it possible that the external criterion of science should be used only in the natural sciences where it originated? Should it apply only to the world of chemistry, physics, the world·of things, to the concept of closed systems and of reversible processes? Can an external criterion be applied at all to life, the open system (Anderson and Anderson, 1954a), to the system of irreversible processes, the world of nonrecurring processes, the nonrecurring organization and relating, the flow of originality, the process of creativity? In dealing with human creativity have we allowed ourselves to be lulled into thinking that we are "scientific" when we have "conformed" to the dogmas of the physical sciences? We have heard repeated self-criticisms of behavioral scientists that the biological and social sciences have borrowed ill-adapted methodologies from physics and chemistry and that they should instead develop their own methodology.

Cronbach (1957) presented an argument that within the field of psychology the "two disciplines of scientific psychology" (i.e., correlational and experimental) need new methodologies. "Correlational psychology studies only variance among organisms; experimental psychology studies only variance among treatments. A united discipline will study both of these, but it will also be concerned with the otherwise neglected interactions between organismic and treatment variables. . . . From observations we must infer a psychological description of the situation and of the present state of the organism. Our laws should permit us to predict, from this description, the behavior of organism-in-situation."

From another source, Dunn (1958) has reported the struggles of an interdisciplinary group in discovering and defining criteria for a positive concept of *wellness*, a concept in which Dunn includes creativity in the individual person.

It is not clear yet wherein the methodologies of the biological and social sciences should be different. The several branches of the biological sciences have similar problems. Uncertain validities of criteria are found in assessing physical growth and development, nutritional adequacy, and physical and mental health.

There is a real question whether it is possible by any of our methods or by methods to be derived from our traditional concepts of science, to measure what is referred to as an open system. It is possible to measure specifically and reliably environmental factors which contribute to a closed system. Anderson (1946) drew attention to the differences in research approaches to positive and negative aspects of behavior in his own and other researches. Gough, *et al.* (1952), reported it easier to construct negative items for a measure of responsible behavior than to find positive items. This problem of negative and positive approaches was discussed by Anderson and Anderson (1954a) in connection with social development and with a concept of psychological entropy as the environmental degradation of the quality of behavior. There they pointed out that negative entropy, a double negative concept recently introduced into physics, cybernetics, and communications theory, becomes a synonym for increase in information, enhancement of the quality of behavior, creativity.

THE SOCIAL NEED FOR CREATIVITY

Most of our authors have mentioned a social as well as individual need for creativity. These authors were not perfunctory in their citation of this problem. Rather have they presented the need for creativity as a national crisis, a desperate situation for the military forces, for industrial leadership, for humanitarian living. In viewing creativity in perspective it seems rather futile to expect to meet our declared national need for creativity by identifying those adults in whom the spark of individuality has been kept alive. There are not enough such adults. If our need were only partly as great as our dedicated authors have represented, there would seem to be one feasible method. It would be difficult and it would take time. Why not take any generation of small children, already creative, and find out how to cultivate them?

REFERENCES

ADAMSON, R. E. 1952. Functional fixedness as related to problem solving: a repetition of three experiments. *J. exp. Psychol.*, *44:* 288–291.

——— and TAYLOR, D. W. 1954. Functional fixedness as related to elapsed time and to set. *J. exp. Psychol.*, 47: 122–126.

ALLPORT, G. W. 1955. *Becoming: Basic Considerations for a Psychology of Personality.* New Haven: Yale Univer. Press.

ALMOND, G. 1950. *The American People and Foreign Policy.* New York: Harcourt.

ANDERSON, H. H. 1937a. An experimental study of dominative and integrative behavior in children of preschool age. *J. soc. Psychol.*, 8: 335–345.

———. 1937b. Domination and integration in the social behavior of young children of preschool age. *Genet. Psychol. Monogr.*, *19:* 341–408.

———. 1939. Domination and social integration in the behavior of kindergarten children and teachers. *Genet. Psychol. Monogr.*, *21:* 287–385.

———. 1940. Educational implications of research in dominative and socially integrative behavior. *J. educ. Sociol.*, *13:* 490–501.

———. 1946. Socially integrative behavior. *J. abnorm. soc. Psychol.* 41: 379–384.

——— and ANDERSON, GLADYS L. 1954a. Social development. In L. Carmichael (Ed.), *Manual of Child Psychology* (2nd ed.). New York: Wiley, pp. 1162–1215.

——— and ———. 1954b. Children's perceptions of social conflict situations: a study of adolescent children in Germany. *Amer. J. Orthopsychiat.*, *24:* 246–257.

——— and BREWER, J. E. 1946. Consecutive studies from fall to winter of teachers' dominative and socially integrative contacts and related changes in the children's classroom behavior. In H. H. Anderson, J. E. Brewer, and Mary F. Reed, Studies of teachers' classroom personalities, III. Follow-up studies of the effects of dominative and integrative contacts on children's behavior. *Appl. psychol. Monogr.*, *11:* 101–156.

ARNOLD, J. E. 1954. *Creative Seminar Notes, Creative Engineering Laboratory.* Cambridge, Mass.: Mass. Inst. Technol.

ASCH, S. E. 1956. Studies of independence and conformity: I. A minority of one against a unanimous majority. *Psychol. Monogr.*, 70 (9) (Whole No. 416).

BARKAN, M., and MOONEY, R. L. (Eds.). 1953. *The Conference on Creativity: a Report to the Rockefeller Foundation.* Columbus, Ohio: Ohio State Univer. Press (Multilith.).

BARNETT, H. G. 1953. *Innovation: The Basis of Cultural Change.* New York: McGraw-Hill.

BARRON, F. 1955. The disposition toward originality. *J. abnorm. soc. Psychol.*, *51* (3): 478–485.

———. 1958. The Needs for Order and for Disorder as Motives in Creative Activity (Unpublished MS and other unpublished papers).

BARZUN, J. 1956. New man in the arts. *The American Scholar*, *25* (4): 437–444.

BATESON, G. 1943. *Bali: The Human Problem of Reoccupation* (Supplementary material on the exhibit). New York: Museum of Modern Art (Mimeogrd.).

——— (with CLAIRE HOLT). 1944. Form and function of the dance in Bali. In *The Function of Dance in Human Society* (A seminar directed by Franciska Boas). New York: Boas School.

——— and MEAD, M. 1942. *Balinese character: A Photographic Analysis* (New York Academy of Sciences Special Publications, Vol. II). New York: New York Academy of Sciences.

BELL, E. T. 1937. *Men of Mathematics.* New York: Simon and Schuster.

BELO, J. 1935. The Balinese temper. In *Character and Personality*, Vol. 4, pp. 120–146. Reprinted in D. Haring (Ed.), *Personal Character and Cultural Milieu* (3rd ed.). Syracuse: Syracuse Univer. Press, pp. 157–180.

———. 1949. *Bali: Barong and Rangda.* Amer. Ethnological Soc. Monogr., No. 16.

———. 1955. Balinese children's drawing. In M. Mead and M. Wolfenstein (Eds.), *Childhood in Contemporary Cultures.* Chicago: Univer. of Chicago Press, pp. 52–69.

BENOIST, C. 1936. *Le Machiavélisme.* Vol. 3. Aprés Machiavel. Paris: Libr. Plon.

BERGER, R. M., GUILFORD, J. P., and CHRISTENSEN, P. R. 1957. A factor-analytic study of planning abilities. *Psychol. Monogr.*, *71* (6) (Whole No. 435).

BIXLER, J. S. 1957. An experiment in undergraduate thinking. *Bull. Amer. Ass. of Univer. Professors*, *43*: 282–287.

BONAPARTE, MARIE, PRINCESS. 1949. *The Life and Works of Edgar Allan Poe; A Psychoanalytic Interpretation.* London: Imago Publ. (English trans., original French publication).

BORING, E. G. 1950. Great men and scientific progress. *Proc. Amer. phil. Soc.*, *94* (4): 339–351.

BREWER, H. M., and ANDERSON, H. H. 1945. The measurement of the behavior of kindergarten children in relation to the teachers' dominative and socially integrative contacts. In H. H. Anderson and H. M. Brewer,

Studies of teachers' classroom personalities, I. Dominative and socially integrative behavior of kindergarten teachers. *Appl. psychol. Monogr.,* 6: 109–152.

BREWER, J. E. 1946. The measurement of the behavior of second grade children in relation to the teachers' dominative and socially integrative contacts. In H. H. Anderson and J. E. Brewer, Studies of teachers' classroom personalities, II. Effects of teachers' dominative and integrative contacts on children's class room behavior. *Appl. psychol. Monogr.,* 8: 33–122.

BRUNER, J. S., GOODNOW, J. J., and AUSTIN, G. A. 1956. *A Study of Thinking.* New York: Wiley.

BUBER, M. 1937. *I and Thou* (tr.). New York: Scribners.

BUCKE, R. M. 1923. *Cosmic Consciousness.* New York: Dutton (16th ed., 1951).

CHILD, I. L. 1954. Socialization. In G. Lindzey (Ed.), *Handbook of Social Psychology.* Cambridge, Mass.: Addison-Wesley, Vol. 2, pp. 655–692.

CHILDE, V. G. 1954. Early forms of society. In C. Singer, E. J. Holmyard, and A. R. Hall (General Eds.). *A History of Technology,* Vol. 1, *From Early Times to Fall of Ancient Empires.* New York and London: Oxford Univer. Press, pp. 58–84.

CHORNESS, M. H., and NOTTELMANN, D. A. 1956. The predictability of creative expression in teaching (*Research Report* AFPTRC-TN-56-130). Lackland Air Force Base, Texas: Air Force Personnel and Training Research Center.

———— and NOTTELMANN, D. A. 1957. The prediction of creativity among Air Force civilian employees. *Research Report* AFPTRC-TN-57-36. Lackland Air Force Base, Texas: Air Force Personnel and Training Research Center.

CHRISTENSEN, P. R., GUILFORD, J. P., and WILSON, R. C. 1957. Relations of creative responses to working time and instructions. *J. exp. Psychol.,* 53: 82–88.

COBB, EDITH. Summer, 1959. The Ecology of Imagination in Childhood *Daedalus, J. Amer. Acad. Arts & Sciences.*

CONANT, J. B. 1947. *On Understanding Science. An Historical Approach.* New Haven: Yale Univer. Press.

CRONBACH, L. J., 1957. The two disciplines of scientific psychology. *Amer. Psychologist, 12*: 671–684.

COVARRUBIAS, M. 1942. *Island of Bali.* New York: Alfred A. Knopf.

DEUTSCH, F., and MURPHY, W. F. 1955. *The Clinical Interview.* New York: Internat. Univer. Press, 2 vols.

DEUTSCH, K. W. 1953. *Nationalism and Social Communication: An Inquiry into the Foundations of Nationality.* Cambridge, Mass.: Technology Press of Mass. Inst. Technol.; New York: Wiley.

DREVDAHL, J. E. 1956. Factors of importance for creativity. *J. clin. Psychol.*, 12: 21–26.

DRIESCH, H. 1929. *The Science and Philosophy of the Organism* (2nd ed.). London: A. and C. Black, Ltd.

DUNCAN, D. D. 1958. *The Private World of Pablo Picasso*. New York: Ridge Press.

DUNCKER, K. 1945. On problem-solving (tr.) *Psychol. Monogr.*, 58 (5) (Whole No. 270).

DUNN, H. L. 1958. Report on the possibility of measuring positive mental health (Prepared by an Ad Hoc Committee of the U.S. National Committee on Vital and Health Statistics Doc. NC 261, Pos. Health 1). Washington, D.C.: U.S. Department of Health, Education and Welfare, Public Health Service.

DYSON, F. L. 1958. Innovation in physics. *Scientific American*, 199: pp. 74–82.

EHRENZWEIG, A. 1953. *The Psycho-analysis of Artistic Vision and Hearing*. New York: Julian Press.

FOLLETT, M. P. 1924. *Creative Experience*. New York: Longmans, Green.

VON FRISCH, K. 1939. The language of bees. In *Smithsonian Institution Annual Report, 1938*. Washington, D.C.: Smithsonian Inst., pp. 423–431.

———. 1950. *Bees: Their Vision, Chemical Senses, and Language*. Ithaca, New York: Cornell Univer. Press.

FROMM, E. 1947. *Man for himself: An Inquiry into the Psychology of Ethics*. New York: Rinehart.

———. 1956. Selfishness, self-love, and self-interest. In C. E. Moustakas (Ed.), *The Self*. New York: Harper, pp. 58–69.

FUND FOR THE ADVANCEMENT OF EDUCATION, New York. 1957. *They Went to College Early*. Evaluation Report No. 2. New York.

GERARD, R. W. 1946. The biological basis of imagination; with biographical sketch. *Scientific mon.*, 62: 477–499.

GERRY, R., DEVEAU, L. and CHORNESS, M. 1957. *A Review of Some Recent Research in the Field of Creativity and the Examination of an Experimental Workshop*. Lackland Air Force Base, Texas: Training Analysis and Development Division, Project 56–24.

GHISELIN, B. (Ed.), 1952. *The Creative Process*. New York: New American Library.

GIEDION, S. 1949. *Space, Time and Architecture: The Growth of a New Tradition*. Cambridge, Mass.: Harvard Univer. Press.

GILFILLAN, S. C. 1935. *The Sociology of Invention*. Chicago: Follett.

GOLDSTEIN, K. 1939. *The Organism*. New York: American Book.

GOUGH, H. G. 1957. Imagination—undeveloped resource. In *Proc. 1st. Conf. Res. Develpm. Personnel Mgmt.* Los Angeles: Univer. Calif. Inst. Industr. Relat., pp. 4–10.

————, McCLOSKY, H., and MEEHL, P. E. 1952. A personality scale for social responsibility. *J. abnorm. soc. Psychol.*, 47: 73–80.

GRANT, D. A. 1951. Perceptual versus analytical responses to the number concept of a Weigl-type card sorting test. *J. exp. Psychol.*, 41: 23–29.

GUILFORD, J. P. 1950. Creativity. *Amer. Psychologist*, 5: 444–454.

————. 1956a. The relation of intellectual factors to creative thinking in science. In C. W. Taylor (Ed.), *The Identification of Creative Scientific Talent*. Salt Lake City: Univer. Utah, pp. 69–95.

————. 1956b. The structure of intellect. *Psychol. Bull.*, 53: 267–293.

————. 1957a. *A Revised Structure of Intellect* (Rep. Psychol. Lab., No. 19). Los Angeles: Univer. Southern Calif.

————. 1957b. Creative abilities in the arts. *Psychol. Rev.*, 64: 110–118.

————, CHRISTENSEN, P. R., FRICK, J. W., and MERRIFIELD, P. R. 1957. *The Relations of Creative-Thinking Aptitudes to Non-aptitude Personality Traits* (Rep. Psychol. Lab., No. 20). Los Angeles: Univer. Southern Calif.

HANDLIN, O. 1957. Textbooks that don't teach. *Atlantic Monthly*, 200 (6): 110–113.

HARLOW, H. F. 1949. The formation of learning sets. *Psychol. Rev.*, 56: 51–65.

HARRISON, H. S. 1954. Discovery, invention and diffusion. In C. Singer, E. J. Holmyard, and A. R. Hall (General Eds.), *A History of Technology*, Vol. 1, *From Early Times to Fall of Ancient Empires*. New York and London: Oxford Univer. Press, pp. 58–84.

HEIDBREDER, E., BENSLEY, M. L., and IVY, M. 1948. The attainment of concepts: IV. Regularities and levels. *J. Psychol.*, 25: 299–329.

HERTZKA, A. F., GUILFORD, J. P., CHRISTENSEN, P. R., and BERGER, R. M. 1954. A factor-analytic study of evaluative abilities. *Educ. psychol. Measmt.*, 14: 581–597.

HILGARD, E. R., EDGREN, R. D., and IRVINE, R. P. 1954. Errors in transfer following learning with understanding: further studies with Katona's card-trick experiments. *J. exp. Psychol.*, 47: 457–464.

————, IRVINE, R. P., and WHIPPLE, J. E. 1953. Rote memorization, understanding, and transfer: an extension of Katona's card-trick experiments. *J. exp. Psychol.*, 46: 288–292.

HILLS, J. R. 1955. *The Relationships Between Certain Factor-Analyzed Abilities and Success in College Mathematics* (Rep. psychol. Lab., No. 15). Los Angeles: Univer. Southern Calif.

HORNEY, K. 1937. *The Neurotic Personality of our Time*. New York: Norton.

————. 1945. *Our Inner Conflicts*. New York: Norton.

HOUSMAN, A. E. 1933. *The Name and Nature of Poetry*. New York: Macmillan; Cambridge, England: Cambridge Univer. Press.

HOVLAND, C. I., and WEISS, W. 1953. Transmission of information concerning concepts through positive and negative instances. *J. exp. Psychol.*, 45: 175–182.

HUNT, M. V. n.d. The Natural History of Love (Unpublished MS.).

HUTCHINSON, E. D. 1949. *How To Think Creatively*. New York: Abingdon.

HUXLEY, A. 1924. *The Young Archimedes*. New York: Doran.

JONES, E. 1953–57. *The Life and Work of Sigmund Freud* (3 vols.). New York, Basic.

————. 1957. How to tell your friends from geniuses. *Sat. Rev. Lit.* (Aug. 10), 40: 9–11, 39–40.

KATONA, G. 1940. *Organizing and Memorizing*. New York: Columbia Univer. Press.

KRIS, E. 1952. *Psychoanalytic Explorations in Art*. New York: Internat. Univer. Press.

KROEBER, A. L. 1957. *Style and Civilizations*. Ithaca, New York: Cornell Univer. Press.

KUBIZEK, A. 1955. *The Young Hitler I Knew* (tr.) Boston: Houghton, Mifflin.

LASSWELL, H. D. 1950. *World Politics and Personal Insecurity*. New York and London: McGraw-Hill and Whittlesley House, 1935. Re-issue, Glencoe, Ill.: Free Press, 1950.

———— and KAPLAN, A. 1950. *Power and Society*. New Haven, Conn.: Yale Univer. Press.

LEWIN, K., and LIPPITT, R. 1938. An experimental approach to the study of autocracy and democracy: a preliminary note. *Sociometry*. 1: 292–300.

LILLIE, R. S. 1945. *General Biology and Philosophy of Organism*. Chicago: Univer. Chicago Press.

LIPPITT, R., and WHITE, R. K. 1943. The "social climate" of children's groups. In R. G. Barker, J. D. Kounin, and H. F. Wright (Eds.), *Child Behavior and Development*. New York: McGraw-Hill, pp. 485–508.

LIVINGSTONE, R. W. 1944. *The Future in Education*. Cambridge, England: Cambridge Univer. Press.

LOWENFELD, M. 1935. *Play in Childhood*. London: Gollancz.

————. 1939. The world pictures of children—a method of recording and studying them. *British J. Med. Psychol.*, 18 (Part I): pp. 65–101.

————. 1958. *The World Book*. In press.

McGEOCH, J. A. 1952. *The Psychology of Human Learning* (2nd ed.). New York: Longmans, Green.

McPHEE, C. 1936. The "absolute" music of Bali. *Modern Music*, 12: 165.

————. 1944. *A house in Bali* (An Asia press book). New York: John Day.

————. 1955. Children and music in Bali. In M. Mead and M. Wolfenstein (Eds.), *Childhood in Contemporary Cultures*. Chicago: Univer. Chicago Press, pp. 70–94.

MASLOW, A. H. 1954. *Motivation and Personality*. New York: Harper.

———. 1959. Cognition of being in the peak-experiences. *J. Genet. Psychol.*, in press.

MEAD, M. 1928a. The role of the dance. In *Coming of Age in Samoa*. New York: Morrow.

———. 1928b. The role of the individual in Samoan culture. *J. Royal Anthrop. Inst.* (July–Dec.) *58*: 481–495.

———. 1930. *Growing up in New Guinea*. New York: Morrow.

———. 1931a. Two South Sea educational experiments and their American implications. *Univer. of Pa. Bull.* (18th Annual Schoolmen's Week Proc.), *31* (36): 493–496.

———. 1931b. The meaning of freedom in education. *Progr. Educ.*, 8 (2): 107–111.

———. 1935. *Sex and Temperament in Three Primitive Societies*. New York: Morrow.

———. 1938. *The Mountain Arapesh, I. An Importing Culture*. (Anthrop. Papers of the Amer. Museum of Natural History, Vol. 36, Pt. III). New York: American Museum of Natural History, pp. 139–349.

———. 1941. The arts in Bali. *Yale Rev.* (Winter 1941) *30* (2): 335–347.

———. 1942. Community drama, Bali and America. *Amer. Scholar* (Winter 1941–42) 2 (1): 79–88.

———. 1949. *The Mountain Arapesh, V. The Record of Unabelin with Rorschach Analysis* (Anthrop. Papers of the Amer. Museum of Natural History, Vol. 41, Pt. III). New York: American Museum of Natural History, pp. 289–390.

———. 1950. Experience in learning primitive languages through the use of learning high level linguistic abstractions. H. von Foerster (Ed.), *Cybernetics—Transcription of the 7th Conference*. New York; Josiah Macy, Jr., Foundation.

———. 1952. Some relationships between social anthropology and psychiatry. In F. Alexander & H. Ross (Eds.), *Dynamic Psychiatry*. Chicago: Univer. of Chicago Press.

———. 1955. Children and ritual in Bali. In M. Mead and M. Wolfenstein (Eds.), *Childhood in Contemporary Cultures*. Chicago: Univer. of Chicago Press, pp. 40–51.

———. 1956a. *New Lives for Old: Cultural Transformation, Manus 1928–1953*. New York: Morrow.

———. 1956b. The concept of mental health and its international implications. *Mental Health in Home and School* (Paper presented in Berlin, Aug. 1956, at Ann. Meeting of World Federation for Ment. Health). London: World Federation for Ment. Health, pp. 10–13.

————. 1958. Bali in the market place of the world. To be published by the Nat'l. Inst. of Arts & Letters in Proc., 1958.

————. 1959. *Cultural factors basic in fundamental education programs.* To be published in 1959 Yearbook of Nat'l. Soc. for Study of Educ.

———— and BATESON, G. 1938. Films, *Karba's First Years* and *Trance and Dance in Bali.* New York: New York Univer. Film Library.

MEER, B., and STEIN, M. L. 1955. Measures of intelligence and creativity. *J. Psychol.,* 39: 117–126.

MEINECKE, E. F. 1957. *Machiavellism: The Doctrine of Raison d'état and Its Place in Modern History.* New Haven, Conn.: Yale Univer. Press.

MERTON, R. K. 1957. Priorities in scientific discovery: a chapter in the sociology of science. *Amer. sociol. Rev.,* 22: 635–659.

MILLER, G. A. 1956. The magical number seven, plus-or-minus two: some limits on our capacity for processing information. *Psychol. Rev.,* 63: 81–97.

MILNER, MARION B. 1958. *On Not Being Able to Paint* (2nd ed.). New York: Intern. Univer. Press, 1958; Chicago: Heinemann, 1957.

MILTON, G. A. 1957. The effects of sex-role identification upon problem-solving skill. *J. abnorm. soc. Psychol.,* 55: 208–212.

MOONEY, R. L. 1956. Cultural blocks and creative possibilities. *Educ. Leadership,* 8: 273–278.

MORGAN, G. A. 1941. *What Nietzsche Means.* Cambridge: Harvard Univer. Press.

MORRIS, C. W. 1956. *Varieties of Human Value.* Chicago: Univer. Chicago Press.

MOUSTAKAS, C. E. (Ed.), 1956. *The Self.* New York: Harper.

MURPHY, G. 1947. *Personality: A Biosocial Approach to Origins and Structure.* New York: Harper.

MURRAY, H. A., and KLUCKHOHN, C. 1948. Outline of a conception of personality. In C. Kluckhohn and H. A. Murray (Eds.), *Personality in Nature, Society, and Culture.* New York: Knopf, pp. 3–32.

NAKAMURA, C. V. 1955. The relation between conformity and problem-solving. (CONR Tech. Rep. No. 11, Contract N6 onr 25125, Dept. Psychol.). Stanford, Calif.: Stanford Univer.

NEF, J. U. 1950. *War and Human Progress: An Essay on the Rise of Industrial Civilization.* Cambridge, Mass.: Harvard Univer. Press.

NOYCE, W. 1958. Why men seek adventure. *Horizon,* 1 (1): 7–12, 135–139.

OSBORN, A. F. 1953. *Applied Imagination: Principles and Procedures of Creative Thinking.* New York: Scribner.

————. 1957. *Applied Imagination: Principles and Procedures of Creative Thinking* (rev. ed.). New York: Scribner.

PLANCK, M. K. E. L. 1949. *Scientific Autobiography, and Other Papers* (tr.). New York: Philosophical Library.

POINCARE, H. 1913. Mathematical creation. In *The Foundations of Science; Science and Hypothesis; The Value of Science; Science and Method* (tr.). New York and Garrison, New York: Science Press, pp. 383–394.

RANK, O. 1932. *Art and Artist.* New York: A. A. Knopf.

REED, M. F. 1946. Consecutive studies of the schoolroom behavior of children in relation to the teachers' dominative and socially integrative contacts. In H. H. Anderson, J. E. Brewer, and M. F. Reed, Studies of teachers' classroom personalities, III. Follow-up studies of the effects of dominative and integrative contacts on children's behavior. *Appl. psychol. Monogr.*, 11:15–100.

ROE, A. 1946. The personality of artists. *Educ. psychol. Measmt.*, 6: 401–408.

———. 1953a. A psychological study of eminent psychologists and anthropologists, and a comparison with biological and physical scientists. *Psychol. Monogr.*, 67 (2) (Whole No. 352).

———. 1953b. *The Making of a Scientist.* New York: Dodd, Mead.

Rogers, C. R. 1953a. Some directions and end points in therapy. In O. H. Mowrer (Ed.), *Psychotherapy—Theory and Research.* New York: Ronald, pp. 44–68.

———. 1953b. Toward a theory of creativity. In M. Barkan and R. L. Mooney (Eds.), *The Conference on Creativity, A Report to the Rockefeller Foundation.* Columbus, Ohio: Ohio State Univer., pp. 73–82 (Multilith.).

———. 1954. Toward a theory of creativity. *ETC.: A review of general semantics*, 11 (4): 249–260.

———. 1956. What it means to become a person. In C. E. Moustakas (Ed.), *The Self.* New York: Harper, pp. 195–211.

ROTTER, J. B. 1954. *Social Learning and Clinical Psychology.* New York: Prentice-Hall.

DE SAINT-EXUPÉRY, A. 1939. *Wind, Sand, and Stars* (tr.). New York: Reynal & Hitchcock. Harcourt-Brace. 1949.

DE SANTILLANA, G. 1955. *The Crime of Galileo.* Chicago: Univer. Chicago Press.

SCHACHTEL, E. G. 1947. On memory and childhood amnesia. *Psychiatry*, 10 (1): 1–26.

SCHEINFELD, A. 1950. *The New You and Heredity.* Philadelphia: Lippincott.

SCHWARTZ, T. 1958. The Paliau Movement in the Admiralty Islands, 1946–1954 (Unpublished doctoral dissertation), University of Pennsylvania.

SHARP, E. F. 1950. *Collected Papers on Psychoanalysis*, Marjorie Brierley (Ed.). London: Hogarth and Inst. of Psycho-anal.

SPRECHER, T. R. 1957. An Investigation of Criteria for Creativity in Engineers. (Doctoral dissertation), University of Maryland.

STEIN, M. I. 1956. A transactional approach to creativity. In C. W. Taylor (Ed.), the *1955 University of Utah Research Conference on the Identification of Creative Scientific Talent*. Salt Lake City: Univer. Utah Press, pp. 171–181.

―――. 1958. The Cultural Context of Creativity. On the Role of the Industrial Research Chemist and Its Relationship to the Problem of Creativity (Unpublished MSS.).

STODDARD, G. D. 1950. *On the Education of Women*. New York: Macmillan.

STRUIK, D. J. 1948. *Yankee Science in the Making*. Boston: Little, Brown.

SULLIVAN, H. S. 1947. *Conceptions of Modern Psychiatry*. Washington, D.C.: Wm. Alanson White Foundation.

TAGIURI, R. and PETRULLO, L. 1958. *Person Perception and Interpersonal Behavior*. Stanford, Calif.: Stanford Univer. Press.

TANNER, J. and INHELDER, B. 1956. *Discussions of Child Development*. New York: Internat. Univer. Press, Vol. 1 passim.

TAYLOR, C. W. (Ed.), 1956. *The 1955 University of Utah Research Conference on the Identification of Creative Scientific Talent*. Salt Lake City: Univer. of Utah Press.

―――― (Ed.). 1958. *The Identification of Creative Scientific Talent. Proceedings of the 1957 Research Conference, Univer. of Utah*. Salt Lake City: Univer. of Utah Press.

TAYLOR, D. W., BERRY, P. C., and BLOCK, C. H. 1957. Does group participation when using brainstorming facilitate or inhibit creative thinking? Dept. of Industrial Admin. & Dept. of Psychol., Yale University (Technical Report 1, Contract Nonr 609/20).

―――― and McNEMAR, O. W. 1955. Problem solving and thinking. *Ann. Rev. Psychol.*, 6: 455–482.

THORNDIKE, E. L., et al. 1927. *The Measurement of Intelligence*. New York: Bureau of Publications, Teachers College, Columbia Univer.

THURSTONE, L. L. 1938. *Primary Mental Abilities*. Psychometric Monogr., No. 1.

TOYNBEE, A. J. 1934–54. *A Study of History*. London: Oxford Univer. Press, 6 Vols.

ULICH, R. 1956. In G. D. STODDARD, et al. *The New York University Self Study*. New York: New York Univer. Press, pp. 229–230.

WALLACE, H. A., and BROWN, W. L. 1956. *Corn and Its Early Fathers*. E. Lansing, Michigan: Michigan State Univer. Press.

WEISINGER, H. 1953. *Tragedy and the Paradox of the Fortunate Fall*. E. Lansing, Michigan: Michigan State Univer. Press.

WEISSMAN, P. 1957. Conscious and unconscious autobiographical dramas of Eugene O'Neill. *J. Amer. psychoanal. Assn.*, 5: 432–460.

WERTHEIMER, M. 1945, 1959. *Productive Thinking*. New York & London: Harper.

WHORF, B. L. 1956. *Language, Thought, and Reality*. Cambridge, Mass.: Technology Press of Mass. Inst. Technol.; New York: Wiley.

WILSON, R. C., GUILFORD, J. P., CHRISTENSEN, P. R., and LEWIS, D. J. 1954. A factor-analytical study of creative thinking abilities. *Psychometrika, 19*: 297–311.

WILSON, R. N. 1958. *Man Made Plain: the Poet in Contemporary American Society*, in press.

WITTY, P. 1956. The use of films in stimulating creative expression and in identifying talented pupils. *Elementary English, 33*: 340–344.

ZOETE, B. DE, and SPIES, W. 1938. *Dance and Drama in Bali*. London: Faber & Faber.

INDEX

Abandon, 63, 238
Absorption, 237
Abstract painting, 192
Action and reaction, 39–40, 41, 240
Activated complex concept, 7–8
Adkins, Homer, 10
Adler, Alfred, 56
Admiralty Islands, 225
Aesthetics, 34
Aknaton, 205
Analogies, recognition of, 4–5
Anderson, Ernest, 9
Anderson, Harold H., xii, 237, 239, 249, 252, 262, 263
  quoted, 240
Anxiety, in creative art, 77, 78
  in sense of self, 50
Aptitudes contributing to creative performance, 144, 149, 157
Aptitudes of High-Level Personnel at University of California (research project), 145n, 150, 157
  factors found, 145–149
Arapesh (people), creativity among, 226
  culture, 226, 229–230, 231
Archimedes, 223, 235
Aristotle, 3, 104, 114
Art, attention-getting, 194
  classic, 195–196
  creativity in, 193
  as essence of experience, 194
  nonobjective, 197
  paintings, 195, 196

psychoanalytic theory of, 212n
  and technical proficiency, 190
  as truth-telling, 195–196
Associational fluency, 145–146
  as creative factor, 172
  tests of, 151
Atomic energy, xi
Atomic research, 11
Atoms, Dalton's evidence, 6
  make-up of, 31
  isotopic study of, 15
Authoritarianism, threat of, 200
Automation, 203
Average man, normal adjustment of, 91
Awareness, as characteristic of creativity, 61, 62, 238, 262
  as human attribute, 74
  in psychotherapy, 74

Bali, arts of, described, 227–228
  creativity in, 228, 229, 233
  dance, professional, 228
  originality demanded, 233
  style, 227
Balinese, adjustment to tourists, 233
  contrasted with Samoans, 228–229, 232
Bandurski, Robert S., xiii
Bartley, S. Howard, xiii
Beauty, as path to truth, 196–197
Beethoven, Ludwig von, 163, 174
Behavior, circular, 129–131, 239
  dominative, 131, 136